GENERATION TARANTINO

GENERATION TARANTINO

The Last Wave of Young Turks in Hollywood

Andrew J. Rausch

BLOOMSBURY ACADEMIC
NEW YORK • LONDON • OXFORD • NEW DELHI • SYDNEY

BLOOMSBURY ACADEMIC

Bloomsbury Publishing Inc, 1385 Broadway, New York, NY 10018, USA
Bloomsbury Publishing Plc, 50 Bedford Square, London, WC1B 3DP, UK
Bloomsbury Publishing Ireland, 29 Earlsfort Terrace, Dublin 2, D02 AY28, Ireland

BLOOMSBURY, BLOOMSBURY ACADEMIC and the Diana logo are trademarks of Bloomsbury Publishing Plc

Copyright © Andrew J. Rausch, 2025

Cover design: Sally Rinehart

Cover images: Quentin Tarantino © The Asahi Shimbun/Getty Images; *Pulp Fiction* © Miramax/Photofest; *Clerks* © Miramax Films/Photofest; *Fight Club* © 20th Century Fox/Photofest | Additional cover art © iStock.com/subjug

All rights reserved. No part of this publication may be: i) reproduced or transmitted in any form, electronic or mechanical, including photocopying, recording or by means of any information storage or retrieval system without prior permission in writing from the publishers; or ii) used or reproduced in any way for the training, development or operation of artificial intelligence (AI) technologies, including generative AI technologies. The rights holders expressly reserve this publication from the text and data mining exception as per Article 4(3) of the Digital Single Market Directive (EU) 2019/790.

Bloomsbury Publishing Inc does not have any control over, or responsibility for, any third-party websites referred to or in this book. All internet addresses given in this book were correct at the time of going to press. The author and publisher regret any inconvenience caused if addresses have changed or sites have ceased to exist, but can accept no responsibility for any such changes.

Library of Congress Cataloging-in-Publication Data Available

ISBN: HB: 978-1-4930-7980-3
ePDF: 979-8-7651-5453-3
eBook: 978-1-4930-7981-0

Typeset by Deanta Global Publishing Services, Chennai, India
Printed and bound in the United States of America

For product safety related questions contact productsafety@bloomsbury.com.

To find out more about our authors and books visit www.bloomsbury.com and sign up for our newsletters.

Contents

Introduction   1
1   Richard Linklater: Slacker Turned Auteur   7
2   John Singleton: A Director to Be Reckoned With   29
3   Quentin Tarantino: The Enfant Terrible of American Cinema   49
4   The Tarantino Film Subgenre   69
5   Guillermo del Toro: Stories About the Dark Side of Life   85
6   David Fincher and the Ultimate Magic Trick   97
7   Robert Rodriguez: The One-Man Band   121
8   Kevin Smith: Jersey Boy Makes Good   143
9   The Deeply Personal Cinema of Noah Baumbach   163
10   The Whimsical World of Wes Anderson   177
11   Paul Thomas Anderson: Born to Make Movies   191
12   Christopher Nolan: American Master   209

| 13 | Darren Aronofsky: "The Ripsnorting Bull of American Cinema" | 219 |
| 14 | Sofia Coppola: Cinema of Isolation | 233 |

| References | 243 |
| Index | 269 |

Introduction

This book is about the '90s. And Hollywood. And Generation X. Oops, sorry, younger Boomers, it's *mostly* about Generation X. And it's very certainly about the attitude and swagger that has come to define Gen X.

Because the title contains the name *Tarantino*, you might be under the impression that this book is about Quentin Tarantino. It's not. Not *precisely* about him anyway. It's about what he symbolizes. Like Kevin Smith, Richard Linklater, Robert Rodriguez, and others, Tarantino personifies the *attitude* of '90s filmmaking. Tarantino, like some of the other filmmakers examined in this book, built his career on a foundation of DIY gusto. Instead of waiting for opportunity to come knock on his door, he created his own opportunity.

This book is about a wave of revolutionary filmmakers who seemingly came out of nowhere. A similar wave of revolutionary mavericks had emerged a couple decades before—Scorsese, Spielberg, Coppola, Altman, De Palma—but this generation was different. This wave was uniquely of its time. This group personified the mindset of young adults in the '90s.

Today we associate a lot of things with the 1990s. Woodstock '99, for instance, *was* the '90s. *Beavis and Butthead*, grunge music, "O.P.P.," and *Infinite Jest* were the 1990s. In that same way, *Clerks, Pulp Fiction, Boogie Nights,* and *Fight Club* were the '90s. Like the decade's so-called nu metal (a wave of questionable hip-hop-infused rock), this generation of filmmakers—Generation Tarantino—defied existing norms and conventions. They broke the rules and created new standards. They forged their own paths, mixing tones and genres in ways that no one had before.

This was a generation that wouldn't take no for an answer. I prefer the label "Generation Tarantino," but this movement could just as easily be identified as the "I Don't Give a Fuck" generation. You've heard the phrase *no fucks given*? That could be used to describe this generation of artists—musicians, novelists, painters, playwrights, screenwriters, and filmmakers; they cared about the work, but they didn't give a damn what society or the system deemed acceptable. Generation Tarantino was here to break down doors and bust through barriers.

They were rebels.

Mavericks.

Artists in the truest sense of the word.

They were fueled by angst and ambition.

The 1980s had been filled with flicks that played it safe. That meant less ambiguous characters and less antiheroes. The melancholy storylines that mirrored real life were replaced by escapist fare and happy endings. It was a decade of repression and filmmaking oppression. There were still some pictures made with the artistic sensibilities that the New Hollywood filmmakers had ushered in a decade before, but those types of films were largely stamped out. For every *Blue Velvet*, *Do the Right Thing*, or *Blow Out*, there were twenty *Howard the Ducks*, *Revenge of the Nerds*, and *Friday the 13ths*. It's telling that most lists of the best films of the '80s include *The Shining* and *Raging Bull* in their top five, considering those films had been made in 1979. Despite being released at the onset of the new decade, those pictures personified the '70s filmmaking aesthetic; in much the same way, *The Virgin Suicides* and *Memento* were released in 2000 but personified the '90s filmmaking aesthetic. Of course, the filmmaking attitude and approach don't instantly change when a new decade rolls in; there's no must-adhere-to rule saying, "Films will now be made like *this*." Additionally, these kinds of generalizations don't (and can't) apply to *every* picture made in an era. But by and large, the 1980s were a decade of "high-concept" pictures produced and packaged for mass consumption.

By the 1990s, filmmakers were ready to break their systematic constraints and create films that lived and breathed like the characters who inhabited them, which required filmmakers working outside the system. Many of the filmmakers who came to represent the '90s filmmaking aesthetic financed their own first pictures and found alternate routes of entrance into the industry. Many of them didn't even attend film school. As a result, these filmmakers had never learned what was and wasn't deemed possible, so they pushed through obstacles and did things that were supposedly impossible without even realizing they were doing it.

What made this generation of filmmakers so different? Why were they the way they were, and why did they make the kinds of films they did? In *The Cinema of Generation X*, author Peter Hanson writes,

> The enigma of the cinema of Generation X revolves around a few key facts: Gen-Xers grew up during one of the tumultuous periods of American history, were inundated with popular culture to an unprecedented degree, suffered through social changes such as a rash of divorces, and then created a youth culture anchored in irony, apathy, and disenfranchisement.

What exactly separates these films from the films of other generations? What does a Generation-X film *look* like? *Film Threat* editor Chris Gore says,

> I think when you look at the attributes and things that are common among people who are Gen X, a lot of those attitudes were woven into the films. We were latch-key kids. We don't give a fuck what other people think about us. We don't feel any sense of pushing our morality onto others. We are the generation that questioned everything. And I think when you look at the themes of Gen-X filmmakers, a lot of that is woven in. You see that in contrast to films today that want to push morality and agenda.

It's important to note that, aside from many Generation-X filmmakers skipping film school, there are other aspects of cinema education that helped mold them. Scott Rosenberg, screenwriter of the '90s indie classics *Beautiful Girls* and *Things to Do in Denver When You're Dead*, makes a terrific point, suggesting that the filmmakers who emerged during the '90s were direct descendants of the filmmakers of the '70s. Where most of the American New Wave filmmakers were heavily influenced by the legendary filmmakers who preceded them, Generation Tarantino was heavily influenced by American New Wave. "What do these filmmakers all have in common?" Rosenberg says.

> What were the movies that they grew up with? What were the movies that they were seeing when they were in their formative years? My father was taking me to see *One Flew over the Cuckoo's Nest* and *Dog Day Afternoon* and *Magnum Force*. All those great '70s movies. Sidney Lumet, Sydney Pollack, Marty Scorsese, and Steven Spielberg. So I think if you look at Paul Thomas Anderson and Quentin and Linklater—all those guys, that's what they had in common.

Arguably the most daring, boundary-pushing (and controversial) American film of the decade was Larry Clark's *Kids*. Now, I'm not asserting that *Kids* is the definitive '90s film—I believe *Fight Club* owns that distinction because of both its content and artistry—but *Kids* takes the biggest chances and pushes the cinematic boundaries the farthest. Plus, it does a fine job, by all accounts, of capturing the feel and essence of New York City street life in the '90s. So why then, you ask, is Larry Clark not one of the thirteen filmmakers covered and examined here? For starters, Clark, who was actually *two generations* older than the Gen-X filmmakers, doesn't fit in with the generational movement. (And yes, some of the directors discussed in this volume are a wee bit older, but they're not *multiple* generations older.) But I'm splitting hairs. The primary reason Clark isn't included is because his career after the '90s is far less impressive, and longevity was something I took into consideration while selecting the filmmakers covered here. This is why some truly gifted filmmakers, such as Todd Solondz and the Hughes brothers, aren't included.

There are other directors, such as Steven Soderbergh and Spike Lee, who just narrowly missed the book's time frame. Both are master filmmakers, but I had to draw the line somewhere, or you would now be holding a book that weighed a hundred pounds. And if I were to include those guys, you could say, "Well, what about *these* filmmakers who debuted just a year before *those* guys?" And then if I included them, as well, the cycle would continue, and we'd eventually end up covering D. W. Griffith and Charles Chaplin. Now, I'm aware that that's an absurd statement, but it makes the point.

So the demarcation lines are directors whose feature debuts were released between 1990 and 2000 (2000 because the films released that year were *made* in the '90s). The question of whether to include Richard Linklater caused some deliberation because he'd technically made a feature film in the 1980s. However, that film, *It's Impossible to Learn to Plow by Reading Books*, was shot on Super 8 and never received proper theatrical or video release. (While it's been released as an extra on the Criterion edition of *Slacker*, no one would consider that a "proper" release for a feature.) While the creation of the film is commendable, the general consensus is that it doesn't count as Linklater's feature debut; it's comparable to the early short films of most other successful directors. This is good because there was no way I could have (in good conscience) left Linklater out of a discussion about this generation of filmmakers. He was a trailblazer and, in many respects, the unofficial leader of the movement.

I should be clear: There are a lot of filmmakers who debuted in the 1990s who are not covered here. Some of them are very good, but again, this book could have very easily gotten out of hand and become unwieldy. So these are the thirteen filmmakers I chose to examine. I believe their work and careers do a fine job of representing this generation of filmmakers, their methods, the hurdles they faced, and the adventurous and rebellious spirit that has become associated with them.

So what other criteria was used in selecting filmmakers for inclusion? The filmmakers had to make fiction films, have a substantial body of work, and had to have made a significant contribution to cinema. Additionally, this volume is about filmmakers making *American* films. So while Guillermo del Toro's debut film, *Cronos*, was made in Mexico, most of the films he's made since have been made in the United States. His second film, *Mimic*, was made in the United States and released in the '90s. Additionally, del Toro's ability to craft films with substantial merit in both countries, sliding back and forth as he wishes, is part of what makes him the maverick that he is.

So what exactly is this book? *Generation Tarantino: The Last Wave of Young Turks in Hollywood* is an examination of the films, careers, and artistic styles of the most significant filmmakers to emerge during the 1990s. I believe that by looking at each of these filmmakers and their works and then stepping back and looking at the group (and their works) as a whole, the reader will get a clearer understanding of what elements made this generation unique, what made the films they created special, and what their contributions (both individual and as a collective) to cinematic history are. It's also a book about the '90s that focuses on the films these directors made during that decade. So while there is some discussion of each director's post-'90s career (primarily in terms of their legacy), *Generation Tarantino* is about the foundations on which those careers were built.

This book is the result of hundreds of hours of research. Additional information was obtained through interviews I conducted with directors, screenwriters, producers, cinematographers, actors, and film critics. Interview subjects include such noted film folk as Quentin Tarantino, Guillermo Navarro, Kevin Smith, Richard Linklater, Steven Bernstein, Guillermo del Toro, and Scott Rosenberg. Some interviews were conducted previously, and some were conducted expressly for this project.

The chapters on each director appear in the chronological order their debut features were released. While this doesn't establish precisely when they entered the film industry, it indicates when they entered into the public consciousness.

Now that we've gotten all of that out of the way, one last observation: Since this book is named after Tarantino, it feels appropriate to quote him: "If you love movies enough, you can make a good one." While that statement is an oversimplification, it leads us to something we can agree on: The filmmakers profiled here love movies, and they've made some damned good ones.

1

Richard Linklater
Slacker Turned Auteur

Richard Linklater was born and raised in Houston, Texas. He played baseball and football in high school. After graduation, he attended college at Sam Houston University, where his mother worked as a professor. He left school and spent time working on an oil rig before coming home, where he fell in love with cinema. When he decided that he wanted to make films for a living, he plunked down his savings to purchase filmmaking equipment.

After relocating to Austin, a city with a burgeoning art community, he helped establish the Austin Film Society. He cut his teeth making short films and then a $3,000 Super 8 road film, *It's Impossible to Learn to Plow by Reading Books*. After spending a year and a half working on that, he showed it to legendary filmmaker Monte Hellman. Hellman was impressed by what he saw and noted that it should have been called *It's Impossible to Learn to Make Movies by Reading Books*. Hellman wrote, "With *Learn to Plow*, Rick created a film that was both extremely realistic and painfully poetic. There wasn't a false note, and I never felt as if I were watching acting or actors. These were real people and this was real life, and I cared deeply about them and it." Making that film gave Linklater the tools and confidence to make something larger. He raised money to make his new film by screening *Learn to Plow* for potential backers. If he could do this on Super 8 with no money, imagine what he could do with an actual budget.

Most of the money he used to make the picture was money he'd raised from friends and family. Although he envisioned having a bigger budget for a film he planned to shoot in Galveston, Linklater was forced to readjust his sites. Instead, he made a cheap film in Austin that moved from one set of colorful characters to the next, and he called it *Slacker*. Although a similar film could have been made at that time in just about any American college town, *Slacker*'s culture and vibe was unique to Austin. *The Austin Chronicle*'s Chris Walters later wrote,

> Few of the many films shot in Austin over the past ten or fifteen years even attempt to make something of the way its citizens live. *Slacker* is the only one I know of that claims this city's version of life on the margins of the working world as its whole subject, and it is one of the first American movies ever to find a form so apropos to the themes of disconnectedness and cultural drift.

Slacker began filming in July 1989. At the time, Austin didn't require (or even have) shooting permits, which was good for *Slacker*'s budget. Linklater had a Shell Gasoline credit card, which was used to purchase snacks, drinks, and gasoline for crew members to get from point A to point B. Linklater could afford nothing so luxurious as catered meals; if actors and crew got hungry, they ate peanut butter and jelly sandwiches. If that didn't suffice or more was needed, out came the Shell card. Because Linklater needed to be present wherever the film was being shot that day, he would hand the card to whomever needed it, and they would forge his signature. The young director also managed to convince local businesses to donate outdated food they were going to dispose of.

By the time *Slacker* was finished, Linklater had spent roughly $23,000. He later told *The Austin Chronicle*, "It wasn't about the money, and we never talked about it. There wasn't any, so we had to get by some other way. Everyone who worked on the film did it for reasons other than cash. The fact that it was done so inexpensively says more about the spirit of the people involved in the project than the cost." He also explained, "The initial cash came from where most truly independent films come from: supportive family and friends, credit cards, any savings, additional loans. You sell off possessions, steal, ask others to steal, all kinds of things you're not particularly proud of."

Although the film feels improvisational, hardly any of it was improvised. Linklater wrote down dialogue from real conversations he'd heard, been involved with, or heard about and then tweaked it. The director explained to author John Pierson, "Every line you hear, ninety-eight percent was on a page in rehearsal before we shot it. The camera was never wondering what would happen. We didn't really have that much film stock."

Most of the crew was comprised of members of the Austin Film Society. Linklater's friend and Austin Film Society cofounder Lee Daniel owned an Arriflex 16 mm camera. He also had some experience filming, so naturally Daniel became the film's cinematographer and Linklater's go-to cameraman throughout the rest of decade. According to Linklater, he was the "oldest member of the crew at twenty-eight."

The cast was comprised of amateur actors, many cast because they had an interesting appearance or something quirky about

Richard Linklater and cinematographer Lee Daniel editing Slacker. *Courtesy of Orion Pictures/Photofest © Orion Pictures*

them. Linklater gave out invitations to people he encountered around the city to interview for roles, but many didn't show up or gave half-assed interviews. The director said that he's had numerous people approach him in the years following, saying they would have shown up or given better interviews had they known *Slacker* was going to be good. He cast friends, acquaintances, and even cast himself. Many reviewers have written that the cast just played themselves, but this is inaccurate. This assessment bothers Linklater because it does the performers a disservice by not giving them the credit they deserve.

Juno director Jason Reitman, who credits *Slacker* as an influence on his own work, discussed the film's acting in an interview with *Paste*:

> As a director, I'm watching *Slacker* and I'm thinking, "There are no cuts in this film." Which means there's no cheating. These actors have to nail it. But these are also presumably people who aren't professional actors. The idea that he was able to get all these natural performances his first time out is mind-blowing. I can't quite fathom how he did it. I mean look, I'm sitting here on camera right now, and I'm nervous. It's scary to be in front of a lens. And to get people to open up, and do these kind of walk-and-talk conversations, and have monologues about philosophy for five minutes [is impressive].

The first screening of *Slacker* was held at Austin's Dobie Theater on September 22, 1991. It was wildly successful and led to more screenings. Eventually, Orion Classics picked up the picture for distribution for $100,000. It gained some attention when it screened at the 1991 Sundance Film Festival, and though it didn't win any awards, it got some press and even garnered the praise of filmmaker Gus Van Sant. When it was given a proper theatrical release, *Slacker* earned an impressive $1.2 million. Additionally, it inspired a number of filmmakers, including Kevin Smith and Reitman, to pick up a camera and make their own features. Amy Taubin of the *Village Voice* asserted, "Richard Linklater was the person most filmmakers wanted to be."

Reitman said,

> The thing that's striking about *Slacker* to me is that when you think about American independent cinema, there's this idea that people are just throwing up a camera and letting people talk. That's not what *Slacker* is, even though you do want to describe it as one conversation running into another. It's beautiful. It's beautifully shot. Almost every shot is a dolly shot; it must have been really hard to make. Also, everything was shot at the right time of day. It almost reminds me of the photography of Stephen Shore or Joel Sternfeld; there's this right time of day with this beautiful sideways light. Even the colors of the cars in the background are gorgeous. It was beautiful-looking, and the structure of it was like nothing I'd ever seen before.

The critics liked *Slacker*, too. *Entertainment Weekly's* Owen Glieberman gave the film an A–, writing, "*Slacker* has a marvelously low-key observational cool . . . the movie never loses its affectionate, shaggy-dog sense of America as a place in which people, by now, have almost too much freedom on their hands." Peter Travers of *Rolling Stone* wrote, "What Linklater has captured is a generation of bristling minds unable to turn their thoughts into action. Linklater has the gift of a true satirist: He can make laughter catch in the throat." Hal Hinson of the *Washington Post* knowingly observed, "Linklater's control seems all but invisible here. But this kind of stylistic lucidity can only be the result of determined calculation and planning. The kind of happy accidents he captures don't come about by accident."

After the film's release, the media started tossing around the word *slacker*, applying it to Generation X whenever possible. While the label was frequently misused, generally in ways that demeaned the generation, the film captures a vibe that is distinctively Gen X. Other films, such as *Singles*, try to capture the vibe but fail miserably because they lack *Slacker*'s authenticity. One gets the sense that Linklater is reluctant to accept the position of Generation X's cinematic torchbearer, but in many ways, he truly is that. "He's that Generation X voice," actress Parker Posey observed in 2011. "He really was a voice that a lot of people in my generation felt we could relate to." While the title of this book is *Generation Tarantino*—which Tarantino has earned—it could just as easily have been *Generation Linklater*.

One person who saw *Slacker* at Sundance was producer Jim Jacks. Jacks, along with Sean Daniel, had just established a new production company called Alphaville Films that had a distribution deal with Universal, and they were hunting for Alphaville's first film. Jacks was impressed with Linklater and believed he'd found just the director to make that film. Jacks and Daniel cut a $25,000 check to the young director to write a script for them, which Linklater used to pay his remaining debts from *Slacker*.

But what would the new picture be? Linklater later told journalist Marc Spitz, "I was doing interviews for *Slacker*, and the last question was always, 'What do you want to do next?' And in one interview, I said, 'I want to make this teenage rock 'n' roll spree.'" So that was the film he chose to make—*sort of*. His original concept for the project was that the entire film would take place inside a car with characters just driving around listening to ZZ Top's *Fandango*. The film's running time would be exactly the length of the album. Thankfully, that isn't the picture Linklater ended up making. The film became *Dazed and Confused*, named after a Led Zeppelin song of the same title, and follows several high school students on the last day of school in 1976. Linklater wrote the screenplay in a month. The screenplay contains some events based on his own experiences. Several characters have the surnames of people he'd gone to high school with. Years later, in 2004, three of his classmates—Bobby Wooderson, Andy Slater, and Richard Floyd—tried unsuccessfully to sue him, claiming characters in the film were based on them.

When Linklater and the producers presented the *Dazed and Confused* screenplay to Universal, they loved it. In fact, they loved it so much that they rushed it into production, moving it ahead of most of the films on their slate.

Casting director Don Phillips, who'd previously cast *Fast Times at Ridgemont High*, was hired to help Linklater cast. When the casting call went out, almost every young actor and actress in town tried out for it. Vince Vaughn, Ron Livingston, Elizabeth Berkley, Brendan Fraser, Mira Sorvino, Jon Favreau, Claire Danes, and Ashley Judd were among the recognizable performers who read for parts and didn't get them. One would-be star who auditioned was Renée Zellweger. The future Oscar winner didn't land the part she read for, but the producers still cast her in a blink-and-you'll-miss-it role without dialogue.

Some of the key performers include Jason London, Joey Lauren Adams, Milla Jovovich, Parker Posey, and Wiley Wiggins. Some of the smaller roles were filled by such actors as Cole Hauser, Nicky Katt, Ben Affleck, and Matthew McConaughey. Interestingly, McConaughey, a University of Texas student at the time, was cast after he approached the casting director in a bar.

Linklater began filming *Dazed and Confused* in July 1992 in Austin with a budget of $6 million and a seven-week schedule. Although the film would be a much bigger picture than *Slacker* had been, the director still brought several members of that crew with him. He later said that using much of the same crew allowed him to bring the "little *Slacker* punk spirit" to the bigger film.

Linklater's approach to helping the actors discover their characters was interesting. He made mixtapes of the music he thought each character would listen to. Some contained Joni Mitchell songs, and others had harder mixes with bands like Black Sabbath. Linklater instructed the actors to listen to and study the music. "My mixtapes? I always took umbrage with them," actor Adam Goldberg recalled in 2013. "I was a gigantic Neil Young fan at the time, and I was getting ELO and Foghat."

Linklater also allowed the actors improvisational leeway. In fact, actors were allowed to write their own dialogue and interpret or change their characters as they saw fit. Joey Lauren Adams recalled the director saying, "If you don't like your character, change it. Just know it when you get to Austin." Marissa Rabisi said that Linklater even told her that he wanted her character to have a love interest but didn't know who it should be. He then asked her which character she liked. "You're teenagers," Linklater told his cast. "Be what you are."

Some of the actors later said there was a party atmosphere during the shoot, with much of the cast and crew hanging out together after hours. "Everyone was just drinking and getting stoned the whole time," Goldberg recalled. Ben Affleck remembered "everybody was having sex with each other, except me." For the record, Linklater was not a fan of such rowdiness. "People are surprised how militant I am about that kind of work ethic," he told journalist Marc Spitz. "I set a tone: 'There's going to be no alcohol or drugs. This is set in the '70s, but it ain't gonna be a '70s movie where they're flying in the cocaine.'" But the director had obligations and couldn't babysit the actors after hours.

The shoot wasn't all fun and games; there was tension between Linklater's *Slacker* crew and the "professional" crew members the studio hired. Studio execs voiced concerns throughout the shoot. They didn't understand or appreciate the style in which Linklater was shooting the film. At one point, they demanded that Linklater fire his cameraman (which he did not do). The studio also wanted changes to the script, including the addition of nudity and more comedy. Author Alison Macor said, "Linklater had to negotiate a lot of studio politics in the making of *Dazed and Confused*—preproduction, time for rehearsal, wanting to hire an Austin-based crew. There was a lot he had to deal with when it came to the studio and what they expected from a comedy. They thought of big studio laughs, which they weren't seeing in the dailies coming through."

Music is a big part of *Dazed and Confused*'s feel and appeal. The movie contains wall-to-wall music, with approximately thirty songs appearing in the film, including "Sweet Emotion" by Aerosmith, "School's Out" by Alice Cooper, "Low Rider" by War, "Slow Ride" by Foghat, and "Show Me the Way" by Peter Frampton.

Editor Sandra Adair began editing the picture on the second day of shooting, but the producers wanted more cuts. The first cut was 165 minutes. By the time all was completed, the running time of *Dazed and Confused* had been trimmed to a lean, mean 102 minutes.

The film scored low at test screenings, so no one was sure what they had on their hands. Gramercy Pictures—a joint venture between Universal and Polygram—distributed the picture. Against Linklater's wishes, Gramercy advertised the picture as a stoner movie. When *Dazed and Confused* was released theatrically on September 24, 1993, its box office was relatively poor. It made

$8 million in its brief theatrical run (although its soundtrack would be a hit, selling more than two million copies).

While the general public had mostly missed *Dazed and Confused*, movie critics caught on quickly. *Rolling Stone*'s Peter Travers gave the film four out of four stars, writing, Linklater is a "sly and formidable talent, bringing an anthropologist's eye to his spectacularly funny celebration of the rites of stupidity. His shit-faced [version of] *American Graffiti* is the ultimate party movie—loud, crude, socially irresponsible and totally irresistible." Giving the film an A, *Entertainment Weekly*'s Owen Gleiberman wrote, "If Linklater captures the comic goofiness of the time, he also evokes its liberating spirit. The film finds its meaning in the subtle clash between the older, sadistic macho-jock ethos and the follow-your-impulse hedonism that was the lingering legacy of the '60s." *Time*'s Richard Corliss praised, "Linklater is surely no ham-fisted moralist, and his film has lots of attitude to shake a finger at. But it also has enough buoyant '70s music to shake anybody's tail feather, and a kind of easy jubilance of narrative and character."

In the decades since its release, *Dazed and Confused* has developed a substantial cult following. McConaughey's line "Alright, alright, alright," lifted from a Led Zeppelin tune, is a popular reference (and even became the title of Melissa Maerz's 2020 oral history of the film). *Entertainment Weekly*, a publication that seemingly exists to fashion lists, ranked *Dazed and Confused* high on its "Top 50 Cult Films," "Funniest Movies of the Past 25 Years," "50 Best High School Movies," and "Cult 25: The Essential Left-Field Movie Hits Since '83." Additionally, Quentin Tarantino included it on his own ten greatest films of all-time list for *Sight and Sound* and has repeatedly called it his favorite film of the '90s.

Linklater was one of the busiest, most prolific filmmakers of the 1990s, making no less than five features during the decade. So after *Dazed and Confused*, he wasted no time moving on to his next project, a sort-of love story titled *Before Sunrise* (*sort of* because the earliest draft of the film's script contained very little romance). This film is a departure from the Generation-X pictures he'd become known for. This time, he tackles more mature themes. *Before Sunrise* follows in the tradition of French New Wave director Éric Rohmer and is essentially a conversation between two people rather than something that is plot-driven and traditional.

The film's story was inspired by a romantic encounter Linklater had with a woman named Amy Lehrhaupt, whom he'd met inside a Philadelphia toy store in 1989. Like the characters in *Before Sunrise*, Linklater and Lehrhaupt had spent the night walking around the city, talking, and flirting. During that night, he'd told her that he would make a film about their experience one day in the future. What he was mostly interested in capturing was the *feeling* of the experience. "I wanted to make a film about a feeling that minimal," Linklater said in 2020. "Can you capture that: two people meeting and having a connection? In the romance genre, that's usually just the beginning and then the story picks up and they head to bed pretty quickly. I was in opposition to that. The first kiss is a big deal. It takes a long time to get there, as it often does in real life."

Instead of placing *Before Sunrise*'s story in Philadelphia, Linklater briefly considered both San Antonio and Berlin but decided on Vienna because he'd discovered that the city offered subsidy money for movies shot there. He tapped actress Kim Krizan, who appears in both *Slacker* and *Dazed and Confused*, to assist him with the script. "In my previous films, I felt the male view overwhelmed," Linklater told the *New York Times*. "So my absolute goal was to have a strong female perspective. Kim was the kind of person you'd run into and within thirty seconds you're talking about something substantial." Krizan agreed to cowrite, and the two collaborated for eleven days. The script that emerged was more of a template than anything else, but it was enough for him to pitch the film. One of the people who read this version was Castle Rock Entertainment cofounder Martin Shafer. Shafer liked the concept and had a particular fondness for the "naturalistic element" of *Before Sunrise*, so he greenlit the movie, inking Linklater to a two-picture deal.

"The movie's about crossing paths with someone who needs the same thing you do," Linklater told *Interview* magazine. "The question is, could this really be something more, something bigger, eternal?"

Linklater and Krizan had intentionally written the script without gender so that either part could be female or male. All that was clear and set in stone was that one of the characters was American and the other was European. Linklater and casting director Judy Henderson auditioned a bevy of actors from both coasts. Some of the actors who auditioned and didn't land the roles would eventually become stars, including Jennifer Aniston and Gwyneth Paltrow. In the end, the potential cast list was whittled down to two actors and two actresses: Ethan Hawke, Michael Vartan, Julie Delpy, and Sadie Frost. Linklater and Henderson liked all four of the performers but ultimately selected Hawke and Delpy because of their undeniable chemistry.

Linklater and the two actors traveled to Vienna to rehearse and revise the script before the shoot. The director allowed Hawke and Delpy to be creative collaborators, making suggestions and devising new lines of dialogue. Hawke later said that

Julie Delpy and Ethan Hawke in Richard Linklater's Before Sunrise. *Courtesy of Castle Rock Entertainment/Photofest © Castle Rock Entertainment*

only about one out of every seventeen scenes they wrote made it into the final script. In a 2019 interview with the *Guardian*, Delpy recalled, "The process was totally collaborative: all three of us had to agree on ideas for scenes. . . . If one of us hated something, it wouldn't make the film." Linklater later explained to journalist Simon Bland,

> It was only when I got with Julie and Ethan in three really intensive weeks of rehearsal and rewriting the script [that I figured out how to write it]. I was going to do what I did on my first two films: work with the actors and infuse them with the characters to such a degree that they wanted to contribute. Julie and Ethan were very giving, generous, and on-board for the challenge.

With only a few weeks to go until the film began shooting, Linklater received word that Amy Lehrhaupt, his inspiration for *Before Sunrise*, had been killed in a motorcycle accident. He later dedicated the film to her, with her name appearing in the film's closing credits.

The shoot began in summer 1994 and lasted twenty-five days, with a budget of $2.5 million. Linklater shot in chronological order. Although the finished film gave audiences the impression that the conversation was improvised, that wasn't the case. While much of the original conversations and gestures had been improvised in the rehearsals, that improvisation had led to the finished screenplay, which the actors stuck closely to. Delpy later said that remembering and reciting the amount of dialogue she had was "torture."

Most of the shoot took place at night, which in summertime in Vienna are hot. Delpy wasn't sleeping much, so she was miserable, but all three collaborators enjoyed their time together and became close friends. They faced several challenges when they shot the scene in which Jesse and Celine kiss for the first time. Delpy was shy and found it difficult to kiss Hawke, whom she saw as a friend. Making matters worse, the kiss took place on a Ferris wheel, and Delpy was deathly afraid of heights. Plus, Linklater wanted to shoot the scene at sunset, but the people who operated the Ferris wheel would only stop it every ten minutes, so he had to allow it to go around again and again. In the end, the first version of that scene had three different lighting levels and looked dreadful. Linklater convinced the Ferris wheel operators to allow them to return and shoot in the morning when the ride was stopped.

The final scene where Celine boards the train was also challenging. Because he was filming on an actual train operating on its normal schedule, Linklater had only one opportunity to get the shot. He later told journalist Ashley Spencer, "I was like, the train's going to leave here at 8:37:30. I'm going to say action at 8:20. She's going to get on a non-moving train. And then when she gets to her seat, the train is going to be moving. It was tense, but we rehearsed the hell out of it and it worked."

Before Sunrise premiered on January 19, 1995, at the Sundance Film Festival. At the time, Sundance founder Robert Redford hadn't introduced a film at the festival in several years, but he introduced *Before Sunrise* because he believed in it. When the picture was released theatrically a week later, critics mostly gushed. *New Yorker* critic Anthony Lane wrote, "The charm—the midsummer enchantment—never feels forced; it steals up and wins you." He also called the picture a "true romance." Janet Maslin of *The New York Times* wrote, "*Before Sunrise* is as uneven as any marathon conversation might be, combining colorful, disarming insights with periodic lulls. The filmmaker clearly wants things this way, with both of these young characters trying on ideas and attitudes as if they were new clothes." *Entertainment Weekly*'s Owen Gleiberman observed, "Small movies can be as daring as big ones, and Linklater, in his offhand way, is working without a net here. *Before Sunrise* may be the closest an American has come to the discursive talk gamesmanship of Eric Rohmer." *San Francisco Chronicle*'s Mick LaSalle wrote, "*Before Sunrise* is so simple, successful, and timeless that it's hard to imagine it not enduring."

The film earned $1.4 million during its first weekend. It went on to make $5.5 million at the US box office and another $17 million abroad. Its success overseas shouldn't have been a surprise, considering Linklater crafted a masterful film that had a European sensibility. "Ethan was the Gen X actor after *Reality Bites* and I was the Gen X director, and we didn't really deliver a Gen X film," Linklater reflected in 2020. "There's no pop-culture references, no hipster types. You pay the price at the time, but now I'm kind of proud you can go to Vienna and have a *Before Sunrise* walking tour right next to a *Third Man* walking tour."

Despite fairly low US box office numbers, *Before Sunrise* spawned two sequels, 2004's *Before Sunset* and 2013's *Before Midnight* (and the characters make a brief appearance in *Waking Life*). Linklater has consistently stated that he's open to the idea of a fourth *Before* film, but as of this writing, one has yet to materialize.

After *Before Sunrise*, Linklater decided to make a western crime picture called *The Newton Boys*. However, the studio where it was set up lost faith in the picture and pulled the plug, forcing Linklater to find a new studio to make the film. It was during this period that he decided to make *SubUrbia*, his first adaptation of another writer's work. The project marked a change for Linklater. *The Austin Chronicle*'s Marjorie Baumgarten wrote in 1997, "When future biographers write their surveys of the film career of Richard Linklater, . . . they will all cite *SubUrbia* as a transitional key. In terms of working methods and subject matter, [it] represents something of a departure from his previous work."

SubUrbia, about aimless twenty-somethings hanging around outside a convenience store, first found life as a stage play by Woborn, Massachusetts, playwright Eric Bogosian. Bogosian's friend Fred Zollo, a play director, suggested that he write something "based on the stories of all the people we had grown up with." Another friend, Robert Riley, curator at Boston's Institute of Contemporary Art, secured Bogosian grant money to finance its writing. Bogosian toyed with the idea for several years before finally writing "forty-five minutes of guys and girls eating pizza and shooting the breeze" while workshopping at the American Repertory Theater in Cambridge. Bogosian later wrote that the play contained "imaginary conversations between the people who are important in [his] life."

Before Linklater decided to adapt the play, several other filmmakers had already attempted to get an adaptation into production, but none were successful, and Bogosian saw them as wastes of his time. All of that changed when Linklater saw a stage production of *SubUrbia*. In a 1997 introduction to his published play, Bogosian wrote, "By the end of '95, the odds were that the film would never get made the way I had hoped. And then Rick [Linklater] invited me to Austin to perform one of my solos and we took a ride in his pickup."

The one-act, one-man play Bogosian performed in Austin was called *Wake Up and Smell the Coffee*. While the playwright was in town, Linklater conducted an interview with him for *The Austin Chronicle*. That's when Linklater took Bogosian for that ride, giving a tour of the local strip malls and subdivisions while discussing the play. He told Bogosian about his idea for the opening credits and asked if he thought they could produce an adaptation quickly, to which Bogosian replied, "Quick is good."

Linklater made the film for Castle Rock—the second film in a two-picture deal—with a $500,000 budget. The two writers collaborated closely on the script. "We adapted it together," Linklater told *MovieMaker*.

> I felt an incredible responsibility to the characters and to Eric's intentions, because I knew they were my intentions, too. I knew we were on the same page. I think it gets problematic when you're taking something and you're trying to make it something else. In the case of *SubUrbia*, I wanted to stay true to that. It still necessitated change, but it was a good collaboration as far as the writer-director thing goes. Neither of us wanted to let the other down.

Bogosian has stated that he views stage plays as being very different from film screenplays, so he was open to making necessary changes for the script. In their adaptation, the two writers trimmed or completely cut some of the dialogue and longer speeches. The duo also "ironed out some thematic/action aspects" near the end of the film. They made multiple attempts at changing the film's ending, but they ultimately stuck with Bogosian's original ending.

Although the material didn't originate with Linklater, he felt he could relate to the characters to a degree where the final film felt somewhat autobiographical, as much a reflection of him as it was Bogosian. "I'm all the characters," he explained. "I feel like I'm Jeff, but I'm Tim, I'm Pony, and in a strange way I'm Sooz. You end up as all your characters. They're all a reflection of you." In an *Austin Chronicle* interview, Linklater took this a step further, saying,

> Some of our favorite films are obviously not written by the person who directed it. And yet a *Taxi Driver*, or some Nicholas Ray movie, like *In a Lonely Place*, seems so personal or obsessive or whatever. When I saw *SubUrbia* on stage, I started having those feelings inside me. I saw it as a film, and I knew the characters, or I *was* the characters. It really dredged up all this stuff in me that never went away. So I was like, "Okay, this is how this works!" You find your way into something.

The cast of Linklater's film included Giovanni Ribisi, Nicky Katt, and Parker Posey, as well as two holdovers from the stage production, Steve Zahn and Samia Shoaib.

SubUrbia's first screening was at the New York Film Festival on October 11, 1996. It was then released theatrically the following February and earned a disappointing $656,747 at the box office.

While garnering nowhere near the praise *Before Sunrise* had, *SubUrbia*'s criticism was middling but mostly positive. *The New York Times*' Janet Maslin wrote, "Mr. Bogosian's venomously funny play, which he adapted himself for the screen, is given warmth and generosity by Mr. Linklater, whose elegantly fluid direction and great skill with actors are accentuated by the play's spareness." *Variety*'s Godfrey Cheshire observed, "Writer-director teamings seldom mesh as smoothly or suggest so many creative affinities as does the one at the heart of *Suburbia*. . . . The collaboration seems almost preordained, as both artists share a concern with youth's discontent and middle-class anomie, a passion for language and pop culture detritus, and intelligent, discursive comic sensibilities." Peter Stack of the *San*

Francisco Chronicle wrote, "Though some of *SubUrbia* has a feeling of forced angst, its message stings."

In the years that have passed since the film's release, numerous websites and publications have made their own rankings of Linklater's oeuvre. In pretty much all of them, *SubUrbia* ranks somewhere near the bottom. The problem isn't that it's a bad film; it's just one of Linklater's weaker pictures. While he and Bogosian shared a lot of the same ideas and feelings, the result of their collaboration isn't completely successful. It resonates, but it's not as effective as either man's solo works. *SubUrbia* isn't a bad film by any means. It's a testament to Linklater's consistency and talent that his "lesser" films are still qualitative.

After he'd read an article Claude Stanush had written for *Smithsonian* magazine in 1994 about a band of Uvalde, Texas, outlaws, Linklater recognized the potential for a film on the subject. It was one of gang's members in particular, Willis Newton, who'd caught his interest. "I immediately identified with him," Linklater would tell the *Los Angeles Times*. "I'm fascinated with him, because I see parts of myself in him. Someone who will manipulate everyone around him to get what he wants, and do it in a charming way. I mean, what's a film director?"

Although the four-man Newton Gang was relatively unknown outside the Lone Star State, their exploits were significant. The gang robbed a reported seventy-five banks and six trains from 1919 to 1924. It has been alleged that they stole more money than the Dalton Gang, the Wild Bunch, and the James-Younger Gang combined. Remarkably, the Newton Gang never killed a single person during their many robberies.

Stanush had also written an oral history and produced a documentary about the robbers, both titled *The Newton Boys: Portrait of an Outlaw Gang*. These would serve as bibles for his project. Because Stanush had already written his own unproduced script, Linklater decided that it would become the bones around which he would fashion a new script. Linklater tapped Clark Lee Walker, the husband of the film's producer, Anne Walker-McBay, to write the new script. Linklater sought to remain as close to the truth as possible; there would be no Hollywood make-up-your-own-story bullshit here.

Walker listened to audio tapes of interviews with the Newtons that Stanush had recorded in the 1970s. Listening to the bandits detail their own exploits, Walker felt inspired. However, Stanush's original screenplay wasn't very good. In Walker's estimation, the script had failed to capture the outlaws' personalities. Stanush, Walker, and Linklater produced close to thirty drafts of the *Newton Boys* script.

Castle Rock, where Linklater had a two-picture deal, decided they didn't want to make the film. In October 1995, 20th Century Fox chairman Bill Mechanic stepped up and signed on to finance the film. Mechanic liked the idea of the script and loved the idea of working with Linklater even more but believed the screenplay needed more work.

Linklater had envisioned Matthew McConaughey in the lead as Willis Newton. Mechanic appreciated McConaughey's turn in *Dazed and Confused* and thought this was a great idea. The only problem was that McConaughey was now a "name" actor. While McConaughey was considering the offer, both Viggo Mortensen and Sean Penn were considered, but Mechanic and the suits at Fox didn't like either of them for the film. Eventually, McConaughey signed on to play Willis.

Linklater had also envisioned Ethan Hawke in the film from the start. This, however, turned out to be problematic because Hawke wanted to play the role that McConaughey had been cast in. This led to Hawke signing on, then backing out, and then signing on again in a smaller role. Both screenwriter Walker and his wife, Walker-McBay, had issues with the casting; neither believed McConaughey was right for the role. They voiced their concerns, but the director had the final say.

The film went into preproduction in the spring of 1996. A few weeks later, Fox decided not to make *The Newton Boys*, so Linklater made *SubUrbia*. Eventually, Fox decided to move forward with *The Newton Boys*, but they had issues with the script. John Sayles, a gun-for-hire scribe who'd recently worked as a script doctor on *Apollo 13* and *Mimic*, was hired by the studio to tighten up the script.

The actors who played the robbers were McConaughey, Hawke, Skeet Ulrich, and Vincent D'Onofrio. Country singer-turned-actor Dwight Yoakam and Julianna Margulies were also cast in the film.

This time out, Linklater hired a new cinematographer. He'd worked with his friend and former roommate Lee Daniel on all his previous films, but on this one, he hired Peter James. James, Linklater believed, would be better suited to shooting a bigger-budget period film.

Then something unexpected happened. Steven Spielberg approached McConaughey, asking him to appear in *Amistad*. Recognizing what could be a once-in-a-lifetime opportunity to work with Spielberg, McConaughey agreed to do it. Unfortunately, the only way this could work was if Fox delayed filming of *The Newton Boys*, so the picture was delayed.

At the start of April 1997, the cast of *The Newton Boys* began a three-week rehearsal. On April 21, Linklater began filming. Each of the actors was ready, having studied their characters and prepared for their roles. They had listened to the recordings of the real-life outlaws, and Hawke had even visited a house where they once lived.

With a cast and crew of more than two hundred people, a $27 million budget, and more than eighty filming locations, *The Newton Boys* was significantly larger than anything Linklater had done previously. Despite the fact that the shoot was plagued by a series of rainstorms, hailstorms, and even a tornado, Linklater managed to complete the film on time and on budget. It may not have been his finest work (most qualitative rankings of his work list *The Newton Boys* at or near the bottom), but it was a solid, good-looking picture.

Despite the film testing well, the studio ordered that the picture be trimmed. Most troublesome to Linklater and editor Sandra Adair was the removal of an entire scene that would have let the audience get to know the characters. Additionally, Linklater and the studio had different ideas about marketing. Linklater once told me,

> The unfortunate thing with the studios is that they only know one audience, which is a teenage boy. So if you've made a film that appeals to older people—and *Newton Boys* played best

with audiences over fifty—it always has to be seen in terms of a mass-market film, and when you don't deliver that, they will try to sucker in that audience. That simultaneously alienates the real audience because the studio has made it look like this MTV piece of shit, and then it ultimately doesn't appeal to that audience that they're lying to. I had a very traditional old-fashioned movie poster that we had made, which looked like a movie poster from the '20s and '30s. An illustrated poster with all of the action and the characters' faces. It's beautiful. You see that and you say, "Oh my God! That's the movie!" And then Fox didn't want to use that because it was a western and old fashioned and all that kind of stuff. So we ended up with *Young Guns* meets *Mobsters* as their poster. What person with a brain in their head would wanna go see that? I wouldn't.

Audiences agreed; they didn't want to see it either. When *The Newton Boys* was released on March 27, 1998, it tanked, ultimately earning only $10 million.

Critics weren't in love with *The Newton Boys* either. The reviews weren't bad, but the consensus seemed to be that the picture was mediocre. Roger Ebert of the *Chicago Sun-Times* wrote, "It's not an enormous cast, and yet somehow the Newtons are hard to tell apart—not in appearance, but in personality." He went on to write that the "film as a whole seems drained of thrust and energy—especially compared to [Linklater's] earlier films." The *Washington Post*'s Desson Thomson observed, "There are no dramatic peaks and valleys in this story line, just a uniform, dramatic flatness." Owen Gleiberman of *Entertainment Weekly* wrote, "Scored to a disarmingly quaint array of fiddle-and-banjo tunes, *The Newton Boys* has so little in the way of blood or rancor that before long, you begin to notice that there's no real drama in it, either."

By the end of the decade, Linklater had made five very different films. This would be a trademark of his career. In the decades to come, he would make films as disparate as the $35 million mainstream comedy *School of Rock* and the more simplistic "art" film and *Before Sunrise* sequel *Before Sunset*, which he made back to back in the same year.

Linklater proved himself to be a director who could make anything and wasn't afraid to experiment. Some of his more notable experimental films are *Tape*, a chamber piece that unspools in real time; *Waking Life*, an existential rotoscoped "animated" movie; and *Boyhood*, which follows a boy's growth and maturation from age six to eighteen and was shot over a twelve-year span. Not only can Linklater craft highly qualitative films in seemingly any genre with any budget, but he can also make them look completely different from each other. He doesn't push himself to the forefront, drowning out the characters or the story by reminding the audience of his presence.

Linklater is a maverick. He made concessions early in his career, but those experiences taught him how to maneuver through the studio minefield. He told me,

> There are some people with a strong enough will who actually envision what the film they want to make is, and there are others who don't. My experience is that if your vision is strong enough—you really have a strong enough film in your head that you're trying to achieve—you'll do that no matter how many studio notes and bullshit that you get. You're the one making the film. What's your excuse? The day I say [mock whining voice], "Oh, the studio made me do this and this," I'll quit. That's just pretty weak. There's no excuse. You can't blame the system. The system is what it is and what it will always be.

Richard Linklater was the first important American filmmaker to emerge in the '90s. And he had a huge impact on the indie filmmakers who followed by leaving them a template for success.

2

John Singleton
A Director to Be Reckoned With

John Singleton, a self-described "child of *Star Wars*, *Raiders of the Lost Ark*, and *E.T.*," was the product of teen parents. His mother, Shelia Ward-Johnson, a sales exec for a pharmaceutical company, and his father, Danny, a mortgage broker, never wed. Both parents remained positive forces in his life, and he spent periods living with each of them. Most of his childhood he lived with his mother, but when he started acting out at age thirteen, he was sent to live with Danny in South Central Los Angeles. "My father said that he couldn't afford child support, but he could pay moral support," Singleton later recalled.

In a neighborhood where the sounds of gunfire and police helicopters flying overhead were routine, many of Singleton's friends and peers joined street gangs. Singleton was a precocious kid who generally had his nose buried in a book. Books on his early reading list included *The Autobiography of Malcolm X* and Anne Moody's *Coming of Age in Mississippi*. He was also an avid comic book reader and enjoyed reading superhero stories.

His dad was a film buff who idolized Japanese screen icon Toshiro Mifune, and he took his son to see films of every kind. As he continued watching and studying films, Singleton developed his own cinematic idols, but instead of actors, his heroes were filmmakers, including Steven Spielberg, Francis Ford Coppola, George Lucas, Orson Welles, François Truffaut, John Cassavetes, Martin Scorsese, and Akira Kurosawa. Humorously, he told author and friend Michael Dequina,

> I saw *Raiders of the Lost Ark* at the Chinese Theater when I was thirteen years old. I'm watching it, and I had to go to the bathroom. But I didn't want to leave, you know what I mean? So I took this cup—this lemonade cup—and I pissed in the cup. But when I reached down to piss in the cup, it was the first time I noticed I had pubic hair. While I was watching *Raiders of the Lost Ark* I realized I had my first pubic hair! I became a man watching *Raiders of the Lost Ark!*

In middle school and high school, Singleton saw Spielberg's path to success as a blueprint for creating his own. He remembered, "I got the equipment from the junior college; I started taking junior college classes while I was in high school in cinematography just so I could get the equipment, and I started shooting little films. By the time I was in the twelfth grade, I'd made four or five films." In 1986, Singleton graduated from the mostly white Blair High School in Pasadena.

With a goal no less than "making classic movies," he landed a spot in the University of Southern California School of Cinema-Television's Filmic Writing Program. The reason for his decision to attend USC was simple: George Lucas had gone to USC, and if USC had been good enough for Lucas, it would be good enough for him. Just before starting classes at USC, he met Spike Lee, who was then making a splash with *She's Gotta Have It*. Swelling with confidence, Singleton informed Lee that he was going to film school and would soon make a name for himself.

During his time at USC, Singleton wrote a number of scripts. He landed his first industry gig while still attending classes, working as a production assistant and security guard on the children's TV show *Pee-wee's Playhouse*. It was there that he met actor Laurence Fishburne. Despite having already appeared in four Francis Ford Coppola films and Spielberg's *The Color Purple*, Fishburne was slumming it on *Pee-wee's Playhouse* as Cowboy Curtis. Singleton told Fishburne that he was going to write a part in a movie specifically for him. In Los Angeles, wannabe filmmakers are as plentiful as palm trees, so Fishburne smiled and was friendly but figured the kid was full of shit.

Not long after that, Singleton landed a directing internship on *The Arsenio Hall Show*—a job he absolutely *hated*. When he was given menial tasks like getting coffee and making copies, Singleton reminded his bosses that he was a *directing* intern and not a production assistant, and he flat out refused. But working there was significant, just as working on *Pee-wee's Playhouse* had been. While at *The Arsenio Hall Show*, Singleton met rapper Ice Cube backstage. Ice Cube had just left N.W.A and was starting a solo career. Just as he'd done with Fishburne, Singleton told Ice Cube that he was going to cast him in a film. Ice Cube didn't believe he had the acting credentials or talent to star in a film, nor did he believe the young intern had the power to cast him in one, so Ice Cube dismissed the college kid as being just another wannabe filmmaker.

As Singleton made his way through USC's Filmic Writing Program, program director Margaret Mehring assessed,

> John has really blossomed into a writer, a filmmaker, and a person. It is possible that he will receive the [Jack] Nicholson scholarship next year. I hope so. He is very much alive, eager, and so full of hope and promise. He recognized the need to learn screenwriting in order to do what he wants to do in production and has done so. I think that John will make some history, not just for black films but for films per se.

Shortly after that, as Mehring predicted, Singleton was awarded the Jack Nicholson Writing Award for a script titled *Twilight Time*.

In 1989, Singleton was assigned to write a screenplay as his thesis for graduation. He found the inspiration and the title of his script while listening to Eazy-E's song "Boyz n the Hood." At the time, Eazy-E and N.W.A were discussing life and death in impoverished Black neighborhoods in a way no one had done before. He didn't own a computer, so he wrote the script in the USC computer lab. As he wrote, he would read the dialogue aloud so he could hear its flow. Surrounded by straitlaced students working on their theses and dissertations, Singleton, by his own admission, was loud and profane. When someone asked him to be quiet, Singleton erupted, "Shut the fuck up! Don't you know I'm writing a classic movie right here? Get out my face! Mind your own damn business!"

Singleton believed he could do the same thing in a screenplay that Eazy-E was doing with his music. "The film schools always say, 'Write what you know,'" Singleton said. "And what do I know? I know South Central Los Angeles." While the screenplay wasn't autobiographical in a literal sense, many scenes and elements were based on situations he'd lived through, witnessed, or heard about. Additionally, characters were modeled after friends and people Singleton had encountered in his neighborhood. Perhaps the most notable character modeled after someone Singleton knew was Furious Styles, who was based on his father. Like Singleton, who credited his father with "whipping him into shape" by giving him responsibilities that included mowing the yard, taking out the trash, and washing dishes, *Boyz n the Hood*'s protagonist is sent to live with his father.

Years later, after the script became a film, Singleton explained his reasons for writing the script. First and foremost, he'd wanted to tell a "good story" about the Black community "because in the last seventy-five years of American cinema, we've been dogged out." He'd also wanted to examine the impact that parental love and support can have on children's lives. He recalled,

> I did the film to show the difference between what a responsible open-minded black man would do in raising his son, so I can contrast that to the way his son's two friends are being raised just by their mother. What we show in this film—there's a mother in the film, who raises her two sons. One, she overly-loves, and he becomes irresponsible and a teenage father. The other one she doesn't love enough, and he becomes a gangster.

In a 1991 interview with the *Los Angeles Times*'s Patrick Goldstein, Singleton credited the support of his parents for fostering the faith in himself to set high goals and believe he could achieve them. Many of his peers didn't have that. "I've heard the copters all my life," Singleton said.

It's an incredible kind of psychological violence. It makes you not think in terms of the future, because who knows if you'll be around. So you say, "Not next year. Not next week. I'm going to get mine now." The only reason I ever thought about the future was because my Moms and my Pops made me think about it. I didn't get involved with gangs, like some of my friends. If I'd joined a gang, my Pops would've kicked my ass.

Singleton completed the *Boyz n the Hood* script in three weeks. According to the writer/director, he told his instructor Viki King, author of *How to Write a Movie in 21 Days*, that he didn't have time to attend classes and would just write his script and turn it in. He later admitted that he'd enjoyed "scaring the white people" during this period of his life, so he'd laid on the tough-guy act pretty thick for the teacher, saying, "Here's my screenplay, boom! I want an A." As cocky and devil-may-care as Singleton may have been to his instructor, it worked. King recognized his talents as a writer, and she knew that *Boyz n the Hood* was special, so she awarded him the A he'd asked for. Singleton then won the Jack Nicholson Writing Award for the second straight year. Then, at the behest of Paul Lucy, one of his instructors, he landed a spot in the school's graduate program "by the skin of [his] teeth." At that point, Singleton planned to continue his studies and make short films. However, fate would take a hand, and as the best-laid plans of mice and screenwriters often do, his plans changed.

Around this time, Creative Artists Agency (CAA) signed Singleton. He also landed another internship, this time at Columbia Pictures. His job was to read through slush piles of unproduced scripts and assess them. While working there, he told studio exec Stephanie Allain that he'd penned a few scripts himself. When Allain asked to read his work, he handed her *Boyz n the Hood*. Like everyone else who'd read it, she immediately recognized how unique and qualitative it was. She then showed the script to her boss, Frank Price, who also liked what he read. Price scheduled a meeting with Singleton and found himself just as impressed by the writer's cockiness as he was with his script. Price told him that the last young writer he'd met with such a high level of confidence had been Singleton's hero, Steven Spielberg. Columbia then inked Singleton to a three-picture deal.

Singleton fought to direct *Boyz n the Hood* so he could protect his vision. But Price wasn't sold on the idea. However, when Price saw how easily Singleton worked with the actors who were brought in for casting sessions, he reconsidered and hired him to direct. At the time, Singleton had only two short films under his belt.

One of Singleton's first decisions as director was casting Ice Cube, whom he'd envisioned for the role of Dough Boy from the very start. Singleton had promised to cast him one day, and now, years later and armed with a Columbia Pictures deal, Singleton approached him again. The third time was the charm, and Ice Cube agreed to appear in the film. Singleton and the rapper found that they had great chemistry, and the director compared their collaborative partnership to that of legendary director Akira Kurosawa and his go-to star Toshiro Mifune.

Ice Cube (O'Shea Jackson) in a publicity still for John Singleton's *Boyz n the Hood*. Courtesy of Columbia Pictures/Photofest © Columbia Pictures

Singleton's second major casting choice was Laurence Fishburne to play the strong, protective father. Singleton had promised Fishburne that he'd write a part for him, and now, three years later, he delivered on his promise.

Singleton shot *Boyz n the Hood* in South Central during the winter of 1990. The budget for the six-week shoot was $5.7 million. The director shot the picture in sequence, leading him to later observe that the film's camerawork gets better as the film progresses. Singleton later admitted that he'd known very little about film directing prior to the shoot, having had very little experience. As a result, he was forced to learn the craft on his feet. According to Fishburne, the cast trusted Singleton and his vision and tried to form a "protective net around him."

The crew for *Boyz n the Hood* was (in Singleton's estimation) 90 percent Black. Where many Black film personalities had previously stated they didn't have the power to hire that many minority crew members, Singleton pulled it off. But how? In a 1991 interview with Karen Grigsby Bates, he said, "I didn't ask anybody if I could. I just did it." Another point of interest: Singleton later revealed that Columbia Pictures fired two directors from other productions while he was making *Boyz n the Hood*. Singleton, however, was unmoved; in an industry where there were so few Black filmmakers that interviewers at Cannes mistook him for Spike Lee, Singleton knew there was no one else the studio could hire who could direct the picture with an authentic point of view.

Boyz n the Hood debuted at the Cannes Film Festival, where it received a twenty-minute standing ovation. The picture was released theatrically on July 2, 1991, to rave reviews. Roger Ebert of the *Chicago Sun-Times* praised that it was "not simply brilliant, but an American film of enormous relevance." Duane Byrge of *The Hollywood Reporter* wrote,

> The performances are knockdown terrific, led by [Cuba] Gooding as the smart and impressionable Tre and [Laurence] Fishburne as his steely, prideful father. [Morris] Chestnut, as the ball-toting Ricky, and Ice Cube, as the porch-sitting laggard, are similar standouts, while Angela Bassett conveys the

love and anguish of a woman who gives up her child for the betterment of both.

On an episode of *Siskel and Ebert*, Gene Siskel called *Boyz n the Hood* an "exciting first film from a director to be reckoned with." He went on to assess the picture as being one of the finest of the year and compared it to Martin Scorsese's *Mean Streets* before observing, "This director, John Singleton, has a seemingly effortless style that is based more on the content of his characters than any particularly flashy camera moves. . . . I think a major new director has arrived."

Critics fell over themselves to sing the praises of both the film and its director. Unfortunately, the film's audience proved to be problematic. Like *The Wanderers*, *The Warriors*, and *New Jack City* before it—all films focusing, at least marginally, on street gangs—gang members came to screenings in twelve states and caused a ruckus. Two people were left dead, and another thirty were injured. Some theaters canceled screenings, while others implemented such security precautions as guards and metal detectors. Rather than pull the film from release, Columbia offered to provide additional security to any theater that needed it.

These incidents got a lot of coverage and gave the film a bad reputation. Hiding behind print and attempting to disguise the obvious racism in such a question, news outlets began to question whether there was something about *Boyz n the Hood* or even Black cinema itself that had triggered the violence. But Singleton's film didn't condone violence; it carried a message of hope and a plea for peace. *Austin Chronicle* critic Mark Savlov noted, "Singleton's explosive vision ends with the message 'increase the peace.' Judging from the opening-night body count, though, nobody seems to be listening." Despite these incidents, *Boyz n the Hood* made $10 million during its opening weekend. (It earned approximately $60 million in its full theatrical run.)

No artist should be asked to defend their art. Nevertheless, Columbia pressured Singleton to hold a press conference to reiterate that neither he nor his film endorsed violence. Singleton did lots of press, and he tried to explain to reporters that, although his artistic medium was different, *Boyz n the Hood* was discussing the same realities of life in the hood as the stories told by hardcore rappers like Ice Cube. Singleton eventually would be labeled the "first director of the hip-hop generation" because of his use of hip-hop music in his films, his casting rappers as actors, and his unflinching examinations of impoverished Black communities and the hardships the people within them endured.

Despite the negative press, *Boyz n the Hood* received nominations from a wide variety of festivals and governing bodies, including Best Director and Best Original Screenplay nominations for Singleton at the 1992 Academy Awards. He failed to take home either award, but his Best Director nomination was significant because it made him the first African American filmmaker, as well as the youngest filmmaker ever (at twenty-four), to be nominated in that category.

Because he'd been accused of making a misogynistic film with *Boyz n the Hood*, Singleton promised his next picture would focus on strong women. In the beginning, he was unsure what exactly its story would be, going so far as to predict it would be "like *Apocalypse Now* with women." Singleton wrote the script for his sophomore film, *Poetic Justice*, in less than two weeks. He later said he found his inspiration in women who had lost their lovers to gang violence. With his *Boyz* follow-up, Singleton had three primary goals: He wanted to get a second picture out quickly so he could solidify his reputation as a viable filmmaker; he wanted to make a picture that was at least moderately successful; and he wanted to show a lighter, more positive side of South Central.

True to his word, *Poetic Justice* focuses on a strong female survivor named Justice, who cuts hair, writes poetry, and falls in love with an unlikely partner. A character study, the film is more of a love story than an *Apocalypse Now*. Actresses who read for the part included Lisa Bonet, Robin Givens, and Jada Pinkett. Singleton, however, insisted he'd written the part specifically for Janet Jackson, whom he'd met on the Sony lot. Singleton wanted her in the role because he'd recognized a toughness within her that had formed as the result of tragedies and hardships. "When singers want to cross over into something else like acting, they get a part as a singer," Singleton told *Premiere* in 1993. "That shit is easy. But I came at [Jackson] with another vibe. I said, 'I want you to be someone else. I want it so you can be considered a serious actress.'" The person he wanted her to become was a "regular sister." To help her, he gave her a strict three-week daily diet consisting solely of waffles to put a little weight on her. (Jackson gained ten pounds for the role.) Jackson also cut hair in a salon for a day. Additionally, she hung out with (and studied) four women who were similar to Justice. Singleton instructed her to watch Vittorio de Sica's *Two Women* and Martin Scorsese's *Raging Bull*, among others.

Singleton had written the part of Justice's lover, Lucky, for Ice Cube. However, the rapper turned it down, saying he worried that appearing in a love story could damage his image, so Singleton was forced to search for a replacement. He'd previously met rapper Tupac Shakur at a party thrown for Queen Latifah. As he considered actors who might be right for the role, Singleton watched *Juice*. He was so impressed by Shakur's performance that he telephoned him, telling him he wanted to cast him in *Poetic Justice*. Shakur had studied acting in high school, and Singleton thought he possessed a natural charisma that translated well on screen. In fact, Singleton went so far as to advise Shakur to give up music to pursue acting full time. Shakur was, of course, resistant to this, telling him, "Music is my life."

Shakur was interested in making *Poetic Justice* from the get-go, but the prospect of shooting a love scene with Janet Jackson was the cherry on top for him; he enthusiastically signed on to make the picture. Singleton and Shakur became close comrades, and Singleton told Shakur that he wanted him to be the Robert De Niro to his Martin Scorsese. Allen Hughes, who codirected *Menace II Society* with his brother Albert, remembers Shakur telling him, "Me and John Singleton have made a pact that I'm only starring in films directed by him—just like De Niro and Scorsese." Additionally, Singleton and Shakur agreed to teach one another their respective crafts; the rapper would teach the director how to write songs, and in exchange, the director would teach the rapper how to direct motion pictures.

According to Singleton, Columbia Pictures initially had doubts about Shakur, but those doubts dissipated when they saw a screen test showcasing Jackson and Shakur's undeniable chemistry. Once the film was cast and the locations secured, it was time for Singleton's return to the director's chair. Singleton had a $13.5 million budget to work with, and filming began at the end of April 1992, just as the verdict was handed down in the Rodney King trial and rioters were filling the streets. (*Poetic Justice* earned the distinction of being the only film shot in Los Angeles that didn't shut down during the riot.)

As confident as Singleton had been on *Boyz*, he was even more confident now, having learned a great deal more about his craft. Also, having already made a film, there was less pressure, so he could relax a little. This time out, he found himself better able to enjoy the creative experience. He tried to experiment more with the characters, the direction, and the editing so he could become a better director. He allowed the actors more leeway in terms of improvisation. He didn't let them run wild, but he was open to implementing new ideas and things he heard or observed on set.

There has long been a rumor that Jackson refused to kiss Shakur until he agreed to take a test proving he didn't have AIDS. According to Singleton, this rumor was just that—*a rumor*. The story had originated as a joke by the director himself, telling Shakur he wasn't sure he should allow him to kiss his lead.

Interestingly, the poetry that Jackson's character writes and reads in the film was written by Maya Angelou. Singleton attempted to write the poetry first but then decided to approach Angelou, who allowed him to use her poetry. Angelou also makes a cameo appearance in the film. However, the iconic poet was less than enthused about the copious curse words that appear in the film. Singleton would joke that Angelou scolded him like he was her child.

Poetic Justice opened on July 23, 1993. Singleton's second picture was not received by critics as warmly as *Boyz n the Hood* had been. While the majority of reviewers complained about Singleton's script and direction (while lauding the performances

John Singleton and poet Maya Angelou on the set of Poetic Justice. *Courtesy of Columbia Pictures/Photofest © Columbia Pictures*

of Jackson and Shakur), *Chicago Sun-Times* critic Roger Ebert was the one major critic who seemed to really *get* the film, writing,

> *Boyz n the Hood* was one of the most powerful and influential films of its time, in 1991. *Poetic Justice* is not its equal, but does not aspire to be; it is a softer, gentler film, more of a romance than a commentary on social conditions. . . . *Poetic Justice* unwinds like a road picture from the early 1970s, in which the characters are introduced and then set off on a trip that becomes a journey of discovery. By the end of the film, Justice will have learned to trust and love again, and Shakur will have learned how to listen to a woman. And all of the characters—who in one way or another lack families—will begin to get a feeling for the larger African-American family to which they belong.

Audiences appreciated the film more than the critics (audiences surveyed by CinemaScore rated the film a B+), and the picture earned a respectable $27.5 million at the box office.

Singleton later admitted to having "problems with the film." He believed he'd written the script too quickly and wished he'd spent more time on it. However, he assessed that while it wasn't a "great" film, it had "heart." He was also proud of himself for making something that was "thoughtful in a sense, but . . . still street." He later admitted that, despite setting out to make a women's film, he wound up making a "film about women" that was "told from a man's perspective." But the director was proud enough of the picture that he named his first child Justice Maya Singleton.

With his third outing, *Higher Learning*, Singleton wanted to try something different. The film was an idea he'd come up with while he was in film school. It required some changes and retooling, but at its heart, it was essentially the same project. This film wouldn't be a South Central hood picture, but Singleton would still draw from his own experiences. This story would be about three very different college freshmen who encounter their new college through the groups they become a part of. Singleton would later tell students at the American Film Institute that he'd wanted to look at the repression that America has about discussing different kinds of conflicts, including racial, sexual, and economic. He went on to say that "it was a hard movie to get made because I'm dealing with some different kinds of issues here, and to a person at a studio, they see a script and it has the brothers, with their presence on campus, it has a lesbian relationship, and skinheads and all this stuff, and it's like, this is not commercial."

One outlandish request by Columbia was that kiddie hip-hop duo Kris Kross appear in the film. According to Singleton, the studio offered to pay him $1 million if he agreed to shoehorn them into the movie. Singleton put his foot down; there was no place in *Higher Learning* for the prepubescent rappers, and Singleton refused to compromise his artistic vision.

According to the director, he faced far more studio interference on *Higher Learning* than he had on his two previous films. Singleton said that Columbia execs urged him to cut or change literally every scene in the film. Singleton told DJ Sway, "I had to get street with them. 'Y'all motherfuckers trying to mess up my movie,' you know? 'I'm trying to make you some money, and you're trying to fuck my shit up!'" Singleton called his agent at CAA and told him to insist that Columbia leave him alone. "I would act like if they came to my cutting room I'd have a gun," the director said. "I had to act like that just to preserve my vision."

For *Higher Learning*, Singleton had planned to cast Tupac Shakur in the lead role (Malik), but Shakur was embroiled in a legal battle. The studio became worried about Shakur's involvement, and Singleton needed to move forward with the production. He then cast Omar Epps. For the role of Professor Phipps, the writer/director had envisioned Sidney Poitier. Poitier was attached for a while but eventually dropped out of the picture. Samuel L. Jackson was Singleton's second choice, but that didn't work out. Singleton then cast Laurence Fishburne, who'd given him a remarkable performance in *Boyz n the Hood*. At one point, a young Leonardo Di Caprio was attached to play the role of Remy, but that didn't work out. Singleton then decided to switch Michael Rappaport, whom he'd cast to play the role of Scott Moss (which he recast with Cole Hauser), into the role of Remy.

Singleton was living with model Tyra Banks at the time. Seeing cinematic potential in her, he cast Banks in the role of Deja. If this hadn't worked out, he was prepared to cast Vivica A. Fox. He later explained that his primary goal with Banks had been to make her appear credible as an actress, which he believed he did. The first scene he shot with her was a love scene between her character and Epps's. Singleton later admitted that he'd been uncomfortable having to watch Epps simulating intimacy with Banks, but as the director, he couldn't drop his guard and appear as anything less than professional. However, Banks became angry because Singleton didn't act jealous, so she and the director got into a heated argument in her trailer.

Singleton was much more at ease on the set than he had been on previous sets. While he wasn't going to let any bullshit slide—his actors had better be prepared and do what he told them to do—he found himself starting to have a good time. Filmmaking was work, yes, and he took it seriously, but it was becoming something he enjoyed doing a little more with each film.

He had wanted to shoot *Higher Learning* on the USC campus, but to his disappointment, the school wouldn't give him permission to film there. He was forced to shoot the picture at UCLA, with interiors shot on the Sony lot. Despite his inability to shoot on the campus of his own college, the film would be quite personal. Not only were many aspects of the story based on Singleton's own experiences, and not only had he cast his girlfriend in a prominent role, but he also gave his mother, Shelia Ward, a cameo.

Higher Learning was released January 11, 1995, and earned more than $38 million at the box office. Reviews were mixed. *Chicago Sun-Times* writer Roger Ebert remained a strong advocate of his work. In his three-star review of the film, Ebert wrote of Singleton, "He sees with a clear eye and a strong will, and is not persuaded by fashionable ideologies. His movies are thought-provoking because he uses familiar kinds of characters and then asks hard questions about them." *Time Out* similarly observed, "A stylish, intelligent filmmaker, Singleton interweaves the threads of his demographic tapestry with assurance, passion and a welcome awareness of the complexities of the college community's contradictory impulses towards integration and separatism." The contemporary criticisms of the film were mostly leveled at the script; reviewers believed the characters were too one-dimensional and that Singleton's messaging was heavy-handed.

While *Higher Learning*'s reception was mixed from the beginning, its overall aggregate scoring has dropped in the decades since its release. (Its Rotten Tomatoes score is just south of fifty, and its Metacritic score is just a little higher.) This likely has to do with the film's prophetic portrayal of the angry White school shooter. (This was four years before the Columbine shooting kicked off that depressing trend.) In the years since Columbine, society has frowned upon books, films, and television shows depicting school shootings, despite the fact that such shootings are (sadly) a common occurrence in America. There has also been a trend in recent years to reevaluate previously existing works according to current standards. Attitudes and perceptions regarding the depictions of LGBTQ characters have also changed, as have attitudes about straight filmmakers like Singleton crafting films about the experiences of LGBTQ characters.

Singleton later reflected, "If you look at *Higher Learning*, which I was twenty-five years old making it, [it's] chock full of everything that would concern young people: lesbianism and racism and everything I could put in that movie. It was a great movie. A fun movie to do. But you could never get that movie made now. Never. The guy shoots everybody, know what I mean?" But again, if such a film could never be made in today's climate, it's important to remember that studios were afraid to make films like *Higher Learning* even then. Singleton, being the maverick that he was, managed to get the damned thing made anyway.

Singleton's next picture, *Rosewood*, is drastically different from his previous films. For starters, it is a period piece based on a true story. Second, it is the first of his projects that did not originate with him and wasn't written by him. The story of *Rosewood* starts with producer Jon Peters, whose credits include such iconic titles as *A Star Is Born* (both the 1976 and 2018 incarnations), *Caddyshack*, *The Color Purple*, *Rain Man*, *Batman*, and *Ali*. When Peters watched an episode of *60 Minutes* about the Rosewood massacre, he knew at once that the tragic story had the ingredients for a good movie, so he optioned the film rights.

The Rosewood massacre occurred in a small Florida town (gone today) called Rosewood on New Year's Day in 1923. Rosewood's residents were almost entirely Black. The trouble started when a White woman named Fannie Taylor, who lived in the nearby town of Sumner, claimed she'd been assaulted by a Black man. Soon, a lynch mob of angry White men congregated and headed to Rosewood, hell-bent on carrying out vigilante justice. The mob eventually descended on the home of an elderly woman named Sarah Carrier. Carrier's son Sylvester and a number of her grandchildren who'd come to visit were with her inside the house. When the lynch mob shot Sarah Carrier in the head, killing her, Sylvester returned fire. This retaliation angered the White men, who left and then returned with *hundreds* of men. The group set fire to the town and began shooting every Black person they encountered.

While state officials at the time claimed there were only 2 to 6 deaths, eyewitness accounts indicate that there were somewhere between 40 and 150 people murdered. Like many racial atrocities in America's history, the Rosewood story was covered up. Finally, in the early 1980s, a *St. Petersburg Times* reporter named Gary Moore dug up the story and brought it to national attention. A decade later, the Florida legislature paid out $2.1 million in reparations to the survivors and the victims' descendants.

Once Peters had secured the rights to the material, he hired a White former theater director named Greg Poirier to write the script. The specifics behind Poirier's selection and hiring are vague. "The most powerful thing the movie has going for it is that it's true," Poirer later observed. "So it was really important to stick as closely as possible to the real thing, so people [don't say], 'Oh, they made a lot of it up. It wasn't that bad.'"

Once Poirier had written the script and the project was set up at Warner Bros., Peters started looking for a director. Because Singleton was Black and somewhat of a hot commodity, Peters offered him the job. Singleton wanted to shed the label he'd been given as a hood director, so he was intrigued, but he wasn't quite sold. The project was outside his comfort zone, and as he later admitted, he'd long had contempt for the South. However, meeting the real-life survivors and hearing their stories convinced him to sign on.

Early in the production, Singleton and the studio butted heads over the budget. He was so incensed by this that he almost quit. But when Minnie Lee Langley, one of the survivors he'd spoken to, passed away, he was reminded of the importance of the project. Singleton and Warner Bros. then settled on a $28 million budget, the highest Singleton had worked with at the time.

Singleton assessed *Rosewood* as being his "first adult movie." The way he saw it, his first three films had been coming-of-age and coming-of-consciousness movies. But this project reflected his growth as both a man and a filmmaker.

While he would say his biggest cinematic inspiration on the picture was *Schindler's List* (so much so that he hired *Schindler's*

List composer John Williams to score his film), Singleton was trying to make a completely different kind of film than Spielberg had made. "What I'm bringing to this film is a youthful perspective," he explained.

> If I was fifteen or twenty years older, *Rosewood* would probably look more like a documentary. I'm doing this for people in my age range and the audience I've had. The older people, maybe they'll come, maybe they won't. I'm twenty-eight. I want people my age to come. I want this to be a date movie. I've got romance, I've got action, I'm counting off the times that one of my lead characters gets his and kills a couple of crackers. 'Cause I know the brothers on the street ain't gonna sit through a whole movie where there's a whole bunch of black people getting killed and no black folks are fighting back, you know what I mean?

A set resembling Rosewood was built about two hours away from the location of the massacre, and the shoot was logistically complicated. Crew members had to deal with a wide variety of bugs and creepy crawlies. In fact, one AD was sent to the hospital after he was bitten by a rattlesnake.

When the shoot was over, no one knew what to expect for *Rosewood*'s box office. Could this bleak story make money? Would *Rosewood*, as Singleton had suggested, be seen as a "date movie"? One thing the film had working against it was its brutality. Even though much of the heart-wrenching violence in the film takes place off-screen, viewers are still left with the feeling that they've watched something far more violent than it actually is. Singleton said, "At least the violence I'm shooting has a point. Only a few people in this movie get killed on screen, but it's real. It's emotional violence."

Rosewood was released to theaters on February 21, 1997. Although it earned a disappointing $13 million at the box office, it became Singleton's best-reviewed film since *Boyz n the Hood*. Stanley Crouch of *The New York Times* pointed at the film as being the director's finest work, going on to assert that "never in the history of American film had Southern racist hysteria been shown so clearly. Color, class, and sex were woven together on a level that Faulkner would have appreciated." *Entertainment Weekly*'s Owen Gleiberman wrote, "Singleton brings the images and underlying psychological truths of American racial violence to the screen with a brute dramatic force that few directors have matched." *Chicago Sun-Times* critic Roger Ebert gave the film three and a half out of four stars, observing, "*Rosewood* represents an important step in [Singleton's] growth; it's a period picture painted on a large canvas, and he handles his big cast effortlessly, establishing a good sense of community life." Ebert continued, "If the movie were simply the story of this event, it would be no more than a sad record. What makes it more is the way it shows how racism breeds and feeds, and is taught by father to son."

Singleton was an interesting filmmaker. He was a studio-type filmmaker in form, but he brought a new perspective and a new subject to Hollywood. In the first decade of his career, Singleton's cinematic output was inconsistent; it was intermittently great. None of his films were bad, but none came close to reaching the level of quality he'd achieved with *Boyz n the Hood*. While the general consensus is that *Poetic Justice* is the lesser of Singleton's 1990s projects, it is undeniably creative, unique, and driven by Singleton's strong, singular vision. While *Rosewood* is somewhat of a return to form, it failed to make an impression at the box office, making Singleton's road forward a bit more difficult. But for a while in the '90s—when he was given the freedom to be such—Singleton was a creative powerhouse, and his success helped fuel a short-lived period of thriving Black Hollywood filmmaking. Not only that, but *Boyz n the Hood* inspired a brief cycle of imitative hood films.

Singleton's post-'90s filmography kicked off with *Baby Boy* and *Shaft* but then took a hard left turn. Why did he stop making the personal films about the Black experience he had become known for? In 2014, he told an audience at Loyola Marymount University that the studios were

> refusing to let African-Americans direct black-themed films. They ain't letting black people tell the stories. They want black people to be what they want them to be. And nobody is

man enough to go and say that. They want black people to be who they want them to be, as opposed to what they are. The black films now—so-called black films now—they're great. But they're just products. They're not moving the bar forward creatively.

This serves as a good explanation for why he made the far less personal commercial pictures *2 Fast 2 Furious*, *Four Brothers*, and *Abduction*. Singleton's greatest post-'90s cinematic contribution was probably *Hustle and Flow*, which he produced.

Singleton's life was cut short when he died at fifty-one years old on May 6, 2019, from complications following a stroke. American cinema and the world in general are poorer for having lost him.

3

Quentin Tarantino

The Enfant Terrible of American Cinema

Everyone knows that Quentin Tarantino worked at a Manhattan Beach video store called Video Archives in the 1980s. After exploding onto the scene in the '90s, Tarantino became such a mythic figure that even the video store became a part of the lore. Tarantino isn't the only filmmaker to emerge during that decade and find success without having learned his craft in film school, but his massive success made him the poster child for an entire movement of filmmakers who skipped film school and entered the film industry in a nontraditional manner.

The oft-told legend says that Tarantino learned how to make films from working at the video store, where he watched countless movies. There's a degree of truth to that, yes, but there's more to the story. Young Tarantino wasn't just *watching* movies; he was also *making* them. He worked on several no-budget movies with his friends, including a never-completed sci-fi action film directed by one of his pals called *Warzone*. During this period, Tarantino went to work directing his own film, *My Best Friend's Birthday*. He cowrote the 16 mm black-and-white picture with his friend Craig Hamann and financed it with the paychecks from his minimum-wage job (along with a good-sized loan from his mother). Perhaps the most interesting thing about *My Best Friend's Birthday* (considering the kinds of projects Tarantino would become known for) is that it was a screwball comedy. Also of note, three future filmmakers—Tarantino, Hamann, and Roger Avary—worked on it. For many years, there was a story about the film being destroyed in a lab fire that was perpetuated by Tarantino himself. The reality is less interesting: He looked at the footage he'd shot and found it to be far more amateurish than he'd have liked, so he discontinued the project.

In the early '90s, Tarantino worked on a script called *The Open Road* that told the story of a couple who goes on the road and embarks on a killing spree. During this road trip, Mickey, the male protagonist, is writing his own script about a different criminal couple on the road. When the screenplay became too large and unwieldy, Tarantino separated the story and the story-within-a-story into separate scripts that he titled *True Romance* and *Natural Born Killers*. Both screenplays were optioned, and both were directed by established filmmakers (*True Romance* was made by Tony Scott, and *Natural Born Killers* was directed by Oliver Stone). The sales of these scripts established Tarantino in the film industry before he'd even directed his first film.

The story of Tarantino's first completed film as director began with an introduction by his friend Scott Spiegel, who'd cowritten the Clint Eastwood vehicle *The Rookie,* to an up-and-coming producer named Lawrence Bender. The producer had helped Spiegel get his own directorial debut, *Intruder*, made. Bender had read *True Romance*, and he asked Tarantino what else he'd written. The would-be filmmaker then spun him a heist story about robbers holed up in a warehouse who end up turning on each other. Bender liked the concept, so Tarantino went to work on the script, which he titled *Reservoir Dogs*, completing it in three weeks. He found inspiration in several preexisting films, including *Asphalt Jungle*, *The Killing*, and most notably the Ringo Lam Hong Kong action film *City on Fire*. Tarantino showed the finished script to Bender, who loved it. Bender asked Tarantino to give him one year to find financing, and Tarantino agreed. However, Bender soon discovered that not everyone loved *Reservoir Dogs* as much as he did. No one was sure what to make of it; production companies passed on it for a variety of reasons but mostly because it was deemed too violent.

Several producers showed interest and made offers, but most of them wanted to alter key elements of the script that Tarantino wouldn't allow. Finally, just as Tarantino was about to shoot the picture himself on 16 mm for a self-raised $50,000 budget, Monte Hellman, best known for directing the 1971 classic *Two-Lane Blacktop*, expressed interest in making the movie. Hellman told me,

> I had been approached indirectly by Lawrence Bender through a friend of mine. They felt that having a director attached would make it easier to get the picture made. They set up a meeting between me and Quentin. I met with him, and just by coincidence, on the day we met, he had sold *True Romance*. He apologized for making me come to the meeting. He said that as much as he admired my work, he was now going to direct the movie himself. He could afford to do it now that he'd sold his screenplay. I told him that was great, and that he would be the right director for it. He asked me if I would help him get it made, and that's what I did.

Hellman passed the script to producer Richard Gladstein, who worked for video distributor Live Entertainment. They were friendly because they'd worked together on *Silent Night, Deadly Night 3*. Gladstein liked the script and came onboard as an executive producer, but things really started rolling when a mutual friend introduced Bender to actor Harvey Keitel. The actor read the script and was stunned. He loved it and signed on as both an actor and producer. Keitel told *Vanity Fair*, "I couldn't speak about it. I just wanted to sit with it, which I did for a number of days, until I called Lawrence Bender." Keitel found the feel of the script so authentic that he believed it had to have been written by either a real-life wise guy or someone connected to wise guys. After Keitel came onboard, casting the picture was fairly easy. The cast included seasoned actors Chris Penn, Lawrence Tierney, and Michael Madsen. Tarantino, a lifelong fan of crime novels, cast novelist Edward Bunker in a small role. Tarantino workshopped the script at the Sundance Film Institute, and there was a weeklong rehearsal prior to shooting. Filming began on July 21, 1991, and lasted thirty-five days, with a $1.3 million budget.

On *Reservoir Dogs*, Tarantino used long, unbroken shots—a characteristic that became a trademark of his work. The picture also introduced the masses to Tarantino's sharp-tongued dialogue and long-winded monologues. The film is near-perfect, except for Tarantino's decision to cast himself in a brief but nonetheless significant role. Tarantino had studied acting under multiple teachers and had originally dreamed of becoming an actor rather than a filmmaker. Unfortunately (with no disrespect to Tarantino), his acting skills pale in comparison to his writing and directing talents. And while he frequently gets knocked for being a bad actor, his turn in Robert Rodriguez's *From Dusk till Dawn* proves that he can be competent if given the right role. Another flaw in *Reservoir Dogs* is Tarantino's decision to leave a take in the film in which a character's squib explodes prematurely during a shootout, resulting in a visibly untouched character's inexplicable death. Tarantino claimed this isn't actually a mistake, and he left the flawed take in simply to make viewers question and argue how the death occurred. If that claim is true, then Tarantino was right because fans became obsessed with the blunder. Shirts were even printed asking "Who shot Nice Guy Eddie?"

Reservoir Dogs premiered at the Sundance Film Festival in January 1992, and the buzz was instantaneous. The film didn't receive a theatrical release until the following October. While some complained about the picture's startling violence, *Reservoir Dogs* was mostly met with praise. It was clear from the start that Tarantino was on the verge of bigger things.

Although it contains elements borrowed from and mimics other films, *Reservoir Dogs* is unique. One thing that makes the picture both different and important is its realistic depiction of violence. Eli Roth, director of such films as *Hostel* and *Thanksgiving*, observed in a *Vice* interview, "At that time, violence had all but disappeared in movies. It was like there was a huge reaction to the 'Rambo' violence of the '80s. And *Reservoir Dogs* was like this frickin' flare that goes off and being like 'wait a minute, let me show you how it's done.'"

One thing that was interesting and innovative about *Reservoir Dogs* is Tarantino's decision to skip the actual robbery around which the plot is constructed; the movie begins with the robbers planning and discussing the impending job and then jumps to the bloody aftermath of the botched heist. Some

Harvey Keitel and Tim Roth in Quentin Tarantino's Reservoir Dogs. *Courtesy of Live Entertainment/Photofest © Live Entertainment*

viewers couldn't wrap their heads around the absence of these key scenes, while others saw Tarantino's defying expectations as a brilliant move. This leads to the question, What might those scenes have looked like? The answer perhaps can be found in Ringo Lam's film *City on Fire*. That film, obscure in America at the time and known today only because of its connection to *Reservoir Dogs*, shows the full robbery.

If you're wondering why scenes from another film might be helpful in understanding this one, here's the deal: Several publications, most notably *Film Threat*, revealed the fact that *Reservoir Dogs*' storyline is almost, beat for beat, a direct (although stretched out) reiteration of *City on Fire*'s final act. This ignited a huge controversy about whether Tarantino had ripped off Lam. A short documentary directed by Mike White titled *Who Do You Think You're Fooling?* arrived soon after, placing scenes from the two films side by side. These comparisons made it obvious that Tarantino had at the very least *seen* Lam's film. So what? What was the big deal? *Reservoir Dogs* is hands down the better film by a huge margin.

The problem was, Tarantino never admitted to borrowing from the film. He credited other films and filmmakers as being inspirations, but he didn't credit *City on Fire*. The closest he came to an admission was when he told reporters that he loved *City on Fire* and had a poster of it hanging in his living room. Making all of this even worse, he famously said, "Great artists steal. They don't do homages." He also said, "I steal from every single movie ever made." Ironically, the "great artists steal" line was itself lifted from Pablo Picasso's famous quote "Good artists copy, great artists steal."

Borrowing from other works in any medium is as old as art itself. It's not new, and it's certainly not limited to Tarantino. As Rick Rubin observes in *The Creative Act: A Way of Being*, "The Beatles were inspired by American rock and roll, artists like Chuck Berry and the Shirelles. But when they played, it was different. . . . It was different because *they* were different." He goes on to state, "There are countless examples of imitation turning into legitimate innovation." There can surely be no debating the fact that Tarantino improves everything he lifts, which speaks to Rubin's assertion that imitation often results in "legitimate innovation." But Tarantino's glib admission that he "steals" seems to make the act of lifting or, to be more precise, *reinventing* more heinous in the eyes of his detractors. Just as it has been with Stephen King, who once joked that his novels were the literary equivalent of a Big Mac, Tarantino's line will continue to be weaponized to dismiss his work for the foreseeable future.

Despite all the finger-wagging that both Tarantino and the film have endured, *Reservoir Dogs* has become a legitimate cult film. It has been ranked number 2 on the Sundance Film Festival's top ten films of all time, based on the votes of five hundred filmmakers and critics. *Empire* magazine has repeatedly shown *Reservoir Dogs* love, ranking it at number 97 on their list of the five hundred greatest films of all time, as well as calling it the "Greatest Independent Film of All Time."

For his *Reservoir Dogs* follow-up, Tarantino sought to create a hard-boiled crime picture that captures the essence of *Black Mask* magazine. *Black Mask* was a popular pulp rag published intermittently between 1920 and 1951. Tarantino's earliest concept for the film that became *Pulp Fiction* was that he would make individual stand-alone short films that he could piece together into an anthology film. "The thing that was cool about it is that what I wanted to do with the three stories was to start with the oldest chestnuts in the world," Tarantino explained to Manohla Dargis in 1994.

> You've seen them a zillion times. You don't need to be caught up with the story because you already know it. The guy takes out the mob guy's wife—"but don't touch her." And what happens if they touch? You've seen that triangle a zillion times. Or the boxer who's supposed to throw the fight and doesn't—you've seen that a zillion times too. The third story isn't a familiar story but an old familiar situation.

So Tarantino wrote multiple segments taking place in the same universe, with the stories and characters interlocking, à la Robert Altman. The three primary segments of the film are "Vincent Vega and Marsellus Wallace's Wife," "The Gold Watch," and "The Bonnie Situation." Much of "The Gold Watch" (primarily the pawn shop sequence) includes material and dialogue from an unproduced script titled *Pandemonium Reigns* written by Tarantino's pal and video-store coworker Roger Avary.

The first draft of the screenplay was a mammoth five hundred pages. Tarantino eventually cut it down to 159 pages, which is still considered long for a film script. He finished his final draft in May 1993. Humorously, and telling of Tarantino's refusal to compromise his art, the script he handed in was marked "LAST DRAFT."

With the help of Danny DeVito and his Jersey Films, Tarantino had inked a lucrative deal with TriStar Pictures for his second film. TriStar balked, however, when they read the script. The studio was worried that the violence and depictions of drug usage might be too much for audiences, so they allowed

Tarantino to take the film elsewhere. After briefly shopping the project, it ended up at Miramax.

Interestingly, *Pulp Fiction* wasn't always Tarantino's clear choice for film number 2. According to actor John Travolta, Tarantino was trying to decide whether he should direct *Pulp Fiction* or *From Dusk till Dawn* when he met him. Tarantino had asked to meet Travolta, who was one of his favorite actors. Things got off to a bumpy start when Tarantino questioned Travolta's career choices, asking him how he'd started out so strongly only to end up making crappy movies about talking babies. Travolta was initially stung by Tarantino's words but then understood what he was getting at: Tarantino believed Travolta could be great again, and he wanted to help him get there. Tarantino wanted to make a new picture with him.

After convincing Travolta to play the *Welcome Back Kotter–* and *Saturday Night Fever*–based board games with him, the writer/director showed him his *Pulp Fiction* and *From Dusk till Dawn* scripts. Travolta told Tarantino that he had no desire to star in a vampire film, but he'd be interested in making *Pulp Fiction*. Travolta's interest in the project may have helped Tarantino choose his next picture because Travolta received a contract to appear in *Pulp Fiction* soon after.

Tarantino had written the role of Jules Winnfield specifically for Samuel L. Jackson. Jackson had previously read for a role in *Reservoir Dogs* but didn't get the part. He'd also played Big Don, a character who mostly ended up on the editing room floor, in *True Romance*. After informing Jackson that Jules had been written specifically for him, Tarantino briefly flirted with the idea of casting Paul Calderon in the role. This got Jackson fired up, and he came back and read for the part, this time bringing great vengeance and furious anger to his performance. After that, Jackson was, once and for all, cast in the role.

The character Jules Winnfield recites Ezekiel 25:17 in two memorable scenes. Tarantino had seen his beloved action star Sonny Chiba quote the line in *Karate Kiba* (a.k.a. *The Bodyguard*), and he liked it so much that he decided to quote it in his own work. He first inserted the quotation in his *From Dusk till Dawn* script but wound up cutting it and using it in *Pulp Fiction*.

Tarantino was always upfront about his lifting the line from *Karate Kiba*, which is good, considering the passage is misquoted exactly the same way in both films, making the requote obvious.

The casting of Uma Thurman is a curious tale. Initially, Tarantino wasn't interested in her, believing she was wrong for the part. But he met and had lunch with her anyway, and the two hit it off. He then decided he'd been wrong and that she was perfect for the role of Mia Wallace. Thurman, however, had since decided that she was wrong for the role, so she declined the offer. Tarantino would not relent; he asked her repeatedly to accept the role until she finally did.

Tarantino had believed that casting the Winston Wolf character would be simple. After all, he'd written the part specifically for Harvey Keitel. And because Tarantino had revived Keitel's career with *Reservoir Dogs*, it was assumed that casting him was a sure thing. However, the second collaboration almost didn't happen. Keitel had a court date that conflicted with the days when he was supposed to shoot, so Tarantino and Lawrence Bender changed the date. However, the court day was then changed, as well, once again overlapping. Keitel told the filmmakers that he was sorry, but he wouldn't be able to make *Pulp Fiction*. But Tarantino and Bender managed the impossible by convincing the cast and crew to get together to shoot Keitel's scenes on a Sunday. (Studios don't like crews to work on Sundays because the unions make them pay more for weekends.)

Before filming on *Pulp Fiction* began, Tarantino assembled his cast for a week of rehearsal. While working to hone the performances during this process, the script was also tweaked. Travolta expressed displeasure about his character accidentally shooting the Marvin character in the throat and then shooting him a second time to put him out of his misery. He pled for the screenwriter/director to change the scene to a single shot to the head, which led to one of the film's funniest lines: "I just shot Marvin in the face!" Another significant alteration occurred just before shooting and involved the hairdo Jules sports in the film. Tarantino had originally envisioned Jules having an afro, But when a makeup designer mistakenly brought Tarantino a

Tarantino and his production partner, Lawrence Bender. Courtesy of Miramax Films/Photofest © Miramax Films

Jheri-curl wig instead of an afro, Tarantino changed his mind, thus creating the character's iconic appearance.

To prepare Thurman for a scene in which her character overdoses on heroin, Tarantino had her meet with his pal Craig Hamann. Hamann had, of course, cowritten Tarantino's aborted first film. Hamann had also done his fair share of heroin, so he was able to share information and techniques with the actress. Additionally, Thurman met with some street-level junkies to pick their brains.

Filming began on September 20, 1993. The shoot, which took place all over Los Angeles, lasted two and a half months. Although much of the film was shot on location, some sets were built, most notably the Jack Rabbit Slim's '50s-style diner.

One of Tarantino's primary aesthetic concerns on *Pulp Fiction* was getting the colors he wanted. "My idea of color is that you make a color film which is really *in colors*, where the red is red, blue blue, and black black," he explained to *Positif* in 2004.

"Primary colors. But I don't like flat lighting. For my [first] two films, my head cameraman, Andrzej Sekula, and I used 50 AMC film which has the slowest emulsion there is. It requires a huge amount of light, but it's not the least bit grainy and the image is clear as crystal.... The colors [in *Pulp Fiction*] are so bright they jump right out at you!"

When Tarantino and Miramax had first negotiated, studio co-chief Harvey Weinstein made it clear that he didn't want John Travolta playing the lead. He'd suggested Daniel Day-Lewis, William Hurt, Sean Penn, and others, but Tarantino stood his ground. He wanted Travolta, goddammit. Weinstein eventually caved and allowed Tarantino to cast Travolta. Humorously, Weinstein ended up being so pleased with Travolta's performance in the film that he bragged the casting had been his idea.

Pulp Fiction made its debut on May 21, 1994, at the Cannes Film Festival. The film quickly became the talk of the festival, and a jury that included Clint Eastwood and Catherine Deneuve awarded it the prestigious Palme d'Or Award, signifying it as the best picture in competition. The film then screened at the New York Film Festival, where an audience member actually fainted during the infamous needle scene. *Pulp Fiction* was released theatrically the following October. The small $8.5 million picture became a smash hit, eventually raking in $214 million worldwide.

The picture's critical response was overwhelmingly positive. Roger Ebert wrote, "Quentin Tarantino is the Jerry Lee Lewis of cinema, a pounding performer who doesn't care if he tears up the piano, as long as everybody is rocking." Of the film's veteran cast, Ebert wrote, "The movie resurrects not only an aging genre but also a few careers." *Entertainment Weekly*'s Owen Gleiberman heralded the picture as being "nothing less than the reinvention of mainstream American cinema." *The Independent*'s Jon Ronson agreed, writing of Tarantino, "Not since the advent of *Citizen Kane* ... has one man appeared from relative obscurity to redefine the art of movies." *Rolling Stone*'s Peter Travers observed,

> It's Tarantino's compassion that deepens the film and sets it apart from trendy, pud-pulling, cinematic nihilism. It also sets

Tarantino apart as a major filmmaker, worthy of comparison to early Godard (*Bande a Part*) and Scorsese (*Mean Streets*). There's a special kick that comes from watching something this thrillingly alive. Pauline Kael calls it "getting drunk on movies." Whatever you call it, *Pulp Fiction* is indisputably great.

The *Washington Post*'s Desson Howe praised,

> *Pulp Fiction* is everything it's said to be: brilliant and brutal, funny and exhilarating, jaw-droppingly cruel and disalarmingly sweet. Quentin Tarantino, the postmodern Boy Wonder of American crass culture, for whom the only thing to fear is boredom itself, has produced a work of mesmerizing entertainment. To watch this movie (whose two-and-a-half hours speed by unnoticed) is to experience a near-assault of creativity.

Tarantino and the film were nominated for and/or won awards from just about every organization that gives film awards. But the icing on the cake was the seven Academy Award nominations *Pulp Fiction* received: Best Picture, Best Director, Best Screenplay, Best Editing, and acting nominations for Travolta, Jackson, and Thurman. Unfortunately (for Tarantino), 1995 was the year of *Forrest Gump*, which, along with its thirteen nominations and five other Oscars, took home the award for Best Picture.

Following the success of *Pulp Fiction*, Tarantino was a bona fide star. He was the most immediately recognizable filmmaker since Alfred Hitchcock and was such a big deal that *New York Post* critic Jami Bernard penned a Tarantino biography after he'd made a mere two pictures. And his influence on the work of other filmmakers soon became noticeable, although not every talky crime picture that came out in the wake of *Pulp Fiction* was truly inspired by him. But thanks to his success, Hollywood was suddenly interested in producing those kinds of films, so old scripts were dusted off, and new ones were written. In reviews, a new term, *Tarantinoesque*, started popping up. The production of such films or simply the comparisons between his films and others became so prevalent that dictionaries would eventually include *Tarantinoesque* as an actual word.

Not quite ready to make another film of his own yet, Tarantino and some of his new filmmaking pals came up with an idea. They would collaborate on an anthology film! The idea resonated with Tarantino because it was a way for him to continue working and keep his name out there without having to spend too much time making something. No doubt the idea resonated with codirectors Robert Rodriguez, Alison Anders, and Alexandre Rockwell because Tarantino was the hottest young filmmaker in Hollywood. The idea for the anthology, *Four Rooms*, was that each of the stories would take place in the same hotel, on the same night. Each director would write and direct a vignette that took place inside one of the rooms. In the project's earliest stages, Richard Linklater was slated to make a fifth segment but ultimately backed out. Shortly after, Tarantino considered backing out but decided to remain part of the project.

Tarantino's segment, "The Man from Hollywood," tells a story largely borrowed from a 1960 episode of *Alfred Hitchcock Presents* titled "The Man from the South." The episode, which Tarantino's characters erroneously refer to as "The Man from Rio," starred Peter Lorre and Steve McQueen and was adapted from a short story by Roald Dahl. "The Man from Hollywood" features actress Jennifer Beals and reunites *Pulp Fiction* performers Bruce Willis, Paul Calderon, and Tim Roth. (Roth appears in all four of the film's vignettes, tying them together.) The other vignettes feature such actors as Antonio Banderas, Marisa Tomei, Madonna, David Proval, and comedienne Kathy Griffin.

When *Four Rooms* was dropped into theaters on Christmas 1995, it landed with deafening thud. Made for a combined budget of $4 million, *Four Rooms* earned only $4.2 million. And the critical reviews were just as bad as the box office receipts. (At the time of this writing, *Four Rooms* has an aggregate score of 12 percent on Rotten Tomatoes. Additionally, it's critical consensus reads, "*Four Rooms* comes stocked with a ton of talent on both sides of the camera, yet only manages to add up to a particularly uneven—and dismayingly uninspired—anthology effort.") Adding insult to injury, Madonna received a Worst Supporting Actress Razzie Award for her work in the film.

At some point in 1995, Tarantino and Bender optioned the film rights to three Elmore Leonard crime novels: *Rum Punch*, *Killshot*, and *Freaky Deaky*. Tarantino had long been a fan of Leonard's work. As a teen, he was arrested for stealing a paperback copy of *The Switch*. Then, he went back to the store and stole the book again. Leonard's impact and influence on Tarantino's films is evident, particularly Tarantino's use of straight-faced comedic dialogue by characters in serious and often dangerous situations. For a while, Tarantino planned to produce and star (alongside Robert De Niro) in a *Killshot* adaptation that would have been directed by Tony Scott. That incarnation failed to materialize, although Bender eventually produced a John Madden–directed adaptation in 2008.

After the roller-coaster ride that *Pulp Fiction* had been, both in terms of the film and its massive success, Tarantino decided his next picture would be an adaptation of *Rum Punch*. (Interestingly, *Rum Punch* also featured the characters Ordell, Louis, and Melanie, who had appeared in *The Switch*.) This was a notable choice for a number of reasons, the primary being that this would be Tarantino's first (and, to date, only) adaptation of another writer's work. Also, the film would be more laid-back and have a slower pace than the director's previous films have.

Tarantino found the process of adapting Leonard quite different from the scripts he'd written previously. "It was an interesting challenge," he told *The Guardian*.

> It was a very interesting thing to tackle as far as adapting is concerned. I have only written originals. . . . The idea of doing an adaptation, by the sheer fact that the source material is different. . . . It is not the same old thing. It is not exactly what you have become accustomed to. That can just be the difference between night and day. It is still mine, but it does have that once-removed quality by its origin.

Tarantino decided early on that his *Rum Punch* adaptation would be different from the novel, perhaps as a way of making the material as much his as it is Leonard's. One significant change was his decision to move the story from Miami to Los

Angeles. Additionally, Tarantino had an affinity for the blaxploitation flicks of the 1970s, so he decided to mold his adaptation into an homage to those pictures. In order to do this, he had to transform the lead character, a blonde stewardess named Jackie Burke in the book, into a Black woman named Jackie Brown.

By this time, Tarantino had developed a reputation as the patron saint of career resurrections, so it was no surprise that he'd envisioned Pam Grier for the role of Jackie Brown from the start. Grier was a cult star known for her work in such blaxploitation favorites as *Coffy*, *Foxy Brown*, and *Sheba, Baby!* At that period of her career, offers were sparse; Grier had become a forgotten relic from a not-so-distant era. So when she received the script, she had no reason to think Tarantino was offering her the lead role. It would be a small role, she thought. Because of this, she waited several weeks to read the script. When Tarantino called her and said that he'd written the lead role for her, she was stunned.

Max Cherry, the film's second lead, was a White, middle-aged bail bondsman. Tarantino considered a number of actors for the role, including Paul Newman and Gene Hackman. However, the actor he ultimately selected was a seemingly washed-up actor named Robert Forster. Best known at the time for playing the lead in Haskell Wexler's 1969 film *Medium Cool*, Forster had read for the role of Joe Cabot in *Reservoir Dogs*. He hadn't gotten the part, but Tarantino liked his work. He'd been a particularly big fan of Forster's work in the exploitation picture *Alligator*. He even went so far as to tell the audience at his QTIII film festival that he'd envisioned Max Cherry as an older version of Forster's *Alligator* character. In an interview with *Character Kings* author Scott Voisin, Forster said Tarantino approached him in a restaurant where the actor had eaten every day for decades. The director handed him a screenplay and said, "Read this and see if you like it." Forster fell head over heels for the script, but he was skeptical, saying, "This is great, and I'd love to do it, but I'm not sure they're gonna let you hire me." Tarantino assured Forster that he could hire anyone he wanted, and the person he wanted was him.

Casting the role of gunrunner Ordell Robbie was a no-brainer. It *had* to be Samuel L. Jackson. After Jackson's bravura performance in *Pulp Fiction*, Tarantino could envision no other actor delivering Ordell's big, loud monologue about guns. The high point of the monologue—a part that Jackson delivered with fervor and intensity—was this memorable line about the AK-47: "When you absolutely, positively got to kill every motherfucker in the room, accept no substitutes." However, as strange as it may sound, Tarantino didn't want to share the role with anyone—even Jackson, as perfectly suited as he was. "The hardest part to give up in *Jackie Brown* was Ordell," Tarantino told *The New York Times*. "I was Ordell. It was so easy to write Ordell. I was Ordell for the year I was writing the script. I had to really work hard in letting go of Ordell and letting Sam play him and not being a jerk about stuff. Sam was him for ten weeks; I was Ordell for fifty-two weeks. . . . Ordell was all my mentors as a young man growing up. Ordell was who I could have been."

Ordell had a duplicitous "surfer girl" gal pal named Melanie. For this role, Tarantino cast actress Bridget Fonda. Fonda, the granddaughter of Henry Fonda, the niece of Jane Fonda, and the daughter of Peter Fonda, was Hollywood royalty. She appeared in her first film at the age of five as an extra in *Easy Rider*. Tarantino's selection of Fonda proved to be another instance of perfect casting. Everyone in *Jackie Brown* is perfectly cast, but Fonda brings the perfect blend of sexiness and attitude to the role. Rounding out the cast are supporting turns by Chris Tucker, Michael Keaton, and Robert De Niro.

As a fan of director Jack Hill's *Coffy* and *Foxy Brown*, Tarantino chose to pay homage to those films with *Jackie Brown*. "The character has a different name in the book," Hill told me. "[Tarantino] said he gave her the name Jackie, after me, and the name Brown, after Foxy Brown." Because the character's name is Jackie in Leonard's novel, Hill's assertion that she was named after him is erroneous. However, the surname change to Brown as a reference to Grier's titular *Foxy Brown* character is true.

Tarantino uses the same font that appeared in advertising materials for *Foxy Brown* in his *Jackie Brown* title sequence. Additionally, he orchestrated a reunion of sorts for Grier and actor

Sid Haig, who worked together in *Coffy* and *Foxy Brown*, as well as *The Big Doll House*, *The Big Bird Cage*, and *Black Mama White Mama*. Haig had retired from acting, but Tarantino lured him back by offering him an opportunity to work with Grier again.

Tarantino pitched actor Michael Keaton the role of ATF agent Ray Nicolette over drinks on Sunset Boulevard. According to Keaton, he got so drunk that he woke up the next morning confused and unable to remember the night before with any clarity. The only thing he knew was that he'd signed on to make Tarantino's film.

As *Jackie Brown* was filming, Steven Soderbergh went into production on *Out of Sight*, which was also based on an Elmore Leonard novel. Because both films feature the Ray Nicolette character, Soderbergh came to the *Jackie Brown* set to observe Keaton's performance. Satisfied with the actor's portrayal of Nicolette, Soderbergh hired Keaton to reprise the role (in a significantly smaller capacity) in his film.

Tarantino had worked with cinematographer Andrzej Sekula on his first two films. This time, however, he hired Guillermo Navarro to be DP. Tarantino had previously worked with Navarro while acting in the Robert Rodriguez films *Desperado* and *From Dusk till Dawn* and was interested in the cinematographer's style and reasoning for doing the things he did. Navarro recalls Tarantino asking him questions about techniques and methods. On *Jackie Brown*, the cinematographer was impressed by Tarantino's ability to see the shots and visuals he wanted in his head. Navarro also found the relationships between the cast and crew on the film to be quite familial. He remembered,

> The shoot was very complicated. It was challenging. Very tight. We had to work fast, and there were a lot of locations. A lot of adapting to situations. It was thrilling to be actively participating in such a good movie. You had to be quick and be able to react to changes, to think; there were some very complicated, very elaborate shots in tiny spaces. We were trying to [create] a sort of nostalgic vision of Los Angeles, so we worked a lot on the style of the movie with the production designer and the wardrobe to keep that colorful palette.

Jackie Brown opened on Christmas 1997. The film, which had been shot on a budget of $12 million, earned just under $10 million during its opening weekend. Although some reviewers commented on the picture's unexpected slower pacing, critical reception was mostly positive. Marc Savlov of *The Austin Chronicle* praised, "The casting . . . is vintage QT: Both Grier and especially Forster are spot-on in their roles, trading sexy stares and duplicitous grins every other frame, while Jackson proves once again just how commanding a screen presence he is, and Keaton comes out of nowhere with his slyest, coolest turn since he donned Batman's dark cowl." He went on to observe, "Anyone expecting *Pulp Fiction* redux—or even a new litter of *Reservoir Dogs*—is in for a surprise. Totally different in style and tact from both of those films, *Jackie Brown* is nonetheless one cool ride." *Rolling Stone*'s Peter Travers wrote,

> Sorry to disappoint those who longed to see Quentin Tarantino fall on his famously flashy ass, but the overlong, over-indulgent *Jackie Brown*—the Q man's first feature as a writer and director since *Pulp Fiction*, in 1994—scores a knockout just the same. Loaded with action, laughs, smart dialogue and potent performances, *Jackie Brown* is most memorable for its unexpected feeling. Tarantino adapts Elmore Leonard's 1992 crime novel, *Rum Punch*, without losing the author's compassion for compromised characters who defy the reduced options that come with age.

In *The Boston Phoenix*, Peter Keough wrote, "*Jackie Brown* shows steady progress in the maturing of one of America's great filmmakers."

Jackie Brown received a single Academy Award nomination, for Best Supporting Actor for Forster's impressive turn. However, Forster lost to Robin Williams for *Good Will Hunting*.

At the time of the film's release, many fans dismissed *Jackie Brown* because it is a more subdued, mature film than they expected. They wanted *Pulp Fiction 2*, and *Jackie Brown* isn't that. In the decades that have followed, however, *Jackie Brown* has grown in stature. In fact, many cineastes believe that it's Tarantino's finest film. Either way, it's an undeniable classic.

After the decade came to a close, Tarantino continued to crank out iconic films, one after the other, including *Kill Bill, Inglourious Basterds, Django Unchained,* and *Once upon a Time in Hollywood,* among others. Tarantino has repeatedly proven himself to be a maverick, continuing to make the pictures he wants to make. He casts who he wants, gets the budgets he requests, and is given unparalleled leeway to delay or even cancel scheduled projects.

His work features a signature style that's difficult to miss. As *Pulp Fiction* producer Stacy Sher stated in a 2016 interview, "If you were dropped from another planet, you could identify his films as the work of one person." Some defining characteristics of a Tarantino film are his use of violence punctuated with humor; long-winded monologues and slick, quotable dialogue; long, unbroken shots; a lot of f-words and an uncomfortable number of n-words; use of popular music perfectly married with the scenes on screen; and, in several films, the use of chapters to break up the story (something that no one in American film was doing before *Reservoir Dogs*).

As frequent Tarantino partner-in-crime Samuel L. Jackson has noted, there's generally about twice as much dialogue in a Tarantino film than there is in other Hollywood films. Tarantino often uses familiar scenarios and tropes, finding ways to update them and turn them on their heads, and he generally makes them better. His films feature a sort of je ne sais quoi that is uniquely his. His snappy dialogue gives the illusion of sounding like real-life banter but is actually a very stylized version of the way people speak. His dialogue also has a sort of musical quality to it. Oh, yes, and *feet*—there are almost always bare feet on display somewhere in the films.

In recent years, Tarantino has frequently been called a racist or, at the least, someone who makes racist films due to things his characters say. *Film Threat*'s Chris Gore said,

> *Characters* in Tarantino movies have certainly been racist. However, that's not the filmmaker endorsing racism. The purpose of all fiction, whether it be comic books, movies, video games, novels, is to see the world through someone else's eyes.

There is morality in Tarantino's films. Tarantino makes *monster movies*. And the monsters are us. Humans. Regular everyday people, making choices and doing monstrous things to each other. I think that's why his movies have such an appeal. He's never really made a genre movie, in terms of science-fiction, but his movies seem to operate in that realm, of being a monster movie. When you look at movies like *Pulp Fiction*, when you look at the characters [whose eyes] you see the world through—certainly we would never commit murder or cover up a murder or do these horrible things—but we can see the world through the eyes of that kind of person, which gives us a view into the eyes of the monster, that people are capable of those things.

Cineastes often debate whether Tarantino is the best of the filmmakers who emerged during the '90s. One thing that cannot be debated are his contributions to cinema. In addition to changing the course of American cinema, his films set the standard for what was and wasn't cool during the 1990s.

4

The Tarantino Film Subgenre

Following the successes of *Reservoir Dogs* and *Pulp Fiction*, similar films began to pop up, mostly on home video. In fact, so many similarly themed projects emerged in Tarantino's wake that *Tarantinoesque* became an actual word that now appears in the Oxford Dictionary (definition: "Resembling or imitative of the films of Quentin Tarantino; characteristic or reminiscent of these films. Tarantino's films are typically characterized by graphic or stylized violence, non-linear storylines, cineliterate references, satirical themes, and sharp dialogue").

If you do an internet search of phrases like "Tarantino rip-off" or "Tarantino pastiche," you'll find a bevy of articles with lists of assumed copycats. While discussing this, it's difficult not to smile at the irony of film pastiches being made to resemble the work of a filmmaker who is constantly accused of ripping off the work of other filmmakers. And hey, if Tarantino makes a film that is a pastiche of a hundred other films and another filmmaker skips all those films and simply creates a pastiche based on Tarantino's collective pastiche, where's the foul?

One problematic aspect of these Tarantino rip-off/pastiche labels is the question of what does and doesn't fit in that box. For instance, Tarantino's *Pulp Fiction* cowriter Roger Avary made a film, *Killing Zoe*, that people have frequently labeled as being a QT copycat. A 2019 article by Steven Hyden from *Uproxx* titled "The Most Quintessential Tarantino Rip-Offs from the '90s" cites *Killing Zoe* as one of the top offenders. But is it? Is it *really*?

Tarantino and Avary were friends before either of them found success, and as friends, they shared many of the same tastes, interests, and influences (hence the collective effort of *Pulp Fiction*, which is mostly Tarantino, yes, but *some* Avary). So it makes sense that Avary would create a film that is similar, at least in terms of genre, to those of his friend. Plus, Tarantino himself executive-produced *Killing Zoe* with his production partner Lawrence Bender, who also produced *Reservoir Dogs* and *Pulp Fiction*.

So how do we define a Tarantino rip-off? I ask this because, if it had been Avary who found success first, would people then label Tarantino's films being Avary rip-offs? Tarantino's one-time best friend and prefame collaborator Craig Hamann received similar accusations regarding his directorial debut, *Boogie Boy*. Like Avary, Hamann's longtime friendship and creative partnership with Tarantino makes it inevitable that there would be similarities between his work and Tarantino's. Interestingly, *Boogie Boy* was executive-produced by Avary. Claims about Avary's and Hamann's films being copycats of Tarantino's style, story, or structure are absurd.

The same *Uproxx* article sums up the Tarantinoesque films that came after the director's success: "These Tarantino rip-offs were populated by sharp-dressed hitmen and philosophizing petty criminals. They peppered their conversations with pop-culture references before blowing somebody away while an oldie from the '60s or '70s played on the soundtrack." While this isn't precisely accurate, it gives one an idea of what it is I'm talking about.

While the Tarantinoesque films subgenre is very much a real thing, most of the articles and critical reviews by critics and film buffs have missed a key detail: Many of the similarly themed projects that were released after Tarantino's films were actually written before his success. While some of the pictures are likely to be actual Tarantino rip-offs, many of them simply caught the interest of producers and distributors because of Tarantino's success. So Tarantino's work does play a key role in these films getting made. In this way, it can be said that these films may not have existed as actual financed films had his films not been made first, but they are not rip-offs any more than Tarantino's own pictures are rip-offs. (And they're not.)

For a long time, production companies turned their noses up at the scripts Tarantino wrote, seeing them as nonstarters that couldn't make money. But against all odds, Tarantino got *Reservoir Dogs* made, and it became a success. In Hollywood, where almost everything is about making money and following trends, producers and their assistants started combing through the dusty scripts they'd previously rejected, searching for projects that were at least thematically similar.

Most of the Tarantinoesque movies were released in the '90s, the most significant wave between 1994 and 1997. There were still Tarantinoesque pictures in the 2000s—films like *Smokin' Aces*, *Lucky Number Slevin*, and *Bad Times at the El Royale*—but the Tarantino film genre mostly died out at the end of '90s. So, this chapter examines five of the most famous (or infamous) films that have been labeled as Tarantinoesque.

The first of these pictures is *Love and a .45*. This is a lovers-on-the-road crime film similar to the Tarantino-written films *True Romance* and *Natural Born Killers*. Those films were hardly the first pictures of that nature to be made. *Bonnie and Clyde* and *Badlands* are notable preexisting films that fit the bill. *Love and a .45*, directed by East Texas–born C. M. Talkington, came just on the heels of *Pulp Fiction* and *Natural Born Killers*, so comparisons were inevitable.

"The one thing about me is that I am not a thief, and I am not a liar," Talkington said. "I never have been. Much to my detriment; I would probably be much more successful in a capitalistic society if I were. But I'm not, and that's very important to me. And I'm not an imitator or any of those kinds of things. I just do my thing. Where does it come from? The ether. Where does the ether come from? The ether comes from *everything*."

Talkington started writing *Love and a .45* in 1990. He remembered, "I didn't even know what the name Quentin Tarantino was when I wrote that script, so claims that I ripped him off are absurd." If anyone wants to verify Talkington's claim, he openly invites them to investigate, adding, "It would only take an amateur detective about five minutes to prove that."

Complicating the story is Talkington's assertion that screenwriters Oliver Stone and David Veloz lifted elements of his screenplay while they were rewriting Tarantino's screenplay for *Natural Born Killers*. If this is true, then the exact opposite of the claim that Talkington ripped off *Natural Born Killers* is true. Of course, all of that was after Tarantino had already written and sold his draft, but it's an interesting irony to consider.

Further complicating things is the fact that Tarantino himself has praised Talkington as being his "favorite imitator." He also commended the writer for his "gift for really funny dialogue." While any filmmaker would be happy to receive praise from Tarantino, it's a dubious distinction in this instance because it adds fuel to the fire regarding the public's perception that *Love and a .45* is a rip-off.

"We did not talk about Tarantino's movies at all while we were making *Love and a .45*," the film's producer, Darin Scott, said. "But we did find it gratifying later when he said that out of all the 'imitators'—okay, fine, if that's the way he sees it—that he liked *Love and a .45* best. We'll just take that half of it that says that he loves *Love and a .45* the best. . . . We'll just kind of scrub out that word *imitators*!"

"I never talk about this," Talkington explained.

> I never wanted to defend myself, because I didn't give a shit. Why be defensive? I know what the truth is. If somebody asks me, I'll talk about it a little bit, but it was never something I made a big deal about. I don't hold a grudge against one single person. In fact, all of the people involved in this story are actually people who were very important in my life—people I greatly admire and respect. Oliver Stone. Quentin Tarantino. Tarantino was not really involved, but his name is involved. And he's the most ardent vocal supporter of the film! Wow, you know? The thing with Quentin is, I never even knew he existed. Now, after I finished the script and I gave it to a few people to read, I heard what his name was. Immediately. "Wow, this is like Quentin Tarantino. Have you heard of Quentin Tarantino?" "No, no, no." Of course I did after that, but the last thing I wanted to do was read anything that guy wrote!

Talkington posited,

> Was *Love and a .45* a genre film? And was I thinking about all the genre films that I watched as a kid and trying to pay homage to them? Of course I was! But none of that was really running through my mind. I was just trying to have fun with it. So basically, the only scene in that movie that I put down that's a direct homage was for Peckinpah's *The Getaway*. Peckinpah is one of my favorite directors, and I did a little homage to him when they go in the store at the end and they see themselves on the TV, just like McQueen and McGraw did in *The Getaway*. And that's it. That's the only thing.

On the subject of the Tarantino subgenre, Darin Scott observed that Abel Ferrara's 1990 crime film *King of New York* is also similar to these films, although it was released two years before *Reservoir Dogs*. "Abel Ferrara wasn't biting off Quentin," Scott said. "That was just him doing his thing. And if you look back at it, it's a talky gangster movie with a kind of '90s flavor too. So more than one person [did] that. But the financial success of Quentin's movies, particularly *Pulp Fiction*, opened the doors to a lot of these projects that had already been written."

Scott noted that timing is everything and that people should take a look at the timelines during which these films were made before labeling them as being Tarantino pastiches. He elaborated, "For most people, it takes a couple of years to get a script done. So when you see something like that in the six months after this other hit film came out. . . . It's very unlikely that in that six months they wrote a rip-off, got it financed, and got it made and put out."

The second Tarantinoesque picture is 1995's *Things to Do in Denver When You're Dead*. As strange as it may sound, the project grew out of a tragedy in screenwriter Scott Rosenberg's life. He explained,

> My father got sick with cancer and he died. I kind of wanted to deal with it, but I didn't want to deal with it in a traditional movie-of-the-week kind of way. So [*Things to Do in Denver When You're Dead*] was a metaphor for having a terminal

disease. My parents were separated, and my father had met the great love of his life, second to my mom. And I thought that was part of the tragedy. And I was never thinking in a million years that anybody was going to actually make the movie.

When Rosenberg started writing, the whole thing just poured out onto the page, and he completed the first draft in a week. Soon after, Rosenberg showed it to Gary Fleder, who agreed to direct the picture. Rosenberg and Fleder started sending the script out, but no one was interested. But then a couple of rich Lebanese brothers who owned a number of businesses and clubs, including the Roxbury, offered to finance the film. The brothers began showing the script to all the actors who would come into their clubs, and a buzz about it developed within the acting community. After hearing about the project, Miramax co-chief Harvey Weinstein approached Rosenberg and Fleder about making the film. And just like that, *Things to Do in Denver When You're Dead* became a Miramax film.

Rosenberg had written the lead role, Jimmy the Saint, with Alec Baldwin in mind. Unfortunately, Baldwin wasn't interested. Around this time, producer Cary Wood convinced veteran actor James Caan to sign on to play a character known only as the Man with the Plan. Rosenberg says, "All of a sudden, we were legitimate. We were legitimate because we had James Caan." After that, actors started coming out of the woodwork to read for parts. "We passed on every single person who wound up being in *The Usual Suspects*," Rosenberg says. "Everybody wanted to do the movie." Caan ended up dropping out, but in the end, the cast included Andy Garcia, Christopher Walken, Christopher Lloyd, William Forsythe, and Treat Williams, among others.

Rosenberg and Fleder insist that they weren't ripping off Tarantino. In fact, no one at the time was even certain that Tarantino's quirky films could make real money. "Scott Rosenberg and I, we had both seen the *Pulp Fiction* script many, many months before that film was in Cannes," Fleder recalled.

> We saw it in, like, '93. It had gone into turnaround. I remember we read it, and we said, "This is an amazing, amazing script,

but who's gonna see this movie except for us?" It's like a three-hour movie. It's insane with things like the Gimp. . . . It was just batshit, you know? We were like, "We love this movie and can't wait to see this movie, but no one else will see this movie but us." Well, little did we know.

Going into the project, Fleder didn't even consider the possible similarities. But he can pinpoint the exact moment he knew this was going to be an issue. "We shot the movie in 1994," Fleder said. "We shot in the summer, and that was the summer that *Pulp Fiction* went to Cannes and blew up. And Scott and I had this moment, we knew at *that moment* in May 1994 shooting our movie, that we were kind of fucked." Rosenberg recalled the moment well: "We were just like, 'Oh my God.' I always compared it to, imagine if you were shooting a giant squid movie the summer that *Jaws* came out. You were like, this is either really bad for us, or really good for us."

Rosenberg recalled a conversation he had with Tarantino before *Things to Do in Denver When You're Dead* was released: "I remember saying to Quentin, after we wrapped, after we were in post, I remember saying, 'Quentin, I will give you one dollar for every review of my movie that doesn't mention your name. And I guarantee that I will not be paying you a nickel.' And that was exactly what came to pass."

Regarding making a film similar to the films that Tarantino made in the '90s, Fleder explained that he (and many other filmmakers of their generation) had a lot of the same cinematic influences that Tarantino had, including "*Dirty Mary, Crazy Larry* and kung-fu movies and Don Siegel movies."

"The commonality between our movie and Tarantino's was that it had very, very chatty gangsters," Rosenberg said.

> But that was it. *Denver* is about me dealing with my father's death. *Denver* is not fun. You meet five guys, and then you say goodbye to five guys, and then you watch five guys die. Quentin's stuff is fun. Exuberant. And *Denver* was a much darker affair. But I get the comparisons. And again, if you'll recall, there were a million of those post-Tarantino [films], and we just got caught up in all that, you know?

The third Tarantinoesque picture is John Herzfeld's *2 Days in the Valley*. After directing four movies for television, Herzfeld optioned the novel *The Midnight Club*, written by an ad man named James Patterson. Herzfeld wrote twenty-two drafts of the screenplay adaptation but couldn't get the picture made. He realized that *The Midnight Club* was never going to get made and that he had to move on. Feeling frustrated, Herzfeld stacked all the drafts on the barbecue grill on his patio and set them ablaze.

"My wife probably thought I'd lost my mind," Herzfeld recalled. "I got in my car and I started driving from the Valley, where I live. I can't tell you to this day why I did this, but I ended up driving past the Los Angeles National Cemetery. It was quiet and peaceful, so I went in there and I just started walking around and thinking. 'What am I going to do?'" As he walked, Herzfeld found himself in front of a tombstone with the name *Dosmo Pizzo* engraved on it. "That's a weird name, I thought," Herzfeld remembered. "I'd never heard the name Dosmo. And I said to myself, 'Dosmo Pizzo . . . I know! He's a hitman from New York, and now he's out here working in a pizzeria hiding out. He's a has-been. He's washed up.'"

Then Herzfeld turned and saw another marker beside it with the name *Lee Woods* engraved on it. "I said, 'Lee! He's the guy who hires him for the job here in LA and he's really out to screw him; he's got a plan to use him and get rid of him." Excited by this concept, the filmmaker ran to his car and grabbed a miniature tape recorder to dictate his ideas. Herzfeld then returned to the cemetery for the next three days, speaking into the tape recorder, working out the entire story, complete with dialogue. Those brainstorming sessions resulted in the *2 Days in the Valley* screenplay.

"I'd never written a one-draft script before then," Herzfeld said, "and I've never written another one since. That's how it came to be. It was an unbelievable experience." Later, while shooting a scene with James Spader and Charlize Theron, Herzfeld suggested Theron do some improvisation. Spader, however, was not keen on this. He said, "John, we're all in this because we love the script. Don't fuck it up. Don't start improvising and making changes. Stick to the script." Herzfeld took heed and stuck to the script after that.

Herzfeld said Tarantino's work never crossed his mind during the writing of *2 Days in the Valley*. His biggest inspiration was an obscure 1974 Italian film called *Bread and Chocolate*, which he believes is a masterpiece. Not only does he acknowledge the film's tonal influence on his script, but he also believes it has influenced every day of his life since first seeing it.

Despite Tarantino not having any direct influence on *2 Days*, Herzfeld has great appreciation for his work. He said,

> *Pulp Fiction* ripped the margins off for a lot of filmmakers and screenwriters who thought, "I can't do something like this." But he showed them that you can. I'm sure it was liberating when I saw it. I didn't think of doing a movie like it, because I was wrapped up on something else. But I think he blew down the doors. Nobody does it as good as him. Nobody will *ever* do it as good as him.

The picture's distributor, MGM, made the comparison matter even worse by advertising it with a blurb promising that it "out-pulps *Pulp Fiction*." This move did not sit well with Herzfeld. "I fucking hate that," he said. "I didn't want that. I got good reviews, and inherently those comparisons to Tarantino too."

Critics made these comparisons, as well. Stephen Holden of *The New York Times* wrote, "*2 Days in the Valley* lacks the humanity of *Short Cuts* or the edgy hipness of *Pulp Fiction*, but it is still a sleek, amusingly nasty screen debut by [Herzfeld]." Mick LaSalle of the *San Francisco Chronicle* wrote, "[*2 Days in the Valley*] occupies a territory somewhere between the bleakness of *Short Cuts* and the merry excess of *Pulp Fiction*." In a rather scathing review, Jonathan Rosenbaum of the *Chicago Reader* wrote, "The standard line on this actor-heavy, brain-light concoction by writer-director John Herzfeld is that it's *Short Cuts* meets *Pulp Fiction*, but it isn't a tenth as good as either. It does, however, have a good many dog reaction shots, so if you happen to think the other two movies were lacking in those, credit Herzfeld for making up the difference." The *TV Guide* write-up read, "It sounds lazy to say . . . Herzfeld is doing a Tarantino, but it's easier than going through the *Pulp Fiction* checklist, item by item: dense, meandering, self-referential dialogue. Outrageous—perhaps divinely ordained—synchronicity. Chic world-weariness. Sleazy sexual innuendo. Eccentricity as characterization."

The fourth Tarantinoesque picture is 1997's *Suicide Kings*, directed by Peter O' Fallon. (Interestingly, O'Fallon directed an unaired pilot for a would-be television series called *Odd Jobs* that was written by Roger Avary the same year *Suicide Kings* was released.) *Suicide Kings* is about a group of young men who kidnap a mobster and hold him captive so they can get ransom. The film stars Christopher Walken, Denis Leary, Henry Thomas, Johnny Galecki, and Sean Patrick Flanery.

The screenplay was originally titled *Bred and Bored* and was written by Wayne Rice, who also produced the picture. Rice was impressed by O'Fallon's work on the pilot for the television series *American Gothic*, so he contacted him and asked him to direct the picture. O'Fallon agreed before he'd even read the script. When he did read it, he loved it. "I actually didn't think it was anything like Quentin Tarantino's movies," O' Fallon said. "Quentin has his own style, and the guy's a fucking genius."

In addition to being funny, talky crime pictures, *Suicide Kings* and *Things to Do in Denver When You're Dead* both have an element that remind people of Tarantino: Christopher Walken, who appears in *Pulp Fiction* and the Tarantino-penned *True Romance*. O'Fallon believes that Walken's presence in *Suicide Kings* caused his young costars to do better work. He recalled a script reading at which Walken and his younger "cool guy" (O'Fallon's words) costars were present. Apparently, when Walken immediately started asking questions and working from a dog-eared, heavily notated screenplay, the younger actors took notice and thought, "Hey, I'd better show up" (also O'Fallon's words).

The film also benefits from a fine, funny performance by comedian-turned-actor Denis Leary. O'Fallon recalled, "Denis comes in, and we're talking. I wanted him to wear shark cowboy boots. And he didn't want to do it. He says, 'Let me tell you something about acting, Peter. Acting is about comfort, and I'm not comfortable in these.' I laughed and said, 'Let me tell you something about directing, Denis. You're wearing the shoes.'" This soon became a running joke between the two collaborators. Leary agreed to wear the boots but only in scenes where they're visible on camera, so O'Fallon started every scene that features Leary with a shot of the boots. The boots are also the center of a humorous exchange between Leary and Louis Lombardi. After Leary's character shows Lombardi the boots, Lombardi refers to them as "fish boots," leading to a long diatribe by Leary. O'Fallon said, "Everything Denis says, that whole scene, was ad-libbed. And all of it appears in the movie."

When O'Fallon screened the first cut of *Suicide Kings* for some of his friends, no one laughed at the parts that were supposed to be funny, and he couldn't understand why. So he screened it for the renowned editor Pietro Scalia to get his opinion. "He sat down and watched it and said, 'You've got one simple problem,'" O'Fallon recalled. "I said, 'What's that?' And he said, 'You've got to let them laugh earlier so they understand it's supposed to be funny.'" O'Fallon and editor Chris Peppe then went back into the editing room and recut the picture, moving the introduction of Johnny Galecki's character from later in the film to somewhere closer to the beginning. Because Galecki gets a laugh early on, viewers quickly understand that the film is intended to be funny, giving them permission to laugh.

When *Suicide Kings* was released to theaters, many critics identified it as being a Tarantino knock-off. "When they started saying it was another Quentin rip-off, I just thought, critics do what they do because they don't [make movies]," O'Fallon said. "Honestly, I didn't even think about Tarantino when I was making it." He continued, "So many movies got lumped in together as 'Tarantino wannabes.' And from all the other people I was talking to at the time, none of us were even thinking, 'I wanna be like Quentin.' Because again, I think Quentin has a very unique style. I don't even think you could [duplicate] it if you wanted to."

Interestingly, Wayne Rice wrote a screenplay for a *Suicide Kings* sequel that was never filmed. In the sequel, Johnny Galecki's Ira character would have become a mobster himself, but there was one major problem: While everyone else from the first film agreed to come back for the sequel, Galecki refused.

Perhaps the most popular of the alleged Tarantino knockoffs is *Boondock Saints*, the fifth Tarantinoesque film. The story behind the film is the story of its writer and director, Troy Duffy, which has pretty much become Hollywood lore. In 1995, Duffy was working as a bouncer in a West Hollywood pub called J. Sloan's. One night, he returned home to his apartment building, where he encountered paramedics wheeling a dead woman out of a drug dealer's apartment on a gurney. Duffy had been thinking about writing a script for a while, but this macabre scene served as his light-bulb-over-the-head, *voila!* moment. He was inspired. At that moment, he was ready to write. He didn't have a computer nor the money to buy one outright, so he rented one and went to work on what became *Boondock Saints*.

Despite the popular notion that Duffy was trying to craft a Tarantinoesque film, that wasn't so. Duffy doesn't hesitate to admit that he likes and admires Tarantino's work. He even admitted that maybe, *maybe*, on some subconscious level, Tarantino was an influence, but he was just one of many influences. But influences or no, Duffy wasn't trying to imitate anyone.

"What I really wanted to do was write a movie that I would want to go see," Duffy said. "Because I was like, 'Jesus, movies really suck these days.'" Duffy's script tells the story of two brothers who grow tired of the world's nastiness and are moved to pick up guns and become vigilantes. Duffy said, "I always had kind of an edgy, dark sense of humor, and I was like, with all the shit that's going on in the world, why haven't we seen a movie about two regular guys who just decide, 'Hey, let's clean up our neighborhood'? So I decided that was what I was going to write. I knew the story would be super violent, kind of funny, and also have some meaning."

When he was done, Duffy showed his script to a friend who was working as a producer's assistant. The friend read it and loved it, so he showed it to his boss. The producer liked the characters and Duffy's writing but ultimately passed on the project. However, word of Duffy's sharp-tongued vigilante script spread like wildfire, and soon producers were showing up at J.

Sloan's and ordering drinks. "Hey, are you the guy who wrote that script?" they'd ask. Then they'd sit and read *Boondock Saints* cover to cover as they drank their drinks.

Eventually, a producer named Robert Fried darkened the door of the bar, and everything changed. Fried, who'd produced *So I Married an Axe Murderer* and *Rudy*, read *Boondock Saints* and made it his mission to get it filmed. Fried showed the script around at Miramax, and eventually it reached Harvey Weinstein. As the story goes, a lackey at Miramax was so excited about *Boondock Saints* that they faxed the script to Weinstein, page by page, while the mogul was on his private jet to Los Angeles to attend the Academy Awards. Meanwhile, someone at New Line had expressed interest in making the picture. Weinstein dug the script, and being the competitor that he was, he was even more motivated to purchase the script so he could pull the rug out from under New Line.

Weinstein grabbed his phone and called his people, telling them that he wanted Duffy to meet him in his room at the Peninsula Hotel. Duffy went to that meeting. "Harvey is every bit the gangster that people think he is," Duffy later remarked. He went on to say that the Miramax co-chief not only expressed interest in making *Boondock Saints*, but he also made a point of threatening to hamper the film's production if Duffy took it elsewhere. According to Duffy, Weinstein first asked him what actors he envisioned for each of the roles. After that, Weinstein allegedly said, "Let me tell you something. If you don't give *Boondock Saints* to Miramax and make a deal with me, I'm gonna get every actor you just listed in my movies, and you won't get a single one." Duffy told Weinstein that he needed some time to consider his options.

Weinstein and his entourage showed up at the bar the following day to try to convince Duffy. After Duffy told the mogul that he hoped to one day purchase J. Sloan's, Weinstein made him an offer not even the Godfather could have refused; in addition to paying Duffy $300,000 for his script, he would sweeten the deal by adding a cherry on top: If Duffy signed with Miramax, Weinstein said he would help him purchase the bar with himself as co-owner. Today, Duffy doesn't believe Weinstein ever had any actual intentions of buying the bar. Either way, the savvy producer's offer, genuine or not, became the stuff of Hollywood legend. Duffy signed the contract, and suddenly news of this wild deal offered to an unknown first-time writer was *everywhere*.

The plan was that Duffy would direct *Boondock Saints* himself with a $15 million budget. However, the Duffy-Miramax marriage wasn't meant to be. Disagreements over casting led to a huge argument (and an alleged physical altercation) between Duffy and Weinstein. Following that, Miramax dropped the project, and Franchise Pictures picked it up.

Duffy cast Norman Reedus and Sean Patrick Flanery as the vigilante brothers and Willem Dafoe as the detective trying to catch them. The film began shooting in August 1998 with a significantly less $6 million budget. Due to financial considerations, much of *Boondock Saints* was shot in Toronto, even though its story takes place in Boston.

Boondock Saints had the briefest of brief theatrical releases, but when it was released on video, it became an instant cult favorite. It was so big, in fact, that it caused thousands of fans to get inked with the same tattoo the brothers sport in the film. Additionally, an international motorcycle club adopted the *Boondock Saints* name, and a bar with the name has opened in New Orleans. The film spawned the 2009 sequel, *Boondock Saints II: All Saints Day*.

If you believe all the filmmakers I interviewed here, none of their films were intended to be Tarantino clones. While it's very likely that a good number of the other so-called Tarantino rip-offs were crafted to be pastiches of Tarantino's work, many were not. And while these similar films may not have been inspired by Tarantino's work, the Tarantino subgenre is a convenient (if lazy) label by which to identify these kinds of films because it immediately tells you (at least vaguely) what type of film you're talking about without further explanation. If nothing else, it's a testament to the impact Tarantino made on Hollywood in the 1990s that his films resulted in the birth of an entire subset of films.

While people occasionally attempt to place Paul Thomas Anderson's *Hard Eight* and Bryan Singer's *The Usual Suspects* in the Tarantino subgenre box, it's highly unlikely that either of these fine films actually intended to ape Tarantino in any way.

Some other films frequently cited as being in the Tarantino subgenre are *Thursday*; *Go*; *Reindeer Games*; *Smokin' Aces*; *Truth or Consequences, N.M.*; *Lock, Stock and Two Smoking Barrels*; *Way of the Gun*; *Mean Guns*; *The Big Hit*; *Kalifornia*; *Albino Alligator*; *Best Men*; *Normal Life*; *U-Turn*; *Blood Guts Bullets and Octane*; *Grosse Point Blank*; *Bound*; *Another Day in Paradise*; *Mad Dog Time*; *Underworld*; *Freeway*; *The Immortals*; *Guns, Girls and Gambling*; *Bad Times at the El Royale*; *Snatch*; *Amores Perros*; *The Devil's Rejects*; *Palookaville*; *American Strays*; *8 Heads in a Duffel Bag*; *Phoenix*; *Seven Psychopaths*; and *Pawn Shop Chronicles*.

5

Guillermo del Toro
Stories About the Dark Side of Life

Guillermo del Toro was born in Guadalajara, Mexico, in 1959 and grew up in a devout Catholic environment. Throughout his childhood, he experienced lucid dreams, during which he saw monsters all around him. In order to survive and function in the real world, he believed he had to bargain with the monsters so they would allow his passage. He later credited these waking dreams as being the source of his lifelong fascination with monsters.

His first cinematic memory is watching William Wyler's 1939 film *Wuthering Heights* in a theater with his parents. He remembered falling asleep, waking up, and falling back to sleep throughout the film. Despite sleeping through much of it, he credited the "gothic spirit" of the Emily Brontë novel the film was adapted from as being a major influence on his creative work.

Around the age of eight, he started purchasing ten-minute condensed films (the Boris Karloff–starrer *Curse of the Crimson Altar* was one of them) and projecting them onto a screen. His father owned a camera, so del Toro began making films with his toys. These were generally violent pictures about his *Planet of the Apes* action figures engaging in battle with his Universal monsters figures. Blood was frequently spilled in these early films, with del Toro using ketchup for blood. As a kid, he traveled by bus to different theaters, where he would watch Japanese and Italian horror films. He also went to Saturday matinees to watch genre pictures alongside cartoons. Del Toro has said that he sees Disney family fare and bloody horror pictures as being virtually the same.

As a teen, he started making live-action films with his friends. The length of these shoots ranged from thirty minutes to epic two-day extravaganzas. As he grew older, he spent more and more money making the short films. He even convinced his mother, Guadalupe Gomez Camberos, to appear in some of them. In one, *Geometria*, a $2,500 tale of the undead, his mother met her violent demise at the hands of a zombie.

Del Toro loved cinema, and he enjoyed every genre, but he was mostly drawn to horror and dark fantasy. These were the types of films he dreamed of making. "There are only two things you can do in art or in narrative storytelling," he told BBC Film. "You can tell about the good stuff in life, which has always been very boring to me. And you can tell stories about the dark side of life, which has been much more attractive to me."

As a young man, del Toro still felt passionate about cinema and filmmaking, so he worked in a variety of capacities on short films by other directors. After he graduated from high school, del Toro attended the University of Guadalajara, where he studied film. During his time there, he wrote a book analyzing the films of Alfred Hitchcock. He also wrote two scripts for his thesis: *Vampire of the Grey Dawn* and *The Devil's Backbone*. He ultimately made both scripts into films, but the project he wanted to make first was *Vampire of the Grey Dawn*, which he retitled *Cronos*.

Cronos is about a grandfather, who is a vampire, and the granddaughter who loves him. Similar to his later films *Devil's Backbone* and *Pan's Labryinth*, *Cronos* deals with a child being confronted with horrifying circumstances. The relationship between the little girl and her grandfather was modeled after del Toro's relationship with his grandmother, which was rocky at times, and he claimed that she tried to exorcise him with holy water.

According to del Toro, growing up Catholic in Mexico, coupled with the idea of vampirism as both sacrament and addiction, led him to write *Cronos*. He wanted to reinvent vampirism through alchemy, and he worked on drafts "almost every day" for nearly a decade, during which *Cronos* evolved. In del Toro's earliest drafts, a watchmaker is dragged into a dark alley by a homeless man, who bites him, ultimately transforming the watchmaker into a vampire. In these early drafts, there were more plot twists. In one draft, the old man's nose falls off into a bowl of soup he's eating. Then, when he looks into a mirror, his ear falls off. But when del Toro saw David Cronenberg's *The Fly*, he noted the similarities and excised it from his script.

During this period, del Toro worked on other directors' films, creating makeup effects and drawing storyboards. He had heard quite a bit about a cameraman named Guillermo Navarro. Navarro's cinematography and lighting were superb, but he had a reputation for being difficult to work with. Strangely enough, del Toro says it was for this reason that he wanted to meet him and watch him work, so when he was offered a job storyboarding action sequences for a film Navarro was working on, he gladly accepted.

Navarro remembered his early experiences with del Toro, saying, "He was one of the only people I knew who was doing prosthetic makeup in Mexico, so he worked as a makeup guy on several movies that I was doing. So we became friends during that process. That's when he told me the story of *Cronos*." Wanting to help, Navarro introduced del Toro to his sister Bertha Navarro, who was a producer. She then signed on to help get the film made.

At some point, an American producer also signed on. The producer urged del Toro to rewrite his script in English because he believed that would make it an easier sell, so he agreed and wrote an English draft. Two things of note happened regarding the English draft: The first was that *Cronos* still didn't sell. The second was that del Toro realized that the English version didn't work, either. However, he wrote yet another draft, translating the English version back into Spanish and restructuring it into a traditional three-act piece in the process.

Del Toro had conceived the character Jesús Gris with one of his favorite actors, Arturo de Cordoba, in his mind. Because Cordoba was long dead by this time, del Toro had to find a different actor to play the role. He saw Argentine actor Federico

Luppi in *Last Days of the Victim* and was impressed with Luppi's ability to maintain a screen presence while speaking a minimal amount of dialogue. He knew immediately that he was his Jesús Gris. When Luppi came to Mexico to make another movie, del Toro used the opportunity to slip into his dressing room and offer him the part. Luppi accepted.

Del Toro originally envisioned the Angel de la Guardia character as being a Nazi hiding out in Mexico. With this in mind, he considered Max von Sydow and Maria Brandauer for the part. Because the American producer had suggested that del Toro cast an American actor, he went with Ron Perlman. Del Toro then cast the theater-trained Mexican actor Claudio Brook to inhabit the role of de la Guardia's uncle.

Cronos wasn't eligible for state funding because it was a genre picture; these funds required that a film must be deemed artistic in order to be considered. Nonetheless, del Toro and his producers managed to scrape up $1.5 million to make the film—or so they believed. Unfortunately, $600,000 that had been

Guillermo del Toro on the set of The Devil's Backbone. *Courtesy of Sony Pictures Classics/Photofest © Sony Pictures Classics*

promised by the American producer failed to materialize. This led del Toro to take drastic measures to complete the film. He took out a sizable loan on his house, sold his car and almost everything of value that he owned, and took out a hefty second loan with an exorbitant 10 percent interest rate. At one point, del Toro even asked Ron Perlman to work on the picture for nothing more than the promise of payment in the future. Perlman agreed, and the two men became lifelong friends.

Del Toro paid out of pocket or made personal sacrifices for things not allotted in the budgets of multiple projects after *Cronos*. For instance, on his second film, *Mimic*, he paid $120,000 out of his own funds for additional effects. On *Hellboy*, he put half of his salary back into the production. A true artist, del Toro's maxim is, "I have to make films. How much will it cost to make it the way I want to make it?"

Del Toro storyboarded a handful of scenes for *Cronos*, which he later decided to discard, saying they were too rigid. He purchased a leather-bound notebook that he carried with him everywhere. It contained page after page of intricate notes and "scribbles and doodles" regarding scenes in the film. After completing *Cronos*, del Toro loaned his notebook for the film to *Terminator* director James Cameron, who lost it. In the years since, del Toro has continued to carry one of those notebooks with him everywhere he goes. He fills the pages with thoughts, observations, questions, and drawings pertaining to whatever project he's working on. Since *Cronos*, he has filled hundreds of notebooks with ideas and visuals, and he never discards them. To date, the only notebook he cannot account for is the one Cameron lost.

The films of directors Terence Fisher and James Whale proved to be tremendous influences on *Cronos* (and every film del Toro has made since). Fisher's primary influences on del Toro are the color palettes of his films, as well as his framing and camera placement. In Whale's *Frankenstein*, which del Toro watched as a child, the scene in which the little girl is thrown into the lake by the monster deeply affected him. With every film del Toro has made—beginning with *Cronos*—he has sought to replicate the feeling he had when he first watched that scene.

Additionally, such German expressionist films as *Nosferatu* influenced the lighting in *Cronos*.

Del Toro worked closely with Navarro lighting the scenes. The warehouse set where de la Guardia's character lives was difficult to light, and Navarro was forced to light the room from the roof of another building. Another location Navarro found challenging to light was the rooftop, where the neon "DE LA GUARDIA" light was the only light source. Interestingly, after the film was completed, Navarro found that he was extremely happy with the way these scenes turned out. "With that I learned that the best way to really embrace a challenge is by taking it directly from the front and [to] take a big chance," Navarro later said in an interview for the film's 2010 Criterion release. "And we took huge risks on doing that—very, very big risks, and they paid off very well."

Navarro said of del Toro,

> I think he's like clockwork. It's a combination of writing and directing where he is in complete control of his vision. And he knows very well that film language is a tool. So he's not like many other directors, just registering the moment; he builds it shot by shot. That's where we connected very well, because my tool is a film language as well—the camera is telling the story. That's really why I started and continue doing what I do, because I'm a very strong believer of that. With him it's been the perfect combination of building scenes and visual narrative.

Navarro, who lensed several other del Toro films, including *The Devil's Backbone* and *Pan's Labyrinth*, said he and the director have a symbiotic collaborative relationship. "That comes from the prep," he says.

> The preparation process [we do] together, and we can divide the tasks very well so I can take care of my department and push everything forward. Then there's the great ability to react. Because many things we have to shoot are scenes that weren't necessarily planned in that moment, but things are changing constantly. So we can just reconvene and address

the things. But we work, always, very confident about what we are doing and being very observant of the grammar of filmmaking.

The music for the film was important to del Toro, who is a connoisseur of film music. In fact, del Toro is so passionate about film music that he listens to film scores for enjoyment instead of popular music. On *Cronos*, he was as selective as he is passionate. A fan of such iconic Hollywood scores as *Jaws* and *The Godfather*, del Toro said that he'd never heard a single Mexican film score that he'd liked before *Cronos*. Luckily, production designer Tolita Figueroa showed him a sample of music by her friend, composer Javier Álvarez. Del Toro listened to the music and loved what he heard, so he connected with Álvarez. The two worked as collaborators on the *Cronos* score, with del Toro being more involved with the creation of the music than most filmmakers are. Working closely with composers is something del Toro has continued to do on the films he's made since. Not surprisingly, he is involved to some extent in just about every aspect of his films' creation.

Cronos's postproduction proved to be difficult. His first editor, Raúl Dávalos, left after finalizing his cut. At the urging of filmmaker Alfonso Cuarón, whom del Toro had screened the film for, he went back into the editing room to tighten the picture. In the second cut, which took two weeks to complete, del Toro reduced *Cronos*'s running time by twenty-seven minutes. After screening his completed film, he concluded that he needed to be more flexible. He'd had an artistic disagreement with an actor about his interpretation of the character, so much of the actor's scenes were cut. In the end, del Toro believed this did a disservice to the picture.

In early screenings of the film, *Cronos* proved to be a love/hate film, with a good number of the audience walking out. Mexican critics by and large trashed the picture. However, *Cronos* took home a number of awards at festivals. One of the first awards was a sizable cash prize, which caused del Toro to weep, partly because he was proud of the film's success and partly because it meant he would now be able to pay off enough of his loans that he could avoid going to jail.

Cronos eventually was recognized as an artistic achievement, and it elevated the reputation of Mexican cinema. Del Toro was approached about possibly remaking the film for an American audience, but believing *Cronos* is a uniquely Mexican story, he declined. Nevertheless, American film studios wanted to work with him. One of these was Miramax.

In the mid-'90s, Miramax chieftains Bob and Harvey Weinstein came up with the idea to make a science-fiction anthology film showcasing up-and-coming directors they were working with. (This same half-baked "anthology film featuring Miramax directors" concept was used to make the Miramax dud *Four Rooms*.) Each segment would be thirty minutes long, and the directors were Gary Fleder, Danny Boyle, and Guillermo del Toro. It was ultimately decided that Fleder's segment, "Imposter," and del Toro's segment, "Mimic," would be expanded into feature films.

Mimic was an ideal project for del Toro, who had a love for and fascination with insects. The story is about the discovery of a new breed of insect called the Judas breed. However, the experience of making the film was not positive for del Toro. He later pointed to one particular moment as being the point when he'd known there were going to be problems. Del Toro and a producer were sitting at a table talking about the storyline.

In del Toro and cowriter Matthew Robbins's script, the bugs were beetles that were carrying a disease. After the producer took off his shoes and picked at his feet—a move del Toro called "super classy"—the producer said, "Why don't we make them cockroaches?" This suggestion horrified del Toro, who informed the producer that this change would lead to *Mimic* forever being identified as the "giant cockroach movie." Del Toro loved B movies, but he didn't want to make one.

Del Toro's pleas went unheard, and he was, as he later said, "condemned to doing the best giant cockroach movie ever." Knowledgeable about insects—critters he calls "God's favorite creatures"—del Toro worked closely with production designer TyRuben Ellingson to create the Judas breed. They studied copious volumes in del Toro's extensive library of insect books.

Ellingson later called del Toro a "bona fide genius" who is "like a historian mixed with a technologist mixed with a fine artist."

Late in the process, the studio balked at the insect designs and demanded that the creatures' antennae be removed. But through all of this, del Toro's primary goal was to create something that looked natural and believable within the context of the story. In the end, del Toro and Ellingson's creations so impressed experts in the field that scientists later named a fluid released from the defensive gland of a water beetle Mirasorvone (after *Mimic* star Mira Sorvino).

The studio suits continued to complain about the script even after the beetles became cockroaches, so an army of script doctors were brought in to take passes at del Toro and Robbins's script. One of these writers was John Sayles, who'd written the B movies *Piranha* and *Alligator* in the 1980s. Del Toro liked Sayles's draft, although hardly any of it made it into the final film. Steven Soderbergh also contributed a draft, which del Toro called "truly deranged," but it was so radically different from the director's vision that most of it was tossed out, too.

Miramax also took issue with del Toro's casting choices. The director wanted Andre Braugher for the role of Josh Maslow, but the studio said no because they believed an interracial couple would draw ire from some quarters (and, in turn, lose the studio money). So Braugher was out, and Josh Brolin became Josh Maslow. Miramax also took issue with del Toro's plans to use religious symbolism in the film.

The studio hired additional camera crews to shoot second-unit footage, and Robert Rodriguez led one of these crews. Del Toro did not want second-unit crews shooting additional footage, so when the studio took control of the film's editing and included a significant amount of the footage, he was understandably upset. In the years since, del Toro has refused to use second-unit crews on any of the films he's made, and he's proud to be able to say that all the footage that appears in the films was shot by himself and his cinematographer. Interestingly, del Toro managed to sneak a shot of a butterfly with its wings pinned to a board next to his name into the opening credit sequence, alluding to the fact that he'd had very little control over the final film.

When *Mimic* opened on August 22, 1997, *Chicago Sun-Times* critic Roger Ebert wrote that it had been

> stylishly directed by Guillermo del Toro, whose visual sense adds a certain texture that makes everything scarier and more effective. It's not often that a movie like this can frighten me, but I was surprised at how effective *Mimic* is. . . . Del Toro is a director with a genuine visual sense, with a way of drawing us into his story and evoking the mood with the very look and texture of his shots. He takes the standard ingredients and presents them so effectively that *Mimic* makes the old seem new, fresh and scary.

Mimic did lackluster box office business, taking in $25 million against its $30 million budget. It did, however, develop a cult following after it was released on video, leading to two straight-to-video sequels (without involvement from del Toro).

"I do feel a little disappointed that *Mimic* wasn't that thing Del Toro saw in his mind," Ellingson told Inverse. "The one I listened to him talk about was a different film. There's fifty percent of that film in the final cut, but there's also fifty percent of something else representing negotiated studio needs."

"It was a big learning experience for me," del Toro later told the audience at a 2011 Toronto Underground Cinema screening. "I learned a very useful word, which is 'no' . . . and 'Get the fuck away from me!'" In that same discussion, he also called the making of *Mimic* an "endurance test," saying, "I think it's still the worst experience of my life, including the kidnapping of my dad." Del Toro likened the experience to being "gang raped by John Holmes." In a 2018 *Independent* interview, he elaborated further, "It was a horrible, horrible, horrible experience. . . . I was interfered with in plot, in casting, in the type of action. They second-guessed all the time. I never had a single day that was pleasant."

A few months after the film's release, James Cameron nearly came to blows with Harvey Weinstein due to the disservice he felt Weinstein had done to del Toro and *Cronos*. Cameron later told *Vanity Fair* about the exchange, which occurred backstage at the seventieth Academy Awards ceremony. "Harvey came up glad-handing me, talking about how great [Miramax was] for the artist, and I just read him chapter and verse about how great I thought he was for the artist based on my friend's experience, and that led to an altercation." Cameron also claimed he considered hitting Weinstein over the head with the Best Picture Oscar he'd just received for *Titanic*.

In 2009, del Toro revealed that he'd begun work on an expanded director's cut of *Mimic*. To assemble the cut, he went into the *"Citizen Kane*–like Miramax warehouse" and located every piece of unused footage from the film he could find. Two years later, del Toro's director's cut was unveiled, six minutes longer than the theatrical cut. In del Toro's version, jump scares and second-unit material was cut, and more of the original material he'd shot was reinserted. The pace was also slowed, and it better resembled a Guillermo del Toro film than a horror film of the week. Del Toro told everyone who would listen that he loved his new cut and was proud of it. It still wasn't the film he'd set out to make, partially because he'd never been allowed to shoot the original ending he'd written, but it was the best version of the film that could have been assembled with the footage he'd shot.

Del Toro later said that he learned a lot from the experience of making the film. "I'm thankful for *Mimic*," he told IndieWire.

> I learned a lot about technique and new toys and new camera rigs and simple digital effects and I applied all of that in a much smaller budget of less than six million dollars. Most people think that when you do a movie that you're not happy with, it's a bad thing. I think I learned much more from doing *Mimic* than from doing *Cronos*, not only in terms of valuing my creative freedom, but also as being demanded by the studio, to try new stuff. They pushed me to try new stuff, and I realized I was good at certain things that I [had] never tried. It widened my range of camera moves and storytelling. So you can learn more from a hard experience than a nice one.

Interestingly, *Cronos* isn't an American production, and *Mimic* was victimized by studio interference, so neither are *proper* Guillermo del Toro films (in terms of this book's primary focus). Nevertheless, these films are significant because *Cronos* established him as a filmmaker and set a precedent that allowed him to move seamlessly between Mexican and Hollywood productions. This is an unorthodox practice and serves as an example of what makes del Toro a maverick. As he expressed, *Mimic* was important because it made him realize that he didn't want to be someone who compromises his artistic vision. It made him stronger and, in many ways, helped him become the master filmmaker he is today.

Guillermo del Toro's post-'90s filmography includes such artistic triumphs as *The Devil's Backbone*, *Pan's Labyrinth*, *The Shape of Water*, and *Nightmare Alley*. But it also includes some more mainstream films, such as *Blade II*, *Hellboy*, *Hellboy II: The Golden Army*, and *Pacific Rim*. But despite those films being mainstream (or mainstream adjacent), del Toro never sacrifices his vision or his artistry. Simply put, the name *Guillermo del Toro* is synonymous with *cinematic excellence*. If you see his name on a film, you can rest assured that you are in for something daring, unique, and highly qualitative.

6

David Fincher and the Ultimate Magic Trick

David Fincher grew up in the same neighborhood where George Lucas lived. At the age of eight, he watched a documentary about the making of *Butch Cassidy and the Sundance Kid*. Where most kids would be bored to tears watching a making-of documentary, Fincher was mesmerized. "It had never occurred to me that movies didn't take place in real time," he said later.

> I knew that they were fake. I knew that the people were acting, but it had never occurred to me that it could take four months to make a movie! It showed the entire company with all these rental horses and moving trailers to shoot a scene on top of a train. They would hire somebody who looked like Robert Redford to jump onto the train. It never occurred to me that there were hours between each of these shots. The actual circus of it was invisible, as it should be, but in seeing that I became obsessed with the idea of "How?" It was the ultimate magic trick. The notion that twenty-four still photographs are shown in such quick succession that movement is imparted from it—*wow!* And I thought that there could never be anything as interesting as that to do with the rest of my life.

After moving to Oregon as a teenager, Fincher remained focused on becoming a filmmaker. In high school, he did the closest things he could find to filmmaking: He wrote and produced plays, designed sets, worked as a projectionist, and got himself a job as a production assistant at a local television news station.

After graduating, he moved to Los Angeles, where he worked in film in various capacities. He worked as head of production for Academy Award–winning director and animator John Korty. He worked for a time at Industrial Light and Magic (ILM) as an assistant cameraman on *Return of the Jedi* and as a matte photographer on *Indiana Jones and the Temple of Doom*. In 1984, he directed a commercial for the American Cancer Society. After that, he began working in music videos, directing Rick Springfield's *The Beat of a Live Drum* documentary and founding the commercial- and music-video-production company Propaganda Films. Through his company, he worked with other up-and-coming directors, including Spike Jonze, Michel Gondry, Zack Snyder, Antoine Fuqua, and Michael Bay. He directed music videos—fifty-three in all—for such noted musical acts as Michael Jackson, Madonna, Don Henley, Aerosmith, Paula Abdul, and George Michael.

After cutting his teeth making commercials and music videos, Fincher was ready to make a movie. In 1990, he was hired to replace Vincent Ward on *Alien 3*. This was a huge offer, considering he'd be following in the footsteps of Ridley Scott and James Cameron. Unfortunately, the job wasn't all that it appeared to be. While this was the kind of opportunity he'd dreamed of since he'd first watched the *Butch Cassidy* documentary, *Alien 3* caused him great heartache, and in his words to *Empire*, he was "sodomized ritualistically for two years."

The production of *Alien 3* had been problematic from the start. While the public clamored for a third *Alien* film, producers Walter Hill, David Giler, and Gordon Carroll hadn't been all that interested. Their primary hang-up was their desire to make something different from the first two films that could still please fans of the franchise. They finally decided to explore the idea of the aliens being exploited and weaponized by the Weyland-Yutani Corporation. They pitched this concept as two separate installments of the *Aliens* series to the suits at 20th Century Fox. The studio wasn't sold on financing more *Alien* films, but they ultimately greenlighted the films with two stipulations: The producers had to approach Ridley Scott about possibly directing them, and *Alien 3* and *Alien 4* had to be shot back to back. When the producers met with Scott, he was thrilled about the idea but declined due to other obligations. After Scott passed, Renny Harlin was hired.

The first iteration of the *Alien 3* story was written by Hill and Giler. The producers then hired cyberpunk pioneer William Gibson to pen a draft expanding the ideas introduced in their treatment while incorporating new elements. Fearing that a writer's strike was on the horizon, Gibson was given a three-month deadline. His draft had Michael Biehn's Hicks character take over as lead, relegating Sigourney Weaver's Ripley to a secondary role. After that, Eric Red, the screenwriter of *The Hitcher*, stepped in to take a pass. Following Red, a third screenwriter, David Twohy, came in and wrote a new draft. Twohy's script was about the aliens attacking a prison vessel.

Harlin disliked the direction the project was going. He'd wanted *Aliens 3* to be something completely different—no more creeping around in dark corridors. He wanted to explore the idea of going to the aliens' planet, but the producers believed that would be too costly to make. So he quit. "I believe that when you are doing a sequel and you're part of a series, that you want to give the audience . . . the same kind of experience," Harlin explained in the *Making of Alien 3* documentary.

> They expect to see aliens, and they expect to see the heroine and certain types of situations, so I do believe you want to give that satisfaction, but at the same time, I do believe that your job is to invent something new and offer something new because otherwise you're just rehashing what people before you did. That was always my goal. Ultimately, the reason I had to make the hard decision and go to Walter Hill and say, "Walter, I'm really sorry. I think I've been working on this for a year, and we've done illustrations, and we've worked on all of these storylines, but I really feel like somehow we keep circling the same premise, and for me it's not different enough from what the audience has seen before. I just can't get excited about the idea of just having more guns and more aliens."

The second director was New Zealand filmmaker Vincent Ward. The producers approached him several times, but he repeatedly said he wasn't interested in making sequels. Finally, he relented and signed on. He looked at the Twohy script the producers sent him and hated it. On his flight to the United States, Ward conceived an idea and wrote out a rough treatment. He then presented it to the studio suits and producers, and everyone liked it, so the project moved forward. John Fasano was hired to expand Ward's treatment. Soon after, Sigourney Weaver was hired as the lead once again. When the producers decided to rework Ward's story, Ward left the production. Giler and Hill then rewrote the script themselves. After that, *Beverly Hills Cop 2* writer Larry Ferguson came in to polish the script. Fincher became director number 3, and he worked on yet another draft of the script with novelist Rex Pickett.

Aliens 3 finally began filming in January 1991. Because there wasn't a finished script to work from, Fincher found the process to be a nightmare. Additionally, the studio demanded last-minute changes to the schedule throughout the shoot. "It was just miserable," Fincher told journalist Mark Salisbury.

> I don't do the trained dog act, I'm not there to shepherd somebody's idea through. I get very involved in the commercial work I do and rewrite and reconceive a lot of stuff. You make it your own, and I didn't really get to do that in two years of working on *Alien 3*. It was like, "We like your idea, but see if you can do it for $15,000 instead of $150,000?" I had never been a traffic cop and I didn't know how to do that. I don't respond well to people saying "Get more coverage."

Displeased by the studio's constant meddling, Fincher announced to his crew one day, "It's amazing to me that Fox is the number one studio in the country, because they're all such a bunch of morons!" Seemingly nothing went as planned. Additionally, cinematographer Jordan Cronenweth had to leave in the middle of the shoot due to illness, and Fincher spent much of the shoot arguing with 20th Century Fox.

"The most horrifying thing about doing *Alien* 3 was realizing that the more you cared, the more they fucking had you," Fincher later observed.

> It was a very tough lesson to learn. The game that you have to play when you're dealing with that kind of money is that you have to be able to walk away and go "Fuck it." Then if it doesn't work out, say, "I don't give a shit." Then you really are in a position of power. I was totally powerless because I was so possessed to do something that would live up to the other two movies.

Before it was over, *Alien 3* was taken out of Fincher's hands and edited without his participation, leaving much of what he shot on the cutting-room floor. By the time the movie was completed, the budget had soared to $50 million, the largest that had ever been given to a first-time director. Unfortunately, it wasn't the film Fincher wanted to make. When it was all said and done, he was ready to move on and put as much distance between himself and *Alien 3* as he could.

By any measure, the production had been a shit show. Fincher later said, "A lot of people hated *Alien 3*, but no one hated it more than I did." In the decades that followed, the director kept largely tight-lipped about the experience. He refused to participate in commentaries, appear in documentaries about the film, or speak on the film at any length. Finally, in 2023, Fincher broke his silence, summing up his *Alien 3* experience for journalist Nev Pierce:

> There's no one problem with a $65 million fucked up first-time film. Look, I made a crucial error—I listened to the people who were paying for the movie, and they said, "The way to go about this is to not work with your friends. The way to go about this is to work with people who've done this time and time and time again." Basically that translates into "meet a lot of people who are going to resent you and your age and are not gonna want to take instruction from you and allow them to tell you what you can't do." A lot of people who were just like "What the fuck? Who is this twerp?" So I kind of retreated

back to doing television commercials and had no expectation that I would ever be employable again. And I got sent a script and it was *Seven*.

The story of Fincher's next project, *Se7en*, begins with screenwriter Andrew Kevin Walker. Walker, a Pennsylvania native, had relocated to New York City only a few years before. He was working in a menial position at Tower Records and found the city to be bleak, so he was depressed. When he sat down to write, that's what poured out onto the page—a bleaker-than-bleak story about a gloomy crime-filled (unidentified) city. Walker wanted to write something unique about a serial killer who is pure evil but obsessed with the so-called seven deadly sins, which leads him to commit a string of murders. It's also about the two cops trying to catch him.

When Walker was finished with his script, he had no idea what to do with it. On a whim, he mailed an unsolicited copy of it to David Koepp, the screenwriter who had adapted *Jurassic Park*. Usually when screenwriters send unsolicited screenplays to producers and other film professionals, the scripts are immediately tossed into the nearest wastebasket. Walker hoped to avoid this, so he did a second gutsy/stupid nontraditional thing: He cold-called Koepp to make sure he read it. Shockingly, Koepp read the screenplay and passed it to his agent, who then took Walker on as a client.

Soon after, an Italian film production company called Penta Film optioned Walker's script and hired a director to make *Se7en*. The director, Jeremiah Chechik, was and is best known for directing the decidedly un-*Se7en*-like *National Lampoon's Christmas Vacation*. Chechik hated Walker's exceedingly bleak ending in which one cop finds his wife's severed head in a box. Chechik wanted to make something more commercial, so he requested changes to the script.

Penta Film began to crumble, and their option on the screenplay was on the verge of expiring, so they sold it to *Platoon* producer Arnold Kopelson. Kopelson then set the project up at New Line Cinema. At some point in the midst of all this, Chechik quit the production, and a number of directors were approached about directing *Se7en*, including Guillermo del Toro, Ernest Dickerson, and Phil Joanou. All of them declined. At that point, David Fincher was approached. While *Alien 3* had been a mess, Kopelson and the studio liked the dark feel he'd brought to the movie.

Fincher's agent thought *Se7en* could be a good rebound picture for him, but the director almost refused. Fincher read half the script and was unmoved. He called his agent and said, "I'm not interested in this whole last seven days of a homicide investigator." To this, his agent simply said, "Keep reading." "So I went back and I was reading it and I got to the part where John Doe gives himself up, covered in blood, and I'm holding this thing in my hands, so I know there's like eighteen pages left," Fincher told the *Los Angeles Times*.

> Not a lot. There's less than twenty minutes left in the movie. How can you have the guy that everyone's been chasing give himself up? And I remember being in an agitated, elevated state going: Wait a minute. *This can't happen.* I don't have experience with a narrative that can reinvent itself in the last twenty pages. And then I got to the head in the box and I was like: Count me in.

The part that Fincher leaves out is that Kopelson had accidentally sent him the wrong draft of the script, which was the "head in the box" version. Kopelson then sent him the sanitized, watered-down version they were working with at the time, which ended with a chase sequence leading to the cop's house, where the wife is taking a shower. After reading it, Fincher told his agent, "This is just crap. The first one is much better." So Fincher went to Mike DeLuca, the head of production at New Line, and told him he would sign on to make the "head in the box" version. DeLuca concurred that it was the better ending and agreed to finance that version.

However, there was still one problem: Kopelson refused to make that version. Fincher later recalled his conversation with the producer in a 1996 *Empire* interview:

[Kopelson] said, "There is no way there will be a head in the box at the end of this movie, there is absolutely no way that will ever happen, don't even talk to me about that." And I said, "Arnold, in fifty years from now, there's going to be a bunch of twenty-five-to-thirty-five year-olds at a party and one of them is going to say, 'Remember when you were like fifteen and that movie was on TV, I don't even know who was in it, but at the end there's this head in the box and the guy drives up in the middle of the desert,' and everybody's going to go, 'Oh yeah, I loved that movie.' That's how the movie is going to be remembered, so how can you cut the head in the box?" And he said, "You're right."

By convincing Kopelson and DeLuca to make the edgier version of Walker's script, Fincher had already made a significant contribution to *Se7en*, cinema history, and the legacy of '90s filmmaking. Had DeLuca and Kopelson chosen to film the softer version of the script, Fincher would have left, and that safer, blander version would have been directed by another run-of-the-mill gun for hire like Chechik, becoming just another forgotten flick you might vaguely remember seeing on a video store shelf once. It certainly would not have become the classic film that *Se7en* is recognized as today.

After everyone agreed to shoot the "head in the box" version of *Se7en*, it was decided that it would begin filming in just six weeks. When it came to casting Brad Pitt as the lead, Fincher wasn't all that enthused at first. At the time, Pitt was known as a pretty-boy actor. This wasn't what Fincher envisioned. He wanted someone who was "sort of a fuck up." But Creative Artists Agency convinced him to at least meet with Pitt, so Fincher said, "What the hell, sure," and had lunch with him. The two hit it off, and Fincher was impressed with Pitt, particularly because he believed he was the kind of actor who could say anything and the audience would continue to follow him without holding it against him.

Screenwriter Walker had envisioned William Hurt essaying the role of Pitt's older partner, but Hurt was never approached. Several actors turned down the role, including Gene Hackman, Robert Duvall, and Al Pacino. Then Kopelson called Fincher one day and said, "What do you think about Morgan Freeman?" Fincher liked the idea, so he called Freeman. Freeman said, "I would love to be in this." And that was it—the role was Freeman's.

Fincher auditioned approximately one hundred actresses to play Pitt's wife. After finding no one who fit his idea of the character, he was persuaded by Pitt to audition his girlfriend, Gwyneth Paltrow. Fincher believed Paltrow was the perfect actress for the role, and she was cast.

For the role of serial killer John Doe, Fincher and Walker both thought Ned Beatty was the perfect actor. But when they approached Beatty, he was mortified by the darkness he found in the script and passed. Singer Michael Stipe and R. Lee Ermey, who ended up being cast as the film's police chief, were considered and rejected. Fincher fought for Kevin Spacey, who was hot at the time, to play the role. The studio believed Spacey's cost was too high, so another unnamed actor was cast instead. This actor's scenes were filmed, but it was decided that he was wrong for the role, so Spacey was hired. Because Spacey was coming off a streak of hot films (*Swimming with Sharks, The Usual Suspects,* and *Outbreak*), it was decided that his name would be left out of the opening credits and promotional ads so the audience wouldn't figure out who the killer was before they were supposed to. Shooting began on December 12, 1994, and lasted until the following March. The film's final budget was roughly $33 million.

The key to *Se7en*'s success was Fincher's newly developed refusal to compromise his artistic vision. After the *Alien 3* debacle, he'd vowed that he'd never allow that to happen again. As he explained to *Playboy*'s Stephen Rebello, "With my first movie, *Alien 3*, I had to get permission for everything, but my second movie, *Seven*, was my movie. . . . I didn't look to anyone for permission."

Both Kopelson and the studio suggested ways they could tone down the dark mood of the film, but Fincher wasn't having it. If anything, he seems to have doubled down because the finished film is *repellently* dark. Defending the tone and storyline of *Se7en*, he later said, "Some people go to the movies to be reminded that everything's okay. I don't make those kinds of movies. That, to me, is a lie. Everything's not okay."

Much of the film's effectiveness comes from the gritty visual aesthetic Fincher created, working closely with production designer Arthur Max. Fincher has earned a reputation as someone who plans and executes every aspect of his films with incredible precision, and Fincher and Max copied elements of photographs of real crime scenes for the "Gluttony" set. They wanted to give the room a sense of foreboding and the subtle implication that other crimes could have been committed previously in that location.

In another instance, Fincher and Max attempted to evoke a slight feeling of unease by constructing the "Sloth" set inside an office building; the idea was that the audience would be, on some level, confused by the fact that a residence exists inside a space that was clearly constructed to be an office. "What we're saying is, 'This is an abandoned office building that's being occupied by crack-heads, and they live there,'" Max explained in the *Making of Seven* documentary. The details applied to these sets are incredible, considering they're so subtle that they're only meant to imply these ideas; the goals were to evoke feelings and perhaps form these connections in the viewer's mind on a subconscious level. Fincher and his collaborators apply this hyper-focus to the tiniest details wherever possible in his films, and the work he and Max did on these two sets are just two examples.

"He sets up certain rules of the game, and you have to stay within those rules or you get a red card or a yellow card for going out of bounds," Max said in 2020.

> And that goes for everybody in the crew. It has to do with the power of the movie and the atmosphere. In *Seven* he described it very succinctly: "This is a world that's fucked up and nothing works." Everything had to have a patina of neglect in every aspect, and I loved that. You almost wear a designer's whistle and if somebody did something that was too bright—a red or too rich a green—you blow the whistle and say, "Yellow that down and make it gloomier and put some more floor wax on it."

One of the most conspicuous components in the picture's bleak atmosphere is the constant rain. Most people assume that adding the rain was just another way to make the film gloomy. And while the pouring rain certainly does contribute to that, the real reason that the rain appears was a practical one. El Nino ravaged the city at the time of filming, causing an extreme amount of rain. Because of that, Fincher and his crew had to shoot five days' worth of scenes containing rain so they could maintain continuity.

Se7en test-screened in Long Beach, when the movie wasn't quite finished yet, but there was enough of the film for viewers to get a strong sense of its dark atmosphere. Obviously a film as dark and mean-spirited as *Se7en* wasn't going to please everyone. Making the situation worse, the studio offered potential viewers tickets by asking, "Would you like to see a movie starring Brad Pitt of *Legends of the Fall* and Morgan Freeman of *Driving Miss Daisy*?" As a result, the audience contained people expecting to see something similar to those films, which are obviously *very* different from *Se7en* in just about every conceivable way. So as one would expect, the audience reactions were disastrous.

After reviewing the screening's poor numbers, execs at the studio considered pulling the plug on further filming. Fincher then spoke to DeLuca one on one. He later told the *Los Angeles Times* that he told DeLuca, "Dude, we talked about *Klute*. We talked about *The French Connection*. We talked about the kinds of movies that we wanted to make. And I'm telling you, this movie is a *good movie*. It will be if we can complete the intention. And I need the money to finish this, and I'm coming to you and saying if you support this, I know I can make a better movie than what we screened." DeLuca considered this and allowed Fincher eleven extra days to complete shooting.

When *Se7en* was released theatrically on September 22, 1995, it was met with largely positive criticism. Roger Ebert of the *Chicago Sun-Times* wrote, "*Seven*, a dark, grisly, horrifying and intelligent thriller, may be too disturbing for many people, I imagine, although if you can bear to watch it, you will see filmmaking of a high order." He continued, "The material by itself could have been handled in many ways, but the director, David Fincher, goes for evocative atmosphere, and the writer, Andrew Kevin Walker, writes dialogue that for Morgan Freeman, in particular, is wise, informed, and poetic." The *Boston Globe*'s Jay Carr predicted, "When *Seven*, with its velvety world of bottomless evil, taps you on the shoulder, your instinct will be to dive under the theater seat." Michael Price of the *Fort Worth Star-Telegram* took the praise a step further, gushing, "I wouldn't go so far as to call David Fincher's *Seven* the most terrifying film ever, but it's right up there on the top shelf with *Psycho* and *The Silence of the Lambs*." Rene Rodriguez of the *Miami Herald* observed, "Fincher's suffocatingly dark style is the perfect fit for *Seven*: The gloomy nightmarish images communicate a fear that the characters' dialogue cannot, and if *Seven* haunts your dreams, it's thanks to Fincher's post-modern eye."

With the film's reputation being what it is today and your having just read the preceding critical observations and also knowing that *Se7en* ignited Fincher's career, you might guess that all the critics adored the film, but that's not the case. Just as test audiences had been split on the film, so, too, were the critics.

LA Weekly scribe Manohla Dargis eviscerated *Se7en*, but most of her criticisms were directed at its screenwriter: "Because he's working from a screenplay that weighs in as low-end pulp (by first-time Andrew Kevin Walker, who has one sick-fuck imagination), Fincher is forced to bring his staggering gifts to bear on less than worthy material." Despite her opinion of the picture, she praised its director, writing, "As for Fincher, he pierces the heart with genius. Whether he's narrowing his sights on a face gone weary with suffering, or filming one of the great film chase sequences in modern cinema, what he's really doing is taking his place as one of the most important, exciting directors to emerge in years." Some, like Michael Medved from the *New York Post*, held just as much contempt for Fincher as they did the film. In a failed attempt to be cute, Medved called Fincher a "director who seems to feel undisguised Envy for *The Silence of the Lambs*, but will end up inspiring Wrath through overblown Pride in his own intrusive touch."

Se7en became a smash hit, earning a whopping $327.3 million worldwide, making it the seventh-highest-grossing picture of 1995. Despite being nominated for awards at various film festivals and ceremonies around the globe, *Se7en* didn't make much of an impression on Academy Awards voters, who nominated it in only one category (Best Editing), which it didn't win.

After the massive success of *Se7en*, Fincher found himself in the driver's seat. Now one of the hottest and most sought-after directors in Hollywood, he could do whatever the hell he wanted. A lot of people had written him off after the *Alien 3* fiasco, but David Fincher had the last laugh.

In the years that have followed, *Se7en* has been included in a slew of lists ranking the best films of all time, ranging from 15th (*Total Film*) to the 134th (*Empire*). One has to wonder, in hindsight, if the critics who initially trashed the film stand by their assessments.

Fincher's third feature, *The Game*, came from a spec script by John Brancato and Michael Ferris, the writing team responsible for the 1995 hit film *The Net*. The script was sold to MGM, where Jonathan Mostow was attached as director, and Kyle MacLachlan and Bridget Fonda signed on to star. The film was set to begin shooting in early 1993, but the project fell apart, and all the talent dropped out. With *The Game* in turnaround, producer Steve Golin picked up the option. Golin, who'd helped establish Propaganda Films with Fincher, brought the project to his attention.

Fincher liked the script, but he believed it could be tighter, so he brought in Andrew Kevin Walker to perform a rewrite, and they worked together closely to get the script into fighting shape, collaborating on three drafts. Throughout the process, the writers could never come up with an ending they were entirely happy with. Screenwriter Larry Gross, who'd cowritten *48 Hours*, was also brought in to polish the script.

Because of the success he'd enjoyed with *Se7en*, Fincher now found that he could get just about any actor he wanted. He approached Michael Douglas about playing the lead role. Because the character was similar to Douglas's iconic *Wall Street* character, Gordon Gecko, Fincher believed he was a good fit.

Douglas read the script, liked it, and signed on. He was going through a messy divorce at the time, and he believed *The Game* could be a good distraction.

For a brief period, Jodie Foster was attached to costar in the project. Her involvement with *The Game* was even announced at the Cannes Film Festival. She was to play the brother role that eventually went to Sean Penn. There were talks about what exactly their relationship should be: Would she be his daughter, or would she be his sister? In the end, none of that mattered because Foster was unable to appear due to scheduling conflicts. (She was making Robert Zemeckis's *Contact* at the time.)

Fincher hired Harris Savides as director of photography. The two had collaborated previously on a number of music videos. He had asked Savides to shoot *Se7en*, but Savides had declined. He'd had a bad experience making *Heaven's Prisoners* for Phil Joanou and had sworn off shooting features. Savides then shot some second-unit footage for *Se7en*. After that, Fincher convinced him to return to shooting motion pictures.

Fincher wanted to shoot *The Game* in San Francisco, but Polygram Films preferred Chicago or Los Angeles, where filming would be cheaper. (Shooting in San Francisco added an estimated $3 million to the film's budget.) However, Fincher moved forward, insistent that *The Game* be made in the City by the Bay because Fincher and Walker had written it with San Francisco in mind.

With this Hitchcockian thriller, Fincher wanted to subvert the audience's expectations. As he told journalist Ryan Gilbey, "Movies usually make a pact with the audience that says: We're going to play it straight; what we show you is going to add up. But we don't do that. In that respect, it's about movies and how movies dole out information." Elaborating more, Fincher later explained in the film's commentary, "This film, for me, was an interesting study not in human behavior—how people relate to each other, what people want from life or career or any of that. It was, 'What does an audience want or expect or need from a film?' My question was, 'How much will they put up with, and will they go for forty-five minutes of red herrings?'"

The Game and all its twists and turns arrived in theaters on September 12, 1997. It earned $14.3 million during its opening weekend and went on to make an impressive $109 million worldwide. While the critics appreciated Fincher's style and craftsmanship, most expressed problems with the plot. *The New York Times'* Janet Maslin wrote, "Fincher, who has also had considerable experience making videos and commercials, has made *The Game* with impressive craftsmanship and a very high gloss. As photographed by Harris Savides (another stylish veteran of videos and commercials), this film sustains visual allure on several levels." Peter Travers of *Rolling Stone* observed,

> By any fair standard, this lushly produced film is a long, bumpy ride to a major letdown. . . . Fincher's effort to cover up the plot holes is all the more noticeable for being strained. With *Seven* and *Alien 3*, Fincher showed a predilection for dark parables about the human condition. *The Game* has a sunny, redemptive side that ill fits Fincher and ill serves audiences that share his former affinity for loose ends hauntingly left untied.

Desson Howe of the *Washington Post* called *The Game* an "elaborately constructed crock." He continued, "It's formulaic, yet edgy. It's predictable, yet full of surprises. How far you get through this tall tale of a thriller before you give up and howl is a matter of personal taste. But there's much pleasure in Fincher's intricate color schemes, his rich sense of décor, his ability to sustain suspense over long periods of time and his sense of humor."

The Game has the unfortunate distinction of being made and released between two of Fincher's strongest and most enduring films, *Se7en* and *Fight Club*. So while it's seen as being a merely "good" film, it gets lost in discussions of Fincher's other '90s accomplishments.

Fincher later expressed some regret about making *The Game*, saying that his wife, producer Ceán Chaffin, had "vociferously" urged him not to make it. "In hindsight, she was right," he said. "We didn't figure out the third act, and it was my fault, because I thought if you could just keep your foot on the throttle it would be liberating and fun." So despite the picture having been a financial success with at least decent reviews, it didn't live up to the expectations Fincher had for himself. This is telling; this mindset, this constant struggle for absolute perfection is what makes Fincher one of the most respected filmmakers of the last half-century.

Fincher's fourth film, the aforementioned *Fight Club*, found life first as a novel by transgressive author Chuck Palahniuk. In writing the novel, the thirty-something scribe shared selections at a number of Portland, Oregon, writing classes and workshops. Interestingly, one of the groups he read excerpts of the novel to were the patrons of a lesbian bookshop. According to Palahniuk, the reading was wildly successful. By this time, he'd already attempted to sell a novel, which had been roundly rejected, so with *Fight Club*, he'd given up his dream of being published. *Fight Club*, a no-holds-barred, angry, primal scream of a novel, was something he was writing for himself. As such and with no concerns about pleasing an audience, Palahniuk experienced a type of uninhibited freedom he hadn't allowed himself before, and he wrote what pleased him. Without having a literary agent, he managed to get his manuscript read by an editor at W. W. Norton. To Palahniuk's surprise, they accepted the novel for publication, purchasing it for a mere $6,000. The publisher released it as a hardcover with no fanfare, and it initially failed to find readers, selling less than five thousand copies.

One man who did read *Fight Club* was producer Ross Grayson Bell, who at the time had a single production credit under his belt for a picture called *Ice Pawn*. Bell was excited about Palahniuk's novel, wanted to make a movie out of it, and optioned the film rights for $10,000. He then assembled a group of struggling actors to participate in a table read of scenes from the book. He recorded the session and sent the tape to Laura Ziskin, president of the film production company Fox 2000. Ziskin listened to the tape and liked what she heard, so she took on the project.

Before Fincher entered the picture, a number of other filmmakers were approached to direct, including Peter Jackson, Bryan Singer, Danny Boyle, and David O. Russell. All of them passed. Russell later said of the novel, "I read it, and I didn't get it. I obviously didn't do a good job reading it."

Fincher read Palahniuk's novel while he was editing *The Game*, and it resonated with him. "I remember him reading it in galley form and laughing the whole time," Chaffin recalled. "It seemed like exactly the kind of movie he should be making." He wasn't sure how an adaptation could be structured, but he was interested in finding out. He pursued a film option, only to learn that it had already been optioned. To his horror, he discovered that Fox owned the rights. After the *Alien 3* debacle, he'd vowed never to work with Fox again, but he *really* wanted to make *Fight Club*. He met with Ziskin and told her that he was interested but that he envisioned it as a movie with a good-sized budget. Ziskin said she would consider the big-budget version of *Fight Club* if he could put together a good script and a cast. Fincher accepted this challenge.

First he had to find a screenwriter, but who? In Fincher's mind, *Fight Club* was Generation X's finding-yourself, coming-of-age, social-satire equivalent of *The Graduate*. With this in mind, he reached out to *The Graduate*'s screenwriter, Buck Henry, to ask if he might be interested in adapting Palahniuk's novel. But when Henry read the novel, he passed, saying that he didn't find anything funny about it. So Fincher hired Jim Uhls, a writer with no produced screenwriting credits who'd worked throughout the decade on multiple projects that never got made. Uhls immediately felt a connection to the material. A former bartender, he later said, "I knew what it was like to have a bullshit job. It affected how you felt about yourself, in a masculine way. After I read *Fight Club*, my jaw was on the ground for two weeks. But I was bracing myself: 'It will be fun to write this, but it's never going to be made.'" Uhls worked on the first draft for eight months, but Fincher felt that Uhls had removed the narrative voice that he'd enjoyed in the novel, so they then collaborated closely on a new draft.

Fincher went to work looking for actors. He spoke to a number of actors about playing Tyler Durden, who was essentially the flashier sparkplug character. In the end, he decided to cast Brad Pitt, whom he'd enjoyed working with on *Se7en*. One hot summer night, a worn-out Pitt came home to his New York City apartment after a long day of working on *Meet Joe Black*. When he arrived at his door, he found Fincher waiting for him with the *Fight Club* script in his hand.

For the role of the unnamed protagonist, Fincher considered a number of candidates, but no one seemed quite right. Then Fincher watched Milos Forman's *The People vs. Larry Flynt* and found himself fascinated by the young actor playing Flynt's lawyer, Edward Norton. Watching him onscreen, Fincher said, "That's the guy." Norton read the script in a single sitting, and he fell in love with it, calling *Fight Club* the Gen-X *Catcher in the Rye*. Additionally, he saw the same thematic parallels to *The Graduate* that Fincher had.

Fincher still wasn't happy with the screenplay, so he called *Se7en* scribe Andrew Kevin Walker and asked him to work on it. Walker agreed. The process of Walker's rewrite was an unorthodox one. Fincher, Pitt, Norton, and Walker would hang out, sometimes at Pitt's Los Angeles home and sometimes in a production office across the street from Grauman's Chinese Theater, where they played Nerf basketball and talked through the script's ideas, story, and characters. Pitt later said they broke down every line of the screenplay, analyzing it "like it was Shakespeare." According to Fincher, Walker contributed 20 percent of the final script. Despite this, the Writer's Guild decided it wasn't enough for him to receive a writing credit.

Fincher was now ready to take the project back to 20th Century Fox. He handed them the script, complete with a scene-by-scene breakdown of what he planned. He told them Brad Pitt and Edward Norton were attached to play the leads. Then he gave them an ultimatum: "You've got seventy-two hours to tell us if you're interested." Studio head Bill Mechanic liked what he read and agreed to finance the film. According to Fincher, upon hearing the news, he laughed and said, "Those idiots just greenlit a $75 million experimental movie."

Fincher began looking for the actress who would play the role of Marla Singer, the angry, chain-smoking, foul-mouthed, mentally ill gal pal of Tyler Durden. He considered a number of actresses, including Janeane Garofalo and Winona Rider. For a while, he toyed with the idea of casting Courtney Love, who had appeared with Norton in *The People vs. Larry Flynt*. But he knew he'd found his Marla after watching Helena Bonham Carter in *The Wings of the Dove*, so he sent her the script. When the actress read it, she didn't really understand it. Additionally, her mother was deeply offended by its contents. After meeting Fincher in person and sharing her concerns about the project and the role, the director addressed them one by one, and Bonham Carter accepted the role.

Fincher and the actors studied videos of raw backyard-style fights so they could get a better understanding of the fights they would enact in the movie. Pitt and Norton also took boxing and martial arts classes to prepare. Fincher was so much of a detail-oriented filmmaker that he had the actors learn to make soap because their characters discuss making soap in the film. Prepping for the shoot, the actors became as devoted as Fincher was to making *Fight Club* the best it could be. In an effort to make his character as authentic as possible, Pitt intentionally chipped one of his teeth.

Filming began in July 1998 and lasted 138 days, during which Fincher shot more than 1,500 rolls of film. The film was shot in locations around Los Angeles. Additionally, there were more than seventy sets built for the production. The budget of *Fight Club* increased exponentially.

Fincher and Norton disagreed about what the tone of the film should be throughout the shoot. Fincher later said that Norton wanted to make it an obvious comedy, whereas he wanted the comedy to be subtle. Norton later recalled one interaction while speaking to author Brian Raftery: "I was doing something in one of those office moments, and I looked at Fincher, like, 'Is this what you're thinking?' And he goes, 'A little less Jerry, a little more Dean.'"

Fincher is known as a director who shoots dozens upon dozens of takes. He explained, "Part of the promise when I work with actors is that we may be on take eleven and I'll say, 'We certainly have a version that we can put in the movie that will make us all happy. But I want to do seven more and continue to push the idea. Let's see where it goes.'" On *Fight Club*, that number of takes sometimes increased because Bonham Carter kept breaking into fits of laughter in the middle of scenes. Another problem arose when she insisted on chain-smoking nonstop so she could better become her character; because of the high number of takes, the actress smoked an inordinate number of cigarettes, causing her to develop bronchitis. Pitt, Norton, and some of the other actors also jammed their fingers and joints repeatedly during the fight scenes.

After Fincher filmed a scene in which Bonham Carter says, "I want to have your abortion," Laura Ziskin asked him to remove the line to avoid making waves with anti-abortion groups. Fincher told her he would remove the line as long as she and the other concerned studio execs agreed to leave the replacement line in the film, no matter what. Ziskin agreed, so Fincher replaced the abortion line with an even more incendiary line: "I haven't been fucked like that since I was in grade school." Humorously, after Ziskin saw this version of the scene, she begged Fincher to put the original line back in.

After *Fight Club* wrapped in December 1998, Fincher simultaneously worked with the Dust Brothers, whom he'd hired to score the picture, and editor Jim Haygood. During this period, one scene that Fincher's team of visual effects artists had worked on frame by frame for more than a year was finally completed: the scene in which Project Mayhem destroys the credit card companies' headquarters.

On April 20, 1999, three months before *Fight Club* was scheduled to be released, the Columbine tragedy occurred. Suddenly, Fox executives were nervous that *Fight Club* would get tossed onto the pile of pop-culture targets like Marilyn Manson and *The Basketball Diaries* that were being blamed by the media. Sure, *Fight Club* would come out *after* the massacre, but the studio execs knew it would likely be cited as one more example of the kind of entertainment that was driving innocent kids to take up arms and attack the world. Never mind that this idea was complete bullshit; it was negative press, and negative press damaged profits, so Fox backed up the film's release date by three months. During this time, the studio attempted to convince Fincher to tone down the film, but Fincher did not relent.

Fight Club held its premiere screening at the Venice Film Festival in September, where it received a fair amount of boos and walk-outs. Studio head Bill Mechanic, who had supported the picture from the start, called Fincher and warned him that the film could perform badly; he also told him that history would likely have the last word on the film.

When *Fight Club* hit theaters on October 15, 1999, Fincher and his wife went on vacation to Bali to escape. On opening weekend, the film underperformed, despite earning $11 million and coming in first. A few of the critics got it, such as *The Philadelphia Inquirer*, who raved that it was a "knockout. . . . So feverish is *Fight Club* . . . that thermometer contact might make mercury shatter." Peter Travers of *Rolling Stone* called the film an "uncompromising American classic." Janet Maslin of *The New York Times* called the film "visionary and disturbing," writing that Fincher "for the first time finds subject matter audacious enough to suit his lightning-fast visual sophistication, and puts that style to stunningly effective use."

Despite the praise, there were plenty of critics who hated it. *Chicago Sun-Times* critic Roger Ebert called the film the "most frankly and cheerfully fascist big-star movie since *Death Wish*, a celebration of violence in which the heroes write themselves a license to drink, smoke, screw, and beat one another up." He went on to label *Fight Club* "macho porn" and said that midway through the picture, it "turns to some of the most brutal, unremitting, nonstop violence ever filmed." The *Los Angeles Times* called it a "witless mishmash of whiny, infantile philosophizing and bone-crunching violence." *Entertainment Weekly* called the film a "dumb and brutal shock show."

Despite earning $101.2 million worldwide, Fox considered it an underachiever. It ultimately played a role in Bill Mechanic's resignation from the studio the following year. In the decades that have followed, *Fight Club* has gained a massive following. Unfortunately, the film's poster has become a dorm-room staple alongside *Scarface*, giving it a reputation as being emblematic of toxic masculinity in some circles. Additionally, it has been co-opted by the alt right, who accept it at face value, not understanding that it's satire.

In some ways, *Fight Club* is the most important film in Fincher's filmography because it stands as a testament to his unwillingness to compromise his artistic vision. And like his other films, it's a project that achieved its greatness and perfection—although Fincher himself doesn't believe in perfection—because of his hard work and obsessing over the tiniest details. Fincher is a craftsman of the highest order. He *bleeds* for his art. He drives himself half-mad scrutinizing minute details that will likely go unnoticed. The audience may not see them, but he does, and he knows these details add to the overall effectiveness of the films.

After the release of *Fight Club*, Fincher told Andrew Pulver,

> I find when I read interviews with directors I love, that they often say, "I had the whole movie in my head." Well, my hat's off to you, pal, because I don't know how the fuck you do that. I can barely keep four-and-a-half seconds of screen time in my head at any given time. At the start, there's the excitement of all the possibilities; then as you define it, you crush all the life out of it. You're picking paint samples and deciding where the stains on the ceiling are, you're working on minutiae; then you go shoot the fucking life out of it; and then you cut it and say, "Oh, that's not what it's supposed to be."

David Fincher is one of the great directors of his generation. Courtesy of Columbia Tristar Pictures/Photofest © Columbia Tristar Pictures, Photographer: Merrick Morton

How, you might ask, can Fincher enjoy the process when his obsessiveness becomes overwhelming? The answer is simple: "I don't enjoy it at all," he revealed to journalist Gavin Smith. So the next question is, If he doesn't enjoy filmmaking, then why does he continue to do it? Like most true artists, it's likely that Fincher doesn't have a choice. He creates because *he must*. It's a calling, if you will, and he's damned good at it. His filmography, which includes such noted post-'90s films as *Zodiac*, *The Curious Case of Benjamin Button*, *The Social Network*, *Gone Girl*, and *Mank*, stands as indisputable proof. These films also prove that he's not only one of the greatest cinematic craftsmen of his era but also one of the greatest of all time.

7

Robert Rodriguez
The One-Man Band

Robert Rodriguez was born in San Antonio, Texas, the son of a nurse and a salesman. He began toying with filmmaking at the age of eleven. "I started before camcorders were introduced," he told *Video Magazine*. "Back in '79 or '80, my dad got a JVC VCR, and it had a camera that attached with a cable. It didn't have a viewfinder, so you had to watch your TV to see what you were focusing at—real crude stuff, real manual. . . . We had to shoot mainly inside my house because we only had a twelve-foot cable."

While attending St. Anthony Catholic High School, Rodriguez met and befriended a fellow student named Carlos Gallardo, who also wanted to make movies. One day during their freshman year, Gallardo visited Rodriguez's home, which was just down the street from the school, and Rodriguez showed Gallardo something that would make him a true believer. "He showed me a little 8 mm film that he worked on. It was a little cartoon made out of clay like Gumby," Gallardo recalled. "That fucking shit blew me away! I knew, right there, at that moment, that was the place I needed to be, and he was the guy I needed to hold onto and always go and look for."

Rodriguez and Gallardo hung out at Rodriguez's house and watched movies like *First Blood*, *Escape from New York*, and *The Road Warrior* over and over again. These films were entertaining, yes, but they also served as creative inspirations. While in high school, the two boys worked together on a number of movies.

One of them was an action film called *The Guy from Down Under*, which started as a solo project by Gallardo and was later reshot in an extended form by the duo. Gallardo says the idea came from the Men at Work song "Down Under." Another film they collaborated on was a thirty-minute Indiana Jones pastiche called *Ismael Jones and the Eyes of the Devil*, which they filmed on Gallardo's parents' ranch in Mexico. In another of these films called *Street Cop*, Gallardo played the world's youngest undercover cop.

The duo also made fake movie trailers (similar to the ones Rodriguez and Quentin Tarantino created for their 2008 collaborative film *Grindhouse*). Two of the fake trailers were *Rambo Is Back*, featuring a Black Rambo played by a football player from their high school, and an action picture called *The Soldier* that featured the Bob Seger song "Old Time Rock and Roll."

"We didn't have a script or anything [for those films]," Gallardo says. "We would go and kind of structure the story. There was very little dialogue. It was mostly just action and music. Robert used to love *Miami Vice*, so the movies were very musical and action-oriented." The two would-be filmmakers took turns behind the camera, and Rodriguez would edit them using two VHS recorders.

While Rodriguez was attending the University of Texas, he tried to get into the school's film program but was rejected because his grades weren't high enough. "I wanted to be in the film department for the free equipment," Rodriguez later said. After crafting a compilation of short films he titled *Austin Stories*, Rodriguez entered and won first prize at the Third Coast Film and Video Competition. On the strength of that, he was finally accepted into the film program. Using the school's equipment, Rodriguez made a 16 mm short starring his younger siblings titled *Bedhead*, which won a number of awards at a variety of film festivals. This gave him the courage to try to make a proper feature. "Robert's movie *Bedhead* was made for $800, and it was eight minutes [long], so we came to the conclusion that if we made a movie that was eighty minutes, it could be done for $8,000," Gallardo recalled.

Robert Rodriguez set the standard for the DIY filmmaker. Courtesy of Dimension Films/ Photofest © Dimension Films

Rodriguez and Gallardo, who had been collaborating for eight years by then, both dropped out of college in the middle of their senior years to make a feature film. The film, *El Mariachi*, features Gallardo in the titular role as a mysterious musician carrying a guitar case filled with guns. Gallardo also coproduced while Rodriguez wrote, directed, produced, scored, shot, and edited.

Rodriguez planned for the film to be the first installment in a trilogy about his mysterious mariachi gunslinger. The idea was that each film he made at this point would be a practice film that would help him become a better filmmaker. Rodriguez set out to make this practice film so he could sell it to a Mexican video distributor. He later said that his thinking had been, "I'd be the king if I could just make money doing what I love." *El Mariachi* was partially financed with prize money that Rodriguez received for *Bedhead*. The director then raised more money for the production by participating in clinical trials. He wrote most of the screenplay in English while he was in the hospital being a human lab rat. He then handed it over to Gallardo, who translated it to Spanish.

Rodriguez's goal with *El Mariachi* was to make a hybrid film that had the action of a John Woo flick but was also filled with comedic moments. He wanted his film to include a strong female. Another goal was to create a clean-cut action hero who was Mexican, challenging the Hollywood tradition that Mexicans are the bad guys.

El Mariachi was shot chronologically on 16 mm beginning in August 1991 in Gallardo's hometown of Acuna Coahuila, Mexico, and lasted for two weeks. Rodriguez filmed without sound and later added on-set recorded voices in postproduction. Because of the tight budget and schedule, most scenes were shot in a single take, and instead of a dolly, Rodriguez used a wheelchair for tracking shots. The film was made with a three-man crew, but Rodriguez convinced the actors to work as additional crew members when they weren't acting. Clip-on desk lamps were used for lighting.

"If you want to make a movie for a really low budget, you can't spend on anything," Rodriguez said in *The Making of El Mariachi*. "You have to refuse to spend. Think of a creative way to get around your problem and keep your money in your pocket."

Rodriguez devised a number of creative ways to stretch his shoestring budget on *El Mariachi*. One of his smartest ideas was writing scenes that take place in locations that were available to him. For instance, Gallardo told Rodriguez he could get access to the local jail, so the film's opening scene takes place there. Taking his cost-cutting ingenuity a step further, Rodriguez cast the real-life warden and the jailer. By doing this, he was able to have authentic-looking actors in those roles who also wore authentic garb. Rodriguez borrowed guns from the police department, but because the guns were made to shoot blanks, they could only be fired once. To compensate for this, Rodriguez used editing tricks to give the impression that the guns fired multiple times.

Where had this ability to stretch a dollar so far come from? Rodriguez told MSNBC, "I came from a family of ten kids. I know how to survive."

In the end, *El Mariachi* cost only $7,225 to make, less than the $8,000 he'd envisioned. After being rejected by a number of Mexican distributors, Rodriguez sent a videocassette to an ICM agent, who passed the video to a couple of studios. Rodriguez ultimately chose to go with Columbia, who inked him to a two-year development, writing, and directing deal. Columbia also picked up *El Mariachi* for theatrical release, and Rodriguez became the toast of the town. He even got a write-up on the front page of *Variety*. Rodriguez later told Seth Kelley, "Joe Funicello, who was Jodie Foster's agent said, 'Front page? When Jodie got her deal, all I could get was third page. It was a big deal. And that was the beginning of my whole life changing.'"

El Mariachi screened at Sundance in January 1993 and won the Audience Award. It was released theatrically the following month, earning $2 million. Most critics praised the film, primarily because of its budget. This "little film that could" successfully established Robert Rodriguez in the film industry.

That December, Rodriguez took a brief detour to make a film for Showtime. He's spoken occasionally of his early films being intended as "practice films," and he probably saw his Showtime movie, *Roadracers*, as a practice movie, as well. The made-for-television B-movie homage was created as part of Showtime's original movie series *Rebel Highway*, a ten-part revival of American International Pictures (AIP) that was created and produced by AIP chief Samuel Z. Arkoff's son Lou Arkoff and *Halloween* cowriter Debra Hill. According to Lou, the films in the series were, basically *Rebel without a Cause* if it was made in the '90s. He explained, "It would be more lurid, sexier, and much more dangerous." Arkoff had wanted to call the series *Raging Hormones*, but Showtime nixed that, concluding that it was an awful title. Ken Tucker of *Entertainment Weekly* summed up the series: "It is the whimsical notion behind the *Rebel Highway* series to take a group of mostly grade-D exploitation films from the '50s and remake them, with good actors and directors, in the '90s."

The list of directors who fashioned these pictures was a veritable who's who in filmmaking, including such notable talents as John Milius, Joe Dante, John McNaughton, Allan Arkush, William Friedkin, and Jonathan Kaplin, among others. The series stipulations were that each director would select and use a title from an old AIP film. They could then write or hire a screenwriter to fashion a story that was in some way similar to that of the title. The filmmaker could also use the cinematographer and editor of his choice. Each film would have a $1.3 million budget and would feature new, fresh-faced actors.

"[*Roadracers* is] a really lame title," Rodriguez told *MovieMaker*. "The only stipulation was that we had to use it. We could do whatever else we wanted, as long as it was about teen angst some way. So we made, like, *Happy Days* or *Grease*—but imagine Fonzie flipping out and shooting everyone in the end with a shotgun and everybody dies."

Rodriguez told author Michael Singer that the original *Roadracers* had been so terrible that the series' producers weren't sure he could make a film out of it:

> They sent me the tapes of the movies that we were remaking. In fact, they wouldn't send me *Roadracers* because it was so terrible. I wanted to live up to the old posters, which said stuff like, "Some have to dance, some have to kill!" Then you'd watch the movie and they were lame, you know? So it was like, we're going to do the poster beyond the poster. Make it as sordid and crazy as they promised, and then some.

Rodriguez's casting for the film is significant because he cast Mexican actress Salma Hayek, who became a staple of his films. Additionally, the cast included David Arquette, John Hawkes, and William Sadler. Arquette had seen *El Mariachi* prior to making *Roadracers*, and was a fan of Rodriguez, but that was nothing compared to the thrill he experienced working with him. "He's just the coolest fucking guy ever," Arquette said.

> Do you know what I mean? The guy is just cool, tall, macho, just a really cool cat. When we were filming, there was one time where he grabbed the camera himself and held onto the hood and just yelled, "Okay, go!" And we were off and running. He's wild, so full of energy and creativity and he's still like that. I'd be barreling down the street with Salma, and there

would be Robert, holding on and not strapped into *anything*. He's just the biggest badass around, man.

Hayek's assessment of Rodriguez is similar. As she told Michael Beeler, "Robert is the best. He's so relaxed, I've never heard him scream—and I've been in quite a few movies with him. He's just creative, and he's always surprising you with new ideas. He's also exciting and he always knows exactly what he wants."

Rodriguez's love letter to B movies of the 1950s is the first entry in the series, airing on July 22, 1994. Louis Black of *The Austin Chronicle* dubbed *Roadracers* the "perfect Roger Corman movie."

So what was next on the horizon for the young filmmaker?

For his next film, Rodriguez returned to familiar territory. After seeing what he'd done with so little on *El Mariachi*, Hollywood wondered what he could do with a proper budget and "real" actors. With this project they found out. His first studio feature, *Desperado*, is the second installment of his Mariachi Trilogy. This time, he had a $7 million budget. In a year that included the $35 million film *The Quick and the Dead*, the $25 million bomb *Tank Girl*, and the $19 million *Bad Boys*, $7 million might not sound like all that big of a budget, but consider this: That $7 million was one thousand times the budget Rodriguez had when he'd made his first picture.

This time the Mariachi was played by Antonio Banderas, whose star was on the rise. Spanish-born Banderas had, by this time, already made five films with Pedro Almodóvar. Additionally, he was coming off the hit films *Philadelphia* and *Interview with the Vampire*. Rodriguez wrote the Mariachi role in *Desperado* specifically for Banderas. Similarly, he'd created the role of Carolina, the Mariachi's love interest, specifically for Hayek, but Columbia wanted someone more bankable in the role. "I remember Cameron Diaz was huge at the time, and her last name was Diaz, so they said she can be Mexican," Hayek later explained. "She was part of the list, and I had to audition again." Rodriguez stood his ground and eventually got his way. Rodriguez cast veteran actor Raul Julia to play Bucho, the chief bad

Carlos Gallardo as the titular character in El Mariachi. *Courtesy of Columbia Pictures/ Photofest © Columbia Pictures*

guy. Unfortunately, Julia fell ill and passed away before the film went into production, so Portuguese actor Joaquim de Almeida replaced him.

Desperado, like *El Mariachi* before, was shot in Acuna. Gallardo returned, only in a smaller role, this time as one of the Mariachi's gun-slinging comrades. *Desperado* also features many notable cameos. Quentin Tarantino pops up as a joke-telling delivery man. Steve Buscemi shares the legend of the Mariachi to the patrons of a bar. Cheech Marin and Danny Trejo, who eventually became Rodriguez movie regulars, also had small roles. Interestingly, by sheer chance, Rodriguez and Trejo, who'd never met one another, discovered that they were related while making the picture. Trejo later told journalist Matt Barbot, "He's my second cousin.... When I was down in Acuna, Mexico, and my relatives came down from San Antonio to visit me, my uncle said, 'Hey, that's your cousin!'"

Although Rodriguez liked to do the camerawork himself, the union forbade him from being his own cameraman, so Rodriguez hired Guillermo Navarro, a talented cinematographer from Mexico who had worked with Guillermo del Toro on *Cronos*. "Robert was a young, very interesting guy who wanted to do things," Navarro recalled. "He was a high achiever. It was an interesting proposition when I met him." As one might expect, Rodriguez, who had done almost everything on *El Mariachi*, had his hand in almost every aspect of the film. "He's very involved on a set," Navarro told me.

> He likes to operate a camera.... He's in the middle of everything. Sometimes it's difficult [working with someone who is so involved], but sometimes it's simpler because it's actually very good to have a director that is facing the problems that you're having, the difficulties you're having, there on the set, not "Oh, he's back in the camper," or "He's back doing interviews." He's actually there in the trenches.

Producer Bill Borden says that shooting a big-budget film was an eye-opener for Rodriguez, whom he called a "really talented guy." Borden recalled Rodriguez looking at the crew one day on set and saying, "What do all these people do?":

> I think he had to learn to work with crews. If you've got a prop master, how do you get the best from your prop master? Robert would have been happy to do everything himself, but you realize on a big production like that, you have to have a prop master, you have to have a special-effects person, you've got to have a wardrobe person, you've got to have a make-up person.... All of those things have to be worked with and coordinated. I think as a director he had to learn that.

Rodriguez was still learning to work with the performers, as well. "He'd never really worked with actors," Borden says. "He'd never had that training or that relationship. It was a great time for him to learn that actors talk back to you, and they want to know things. 'What am I doing?' 'Why am I blocking like this?' They want those answers. So he learned a lot on that set."

The actors loved working with him. "[Rodriguez is an] open person," Banderas observed later. "Open to the ideas coming from the actors, giving options, bringing new fresh air to the set. He doesn't do things like a director. He takes the camera, he puts the Steadicam on, and he's just working with the camera all the time. . . . He loves to improvise." One example of Rodriguez's love of improvisation was his allowing Tarantino to ad-lib the joke he tells in his scene.

Navarro likened the shoot to those he'd experienced in Mexico: "I learned to work in the third world, where you have less resources, you have to be very resourceful, sorting things and doing things not necessarily in a big way. *Desperado* was shot like that. It was really going and running."

Because Rodriguez was trying to stretch the budget, he used only two stuntmen on *Desperado*. He sometimes asked the actors to do their own stunts. "I got hit in every little part of my body," Banderas told film historian Joe Leydon. "It was quite tough, but at the same time, I think it worked for the movie. You can see the guy is the real guy, there's no stunt guys, there is just myself being hit." However, Banderas later concluded that the actors doing their own stunts was dangerous, admitting, "We were playing with our lives." In a 2019 interview, he remembered shooting the film's most iconic scene: "There was an explosion behind us, a fire that has to fill the whole entire screen. There was no CGI. That was real. And I remember the smell of, you know, burned hair . . . my hair, Salma's hair, and everybody that was behind the camera's hair." Hayek was proud of her stunt work in the film, but she would later recall,

> I eventually got hurt, really badly; nevertheless, I went back up on the roof and kept doing it. You can't really see it [in the movie], but I'm bleeding from my knee. I got hurt a lot. You

always get hurt in action films. I'll tell you one of the things that was the most painful. In one scene, Antonio throws me off the bed and I hit the floor; while he's firing a gun, the hot shell casings were striking my bare legs. They really burned me very badly.

Hayek experienced an uncomfortable situation when it came to her love scene with Banderas. She hadn't known there would be a love scene when she'd agreed to appear in the film, and she was terrified. She insisted that she didn't blame Rodriguez, who is the husband of her best friend, producer Elizabeth Avellan, and she believed Banderas was an "absolute gentleman." The exclusion of information about the scene had been part of a misunderstanding. To accommodate Hayek, Rodriguez and Avellan agreed to shoot the scene with a closed set consisting of only four people: Banderas, Hayek, Rodriguez, and Avellan. "When we were going to start shooting, I started to sob," Hayek told Dax Shepard. She recalled saying, "I don't know that I can do it. I'm afraid." Try as they might, the other three people in the room could not get Hayek to drop the towel covering her body for more than a couple seconds. Rodriguez was never able to get what he wanted for the scene, but he managed to make it work by using quick cuts.

Because he could only afford to keep Buscemi and Marin for six and seven days, respectively, he was forced to shoot them out much quicker than he would have liked. The scene in which Tarantino's character goes into the disgusting bar bathroom was shot in the very cramped bathroom of an actual bar. Because of this, Rodriguez had to use a smaller crew to get what he needed. He didn't care to push himself into the cramped space, so he allowed Banderas to go in and direct that short scene.

When *Desperado* was submitted to the Motion Picture Association of America (MPAA), it was slapped with the dreaded NC-17 rating due to its graphic violence. To get the R rating the studio needed, Rodriguez had cut the film substantially. One scene—a giant shootout at the end of the film—required so many elements to be cut that Rodriguez decided to cut the entire scene. The deaths of several characters, including Tarantino's and Trejo's, were trimmed. Two scenes featuring the "codpiece" gun shown in the final version of the film but never fired were also cut completely.

Desperado turned out to be something Rodriguez could have only imagined while making *El Mariachi*. The film, which *Medium* writer Jonathan Simpson later described as being like a "Spaghetti Western shot by the lovechild of Sergio Leone and John Woo," features bigger set pieces, bigger explosions, cartoonlike action sequences, and gallons of fake blood. It was, in essence, the director's dream come true.

Desperado was released on August 25, 1995, making $7,910,446 on its opening weekend. It eventually made $25.4 million in the United States and Canada and $58 million worldwide. Its Rotten Tomatoes consensus reads, "*Desperado* contains almost too much action and too little of a story to sustain interest, but Antonio Banderas proves a charismatic lead in Robert Rodriguez's extravaganza." Its contemporary reviews were generally positive. Bob McCabe of *Empire* observed, "It's big, it's daft, but *Desperado* is confident and hugely entertaining filmmaking." Heidi Strom of *Daily Press* called it a "pure adrenaline rush from start to finish," writing that "*Desperado* will shock, amuse, thrill, and disgust."

So, what was next for Rodriguez? The director had little time to relax; he began working on his next film almost immediately after wrapping *Desperado*. Someone at Miramax had cooked up the half-baked idea to gather some of the hottest young directors and have them collaborate on an anthology film, and Rodriguez was invited to participate. Because one of the other directors was his new pal Quentin Tarantino, whom he'd befriended at the Sundance Film Festival in 1992, Rodriguez happily signed on. The name of the anthology was *Four Rooms*, and each of the four stories takes place inside a different room in a hotel with a single bellboy character tying them together. The directors Miramax enlisted for the film were Rodriguez, Tarantino, Alexandre Rockwell (*In the Soup*), and Allison Anders (*Gas Food Lodging*).

Before *Four Rooms* was released, Rodriguez told *Boxoffice* magazine, "We each had certain elements to make a story around—a hotel room on New Year's Eve, a bellhop—and we didn't tell each other what we were doing. It could easily have been a bad idea, but they all tie together very well."

Rodriguez's segment, "The Misbehavers," is easily the best of the four. It stars Antonio Banderas and Tamlyn Tomita as the parents of some truly rotten kids who, as the segment's title says, misbehave.

When the film dropped into theaters on Christmas 1995, it was a disappointment, earning only $4.2 million on a budget of $4 million. The critics seemed to be the only ones who were excited about it, and they were just excited about having the opportunity to decimate it. Roger Ebert of the *Chicago Sun-Times* wrote, "[*Four Rooms*] comes billed as a film made by four friends. If they are still friends after finishing this film, that says a lot for their friendship." *Variety* called *Four Rooms* "disappointingly tedious." Mal Vincent of *The Virginian-Pilot* called it "one of the more interesting disasters of the waning film year."

Although *Four Rooms* proved to be a semi-interesting experiment that became a critical bomb, it didn't hurt any of its makers' careers, particularly Rodriguez and Tarantino, who owned, or at least co-owned, the decade.

Before *Desperado* and *Four Rooms* were released, Rodriguez was already hard at work on his next film, a vampire flick called *From Dusk till Dawn* that had been written by his buddy, Tarantino. Of his rapid succession of films, Rodriguez wrote, "I knew people would be watching for that sophomore slump, so I figured that instead of making one film and putting all the eggs in one basket, I would simply confuse the marketplace by putting out four films quickly."

The concept for the vampire story originated with special-effects makeup guru Robert Kurtzman, known in the film world as the K of KNB Effects, the company that he, Greg Nicotero, and Howard Berger formed in 1988. Kurtzman wanted to spread his wings and direct a film of his own, so he came up with a rough storyline about criminals who are confronted by supernatural forces. This, he believed, would be something he could direct. A lifelong fan of low-budget horror pics like *Assault on Precinct 13* and *Race with the Devil*, he planned for *From Dusk till Dawn* to be a drive-in movie.

After Kurtzman wrote a treatment, his friend, screenwriter Jon Esposito, was supposed to write a script based on the story, but Esposito got called away to Maine for several months to work on *Graveyard Shift*. It was then decided that another screenwriter would be hired. Kurtzman considered several screenwriters, including Scott Spiegel and David Goodman. Then Spiegel introduced him to an as-yet-unproduced writer named Quentin Tarantino. Kurtzman read Tarantino's (then unsold) scripts *Natural Born Killers* and *True Romance* and hired him to write a script for $1,500. That was Tarantino's first professional sale, and while it might not seem like a lot now, it was enough money for him to quit his job as a video store clerk. Another part of their deal was that if Tarantino ever managed to get *Reservoir Dogs* made, Kurtzman would do the special-effects makeup for free.

Kurtzman read the script he'd commissioned and dug it. There was just one problem—no one else liked it, at least not anyone who could get it made. "It was initially rejected everywhere," Kurtzman told *Backwoods Horror*. "No one wanted to do it. They thought it was too vulgar and too violent." Additionally, no one understood the script's structure. "It feels like two different movies," they would say, noting that the first half of the story is a straight crime story, and then, in the second half, vampires show up and descend on the criminals. "Originally, they thought it was weird," Rodriguez later said. "You turn the page and there's vampires!"

Skip forward a couple years, and Quentin Tarantino was the hottest screenwriter/director in Hollywood. *Reservoir Dogs*, *True Romance*, *Natural Born Killers*, and *Pulp Fiction* had all been released to various degrees of acclaim, and producers were keen to make anything with his name on it. By this time, Rodriguez and Tarantino were friends. They discussed possibly collaborating on something else, and Tarantino mentioned his unproduced *From Dusk till Dawn* script. "What?" Rodriguez presumably said. "You've got a vampire script? Let me read it." So *From Dusk till Dawn* became Rodriguez's next picture. Miramax agreed to finance it and even gave Rodriguez final cut. So in essence, these two wildly creative young collaborators had free reign to do whatever they wanted.

Then it was time to cast. For the badass tough-guy Seth Gecko, Rodriguez and Tarantino cast George Clooney, who'd been a star on the similarly titled series *Emergency Room* and *E.R.* "Since he plays an E.R. doctor on television," Rodriguez quipped, "I wanted him to come and portray someone who sends people to the E.R." Clooney had seen *Desperado* and was chomping at the bit to perform action scenes, so Rodriguez found places in the film where he could insert Clooney's character punching people. For the role of Seth's psychopathic brother Richie, Rodriguez cast Tarantino. While Rodriguez ultimately caught a lot of flak for this casting choice, Tarantino is quite effective in the role.

Then there's Jacob, the faithless minister. Who could play that role? Rodriguez cast the iconic actor Harvey Keitel, with whom Tarantino had worked previously on *Reservoir Dogs* and *Pulp Fiction*. While everyone pointed at Tarantino as being miscast, Keitel, who gives a fine performance, doesn't seem to fit his role particularly well. Again, he's great, but he could have been put to better use playing one of his patented tough guys.

The all-star cast also includes Juliette Lewis, Salma Hayek; Danny Trejo; Fred Williamson; Michael Parks; John Hawkes; and Tom Savini, whose character finally uses the "codpiece" gun cut out of *Desperado*. Savini was originally invited to play Frost, the part Fred Williamson ended up with. "Sex Machine is a little guy, and Frost is a big guy," Savini once told me. "But when I read the script, I said, 'This Sex Machine character is a lot more interesting.' So the audition tape that I sent was for Sex Machine. I didn't even read Frost's lines. From what I understand, I made Quentin laugh, and he switched the body types and gave me Sex Machine."

While unintentional, Rodriguez had put Hayek in a situation where she'd felt uncomfortable on *Desperado*. In that instance, it was a love scene that she'd found traumatizing. In *From Dusk till Dawn*, he did it again when he filmed her dancing with a huge snake. "[He] made me do something that I hated, but I ended up thanking him," Hayek told *Femme Fatales*. "I had a phobia for snakes. I'd have an attack if I even *saw* one. He decided that this character I played should dance with a snake. And he knew

I had the phobia." Rodriguez asked the actress, "Well, can you do it or not?" She responded, "No!" He then said, "Well, I'm the director and I want this character to dance with a snake! Can you do it or not?"

Hayek was intimidated but saw it as a challenge: "That's a 'thing' with me; don't tell me I *can't* do something! So I said, 'Yes, I can do it.'" The actress used hypnosis to overcome her phobia. Eventually, she managed to do the scene flawlessly, proving she was far more than just a pretty face. She later explained to IGN that she'd wanted the scene to appear as organic as possible: "I went to the extent that I created a relationship with this snake. I mean in my mind it had to have a meaning so that I could go into a trance. It was months of preparation for that one dance."

In an effort to trim costs and shoot with less restrictions, Rodriguez and company hired a nonunion crew. When the International Alliance of Theatrical Stage Employees (IATSE) found out that there was an $18 million film shooting with a nonunion crew, they were less than pleased. They attempted to bring the crew into the union, but Bender put a stop to it, saying it would add another $300,000 to the film's budget. The union and the filmmakers continued to quarrel, but the shoot continued without pause. Eventually, Miramax stepped in and made a compromise, agreeing to provide health care for the crew.

Some of the film was shot on a Hollywood soundstage. Other parts were filmed in Austin, Texas, and in the desert near Barstow, California. While shooting in the desert at the Titty Twister bar set, they reached the point where the pyrotechnics crew had to blow it up. It caught fire, but not one to be stopped by something as small as his set being enveloped in flames, Rodriguez continued shooting. He had to stop later that day, however, when a dust storm swept in, pelting and blinding everyone. Then during the final shot of the production, it began to pour down rain, once again slowing things. When the rain finally subsided and the crew was able to set up and match their shots, shooting was completed, and filming wrapped.

Between the fire, the dust storm, and the rain, it seemed like Mother Nature was out to get the production. Guillermo Navarro said those obstacles didn't seem unusual to him.

"That's the story of every film I've done," he explained. "You're there fighting the elements constantly. And then you have to keep this artificial process of making believe that that journey of a day is really two weeks of shooting, so you have to keep control and keep the dynamic that you are in a different kind of clock, building your film. It's very complicated. It's a very particular task."

From Dusk till Dawn was released in January 1996. The critics, like the vampires, were out for blood. Many didn't understand the film's trick of instantly switching from one genre to another, but most just seemed to believe that Rodriguez and Tarantino were wasting their time working in horror or were just plain capable of better work. *Variety*'s Todd McCarthy summed up the movie perfectly in a line that could have been quoted as a blurb: "A deliriously trashy, exuberantly vulgar, lavishly appointed exploitation picture, this weird combo of road-kill movie and martial-arts vampire gorefest is made to order for the stimulation of teenage boys." Jonathan Rosenbaum of the *Chicago Reader* wrote, "On a mindless exploitation level this is pretty good, but on other levels it seems to make promises that it fails to deliver on." *The Hollywood Reporter*'s David Hunter called the film "hyper-kinetic" and "well crafted," but lest you think it was a positive review, he added, "Rodriguez pushes the envelope but fails to make any lasting impression except revulsion at the spectacle of acclaimed independent filmmakers wasting their talents on such trash." In *The Boston Phoenix*, Peter Keough wrote, "The results are inert and pointless. Unless you find the idea of a revitalized [Harvey] Keitel backing down rubber demons with a cross and a shotgun uplifting, or the sight of Juliette Lewis kicking her way through dismembered body parts to drive a pool cue through a malefactor's chest entertaining." Because the film developed a cult following immediately, it's safe to say that a lot of people (myself included) do find those things entertaining.

The late Roger Ebert of the *Chicago Sun-Times* was a pretty savvy critic who appreciated a good exploitation picture as well as anybody. If you're the guy who wrote *Beyond the Valley of the Dolls*, you don't have much room to thumb your nose at the lower-brow stuff. While Ebert didn't care for the horror half of the picture nearly as much as he liked the crime half, he appreciated it well enough to rate it three (of a possible four) stars. "This is one of those movies you might like or you might hate, but you won't be able to deny its crazy zeal," he wrote. He also observed, "The good things in the movie—especially some of the dialogue—are so much better than the rest that you wish Rodriguez and Tarantino had tried to triumph over this material, instead of merely delivering it. It's a pro job, but these guys can do better." *New York Times* critic Janet Maslin was on the same page as Ebert about the second half. She wrote, "The latter part of *From Dusk till Dawn* is so relentless that it's as if a spigot has been turned on and then broken. . . . The film loses its clever edge when its action heats up so gruesomely and exploitatively that there's no time for talk."

From Dusk till Dawn has developed a sizable fan base and has spawned two straight-to-video sequels and a television series that ran for three seasons (on Rodriguez's own El Rey Network). In retrospect, *From Dusk till Dawn* can be seen as a precursor to Rodriguez and Tarantino's *other* B movie double feature, *Grindhouse*.

Having worked on one picture after another since his discovery, Rodriguez was the toast of the town. As such, Warner Bros. offered him what, for most comic and pop-culture geeks, would have been an impossible offer to refuse. The studio had a screenplay for a new Superman film called *Superman Lives*. The script had been written by Kevin Smith, but Rodriguez turned it down, citing exhaustion. "I really, really liked Kevin Smith's script, but I had just moved back to Texas," he told *Cinescape*. "The day after I wrapped *From Dusk till Dawn*, they premiered *Desperado*. My book came out that next week. Then two weeks later, my first child was born. Then Christmas. Then *From Dusk till Dawn* opened, like, two weeks later. I mean, it was great, [but] of course, I totally crashed and burned after that." But Rodriguez also knew it wouldn't be a true Robert Rodriguez movie. He wouldn't have complete control of a huge-budget Superman pic the way he did with his own films. He wouldn't have been able to put his own stamp on it: "I knew it would be a big movie and have big [McDonald's] Happy Meals and stuff, but I also knew it would be like that no matter who made it."

So instead, he made a small horror/sci-fi movie. The project, *The Faculty*, was sort of *Invasion of the Body Snatchers* set in a high school. Actress Clea DuVall correctly described it as being a cross between *Invasion of the Body Snatchers* and *The Breakfast Club*. The screenplay was written by Kevin Williamson, who was red hot at the time. He'd created the TV series *Dawson's Creek*, and he'd written *Scream*. *The Faculty*, like *Scream*, would be a smart movie that deconstructed a particular horror genre: With *Scream* it had been slasher movies; with *The Faculty* it would be alien-invasion pictures.

Rodriguez later described his view of the film to *Femme Fatales*: "*The Faculty* is one of those 'Are you, you?' kind of movies. It's an *Invasion of the Body Snatchers* type of film involving conformity and individuality in high school—the best setting for this kind of movie. I was always a fan of these movies. *The Thing* was one of the best 'Are you, you' kind of movies." In another interview, Rodriguez took this further, saying,

> The best sci-fi movies have an element of reality to them before throwing in the idea that becomes the seed of the sci-fi idea. What this had, it felt like a real high school to me—just not trusting the adults, not knowing who you were, not knowing who your friends were. Everyone's changing constantly. And in this movie, you don't know if it's real change or if it's brought on by some alien seed that's starting to take over.

According to Rodriguez, Bob Weinstein, the head of Dimension Films (and cofounder of Miramax), approached him about making *The Faculty* before the release of *Scream 2*, telling him, "You need to shoot this before you do your other movies." Weinstein wanted the picture, which had originally been intended to be Williamson's directorial debut, ready for a Christmas 1999 release. "[Weinstein] called me up before *Scream 2* and you could tell it was going to be really big because everyone was excited about it," Rodriguez recalled. "He said next year there's going to be everyone ripping off the *Scream* movies so they were going to come out with this one, which is different than all these other ones—it won't be a slasher movie. And I was like sure, Bob, way to think ahead." Rodriguez loved the script from the moment he began reading it, and he realized this was the kind of movie he would have watched over and over had it come out when he'd been a kid.

Rodriguez was initially hesitant to make *The Faculty*, which Miramax very badly wanted him to direct. "I made them a deal," the savvy filmmaker explained to Charles Ramirez Berg.

> When that company wants something bad, you can really put them over a barrel and get anything you want, anything your heart desires. So I thought, what can I ask for? I wanted to make my own stuff, but I didn't want to have to pitch a story to them each time. I didn't want to be at anyone's mercy. So the deal was, I would direct one film for them, and they would do *four* films for me, pay or play.

Once he'd signed on to direct the picture, he sat down with Williamson to figure out ways to flesh out the script because Weinstein thought it was too short, and Rodriguez himself thought it needed a few new scenes. The next thing the young director did was to hire Greg Nicotero, one of the special-effects guys he'd worked with on *From Dusk till Dawn*, to design the aliens who would take over the film's fictional high school. The two of them next decided to enlist legendary comic-book illustrator Bernie Wrightson to assist.

Next came the casting, which turned out to be incredibly difficult. One of the main reasons for this was because *The Faculty* focuses on a dozen primary characters. Rodriguez and casting directors Anne McCarthy and Mary Vernieu met with just about every young performer in Hollywood. The first two actors they cast were Clea DuVall and Josh Hartnett. Rodriguez had difficulty casting young actors because many of them wouldn't work with specific other actors, and the process was so prolonged that it wasn't complete until a week before the cameras were set to roll on the film.

The Faculty, in essence, features two sets of actors: teenagers and adults. The older cast includes such performers as Robert Patrick, Salma Hayek, and Bebe Neuwirth. As Rodriguez later said, he found the Miramax casting process similar to the "old studio casting"—they liked to work with a lot of the same actors. Miramax execs were pushing for *Terminator 2* baddie Robert Patrick, whom they'd worked with on *Copland*. Rodriguez hadn't planned to cast Hayek this time because he didn't see a part in the film that the actress seemed right for. But the actress begged him for a part, so he wound up casting her as the school nurse. Because Rodriguez didn't believe the bombshell actress was believable as a school nurse, he decided to "dress her down," filming her in bland clothes and without makeup.

For the film's soundtrack, Rodriguez assembled a virtual who's who of '90s rockers, including Garbage, the Offspring, Soul Asylum, Oasis, and Sheryl Crow. But most impressive was a cover of Pink Floyd's "Another Brick in the Wall, Part II," created specifically for the film by a one-off supergroup calling themselves Class of '99 and consisting of Layne Staley of Alice in Chains, Tom Morello of Rage Against the Machine, Stephen Perkins of Jane's Addiction, and Martyn LeNoble of Porno for Pyros. Could any group be more representative of the '90s than that?

The Faculty was released on Christmas 1998 and made more than $11 million during its opening weekend. It ultimately went on to earn $40.3 million in the United States and $63 million worldwide. While that amount, for a movie made for $15 million, made *The Faculty* a hit, the take was considerably less than Miramax had expected.

The film's critical reception was mixed. *Variety*'s Dennis Harvey wrote,

> Together, [Rodriguez and Williamson] make a complete lack of socially redeeming value seem so much fun that *The Faculty* might well become a pulp classic. . . . For his part, helmer-editor Rodriguez delivers another hyper-confident feature-length adrenaline rush, albeit one thankfully freed from the more irksome macho-iconatry fixations of his prior studio projects *Desperado* and *From Dusk Till Dawn*.

Salon critic Charles Taylor called the film "subversive," observing that its "honest, good-natured junkiness . . . feels like a relief." Marc Savlov, critic for Rodriguez's hometown paper, *The Austin Chronicle*, wrote, "It's a rush, yes, but sometimes I caught myself wishing for a breather of sorts. Still, no one around these days edits with such sublime accuracy as Rodriguez. A master of the smash-cut, *The Faculty* is overflowing with the director's 'I'll try anything once' spirit, and that's what makes the film such witty, freaky fun."

The Faculty is probably the lesser of Rodriguez's '90s features (not counting *Four Rooms*), but it's a solid effort. However, *The Faculty* isn't a misfire; it's just less qualitative. When a filmmaker churns out as many films as Rodriguez does, the end results are bound to vary in terms of quality.

In the decades that have followed, Rodriguez has stayed busy. His post-'90s pictures include the third *El Mariachi* film, *Once upon a Time in Mexico*; two *Sin City* pictures; two *Machete* films; five *Spy Kids* films; and a lot of children's movies. Additionally, he's established Troublemaker Studios, started the television network El Rey, and created several TV series.

Some filmmakers start out making lighter "fun" movies and eventually evolve beyond them to the more "serious" so-called prestige films. But not Rodriguez. He doesn't feel the need to chase that kind of critical recognition. He remains true to himself. Robert Rodriguez is having a good time making the kinds of movies that he loves, and he makes them exceedingly well.

8

Kevin Smith
Jersey Boy Makes Good

After high school, Kevin Smith bounced around from one dead-end job to the next. He worked first as a bus boy at Long John Silvers. After that, he dug graves in a cemetery. He had a job at Domino's Pizza, which he worked for a grand total of one day. (He quit so he could go to see Tim Burton's *Batman*.) In the end, one dead-end job would ultimately lead him to a prosperous future. He was a cashier at a convenience store that doubled as a video rental store. The place was called Quick Stop/RST Video. Smith and a coworker named Bryan Johnson engaged in a daily pastime that consisted of mocking the customers to make each other laugh. "Our time there was not really spent working as much as it was trying not to work," Smith said.

Smith met and befriended a Quick Stop coworker named Vincent Pereira. The two formed a bond over their mutual love of David Lynch and *Twin Peaks*. Smith had always loved movies, but Pereira was a cineaste with a raging passion for film. Pereira's passion proved to be contagious, and the two coworkers would frequently go to see movies together after their shift. One of the films they watched together was Richard Linklater's *Slacker*. Seeing *Slacker* opened Smith's eyes to the kinds of things that could be made on a shoestring budget, and for the first time, Smith considered making a movie of his own.

Pereira recalled,

> We were driving home on the Jersey Turnpike and the Parkway. And honestly, Kevin's face changed. He had a different look about him. He was like, "I can do that." You could definitely see that something had clicked in his mind. He was like, "I have enough credit cards that I could do a movie for that kind of money." There was definitely a change about him from before we went to the movie to after we got out. The look in his eyes had changed. I remember we were talking about it during the whole ride home. It was just like something had clicked in his mind, and he realized that this was accessible and something you could possibly do.

Soon after his *Slacker* awakening, Smith saw an ad in *The Village Voice* for the Vancouver Film School's eight-month filmmaking program. Smith believed he could go to Vancouver, learn how to make movies, and then come back to New Jersey and direct a movie of his own. He thought if he could learn how to use the filmmaking equipment in the class, he could then teach his friends, thus assembling his own filmmaking crew. The only problem was that the course cost $9,000, which, to a convenience store worker making minimum wage, seemed like a hell of a lot. But Smith wanted very badly to go to the school, so he sold off his CD collection and some of his comic books to pay his way.

Smith traveled to Vancouver and started learning how to make movies. While there, he met and befriended Scott Mosier, who eventually became his production partner. While at the school, Smith and Mosier set about making a half-assed documentary called *Mae Day*, about a pre-op trans woman. When the woman disappeared very early in the production, Smith and Mosier changed gears and started making a half-assed documentary about their failed half-assed documentary. They called this *Mae Day: The Crumbling of a Documentary*. Smith decided to bail on the course midway through so he could go home and make his own film. Mosier remained in school, but the two friends made a pact—they would each write their own scripts, and they would work together to film the screenplay for whichever of them completed a qualitative script first.

When Smith got back to New Jersey, he began writing immediately. Remembering a tip that Robert Rodriguez had suggested in his memoir, Smith decided he would write about the things that were at his disposal. In his case, it was the Quick Stop/RST Video where he returned to work. After asking for permission from the owner to shoot a film inside the store after hours, Smith penned an all-dialogue script about minimum-wage workers toiling in a convenience store. The characters in the film were loosely based on Smith and his friends.

His initial idea was very different from the film he wound up making. Pereira said,

> His original idea was to do a David Lynch horror movie set in the convenience store. So that was what I was expecting. He wrote a one-page treatment called *Inconvenience*. And the one-page treatment was basically saying it was going to be about a guy's first night on the job on the midnight to six a.m. shift. And basically, there's this weird society of people that come into the store overnight. In my mind, if anything, I thought if it was going to be comedic at all, it was going to be like *After Hours*. It would have been a nightmarish comedy, but it was definitely much more the idea of doing a David Lynchian–type weird horror movie. I had read some other stuff Kevin had written prior to that, which was generally serious and dark like that. So when he first handed me a bunch of pages and I started reading it, I was like, "Whoa, hold on a second. This is a *comedy*? *About relationships*?"

The comedic script only took Smith a month to write. After Pereira told him he thought *Inconvenience* was a corny title, Smith changed it. Pereira suggested *Rude Clerks*, which Smith liked but cut down to *Clerks*.

Preproduction began on March 19, 1993. In the beginning, the film had no budget. Smith planned to finance the production with credit cards he possessed and would obtain as the shoot progressed. Because his beloved *Slacker*—the film that had inspired him to make his own film—had cost a mere $23,000 to make, Smith figured he could make *Clerks* for roughly the same amount. When Smith's hometown was flooded, he received a

$3,000 check from FEMA to cover the loss of his comic book collection. Smith was sad to see his comics destroyed, but he was happy to have more money to put into his film.

Mosier assisted, as promised, and produced *Clerks*. He was instrumental in obtaining the equipment and supplies they needed to make the film. Mosier also introduced Smith to a cameraman friend he'd met at the Vancouver Film School named David Klein, who then signed on to shoot *Clerks*.

The initial plan was that Smith and his friend Ernest O'Donnell would play the leads. It made sense for Smith to play Dante because the character was modeled after him. The only problem was that Smith didn't have the chops to carry a film. O'Donnell's read of his character proved him to be wrong for the film, as well. (O'Donnell was then recast in a small secondary role.) Smith went to the First Avenue Playhouse in Atlantic Highlands in search of actors who fit the roles. That's where he discovered Brian O'Halloran, whom he cast as Dante. (Recognizing that he was no actor, Smith cast himself in the mostly non-speaking role of Silent Bob.) Smith then chose a nonactor named Jeff Anderson who'd tagged along with a friend to the audition to play Randal. An actress named Marilyn Ghigliotti was cast in the role of Dante's girlfriend after she stunned Smith and Mosier with her ability to shed tears on cue. Smith had written another key role, Jay, specifically for his pal Jason Mewes.

The cast spent several weeks rehearsing inside the convenience store each night from 10:30 p.m. to 1:00 a.m. During one rehearsal, tension arose when Ghigliotti questioned Anderson's acting chops, leading to his nearly leaving the production. Smith allowed very little ad-libbing, insisting that the actors deliver the lines as he'd written them. Considering that Smith's strength was his writing—particularly dialogue—this should come as no surprise. Furthermore, the actors said that Smith was very precise about their deliveries and pronunciation of the words.

The film was shot in 16 mm black-and-white. Although Smith occasionally claimed he'd used black-and-white film to make *Clerks* look more artistic, he actually used it for the same reason any filmmaker without much money would: because it was cheaper. Cinematographer David Klein shot the film on an Arriflex SR-2 camera.

Clerks shot every night for twenty-one nights straight. Most of the cast and crew worked their day jobs and then on the movie at night. Smith, who continued working evenings in the store, wasn't particularly tired during those three weeks. Everyone else was exhausted and dragging. Ghigliotti was a hairdresser, Anderson worked in the AT&T mail room, and O'Halloran worked at a barware manufacturing company. Despite the lack of sleep, the cast soldiered on. Although the primary actors showed up when they were supposed to, many of the extras did not. As a result, people like Smith's mother and sister had to be recruited at the last minute. This is why Mosier appears in three different roles (most notably Snowball). Smith's coworker buddy Walter Flanagan, who had insisted that he did not want to be in the film, ended up with four roles.

In a scene in which he was supposed to recite a lengthy list of raunchy porn titles, Anderson, fearing what his mother's reaction might be, begged Smith to rewrite his dialogue so he wouldn't have to say the titles. Smith thoughtfully told Anderson to give him five minutes so he could rewrite the dialogue. When he returned and handed the script to Anderson, he'd added three more titles to the already-long list. This was, in essence, Smith telling him to suck it up.

"We'd stay up all night and smoke cigarettes and eat Fig Newtons and drink coffee," Mosier told *Vice*.

> Nobody was eating real food. It was really fun. We were blessed by ignorance. If there was anyone on that set who actually knew how to make a movie, it would have warped the whole experience, because someone would have been like, "What are you doing? This is unorganized, and there's no schedule, and you're making it up as you go along." But for that movie, it needed to be that way. It was a movie that if you made it the wrong way, I don't think it would feel as sincere.

After filming wrapped, Smith and Mosier rented a Steenbeck editing table and went to work cutting the film. Interestingly, all the editing also was done inside the convenience store after hours.

Once the film was locked, Smith screened it for his mother, who said, "You spent $27,000 on this piece of garbage?!" Her reaction did not inspire hope. Smith, however, consoled himself with the fact that *Clerks* was not a film made to be enjoyed by his mother's generation. *Clerks* was a Gen-X film about Gen-X kids that would, hopefully, appeal to a Gen-X audience.

Attempting to follow *Slacker*'s path to success, Smith and Mosier entered *Clerks* into the International Feature Film Market. Smith was crestfallen when the film played to an audience of about five people. Where was the audience? Was this going to be it? Was he doomed to continue languishing in his minimum-wage job, earning just enough money to pay his monthly credit card bills? That's certainly how it looked. Strangely enough, though, one of those audience members was Bob Hawk, a consultant to indie filmmakers. Hawk appreciated the film and started telling people about it. He believed the convenience store was intended to be a metaphor for American society.

Who cares if Hawk's reading was a nonsensical and over-reaching read of a film filled with dick jokes? One of the people Hawk told about *Clerks* was John Pierson, the noted producer's rep who had landed distribution deals for such esteemed indies as *She's Gotta Have It* and—wait for it—*Slacker*. Pierson dug the film, although he wasn't sure there was an audience for it—*yet*. He eventually decided to help Smith and Mosier find distribution with the caveat that Smith rewrite and reshoot the film's downbeat ending.

In the original ending to *Clerks*, the hilarity turns to doom and gloom when Dante is murdered by a stickup man. Smith had taken his cue from Spike Lee's *Do the Right Thing*. In Lee's film, the entire story takes place in a single day containing a light mood and a few laughs before hurtling headfirst into the darkness in its last twenty minutes. Pierson told Smith that Dante *had* to live; *Clerks* could not end with such a colossal downer. If Dante died, then Smith was essentially negating all the fun and laughs the audience had experienced up to that point.

Through maneuvering on the part of Hawk, *Clerks* was accepted into the Sundance Film Festival, where it showed to packed rooms and received glowing reviews. Miramax co-chief Harvey Weinstein was in attendance for the film's last Sundance screening at the Egyptian Theater on January 28, 1994. One of his minions had previously tried to screen the film for him, but Weinstein had walked out early. This time was different; Weinstein not only stuck around for the whole thing, but he also could be heard bellowing with laughter. *Clerks* won the festival's Filmmakers Trophy. Shortly thereafter, Miramax purchased the distribution rights to *Clerks*. In addition to the award the film took home at Sundance, it received the Award of Youth and the Mercedes-Benz Award at Cannes.

The Motion Picture Association of America (MPAA) slapped the film with an NC-17 rating, despite the fact that it contained no violence and no nudity. It was simply the film's copious curse words that earned it the rating. Recognizing that an NC-17 rating would drastically diminish ticket sales, Miramax hired

The half-sheet poster for Clerks. *Courtesy of Miramax Films/Photofest © Miramax Films*

famed civil liberties lawyer Alan Dershowitz to appeal. Eventually, the MPAA relented and gave *Clerks* the R rating the studio wanted.

Clerks grossed more than $3 million while playing on less than one hundred screens in the United States. It earned an additional $1.3 million overseas. These aren't exactly *Jurassic Park* numbers, but that's not too shabby for a movie made inside a convenience store for $27,000. To put a finer point on it, the film earned more than one hundred times its budget during its theatrical run. On video, *Clerks* developed a massive cult following and spawned two direct sequels, a cartoon series, a comic book, and even action figures. Additionally, the characters Jay and Silent Bob have appeared in most of Smith's other films. That level of fan love for *Clerks* began at Sundance in early 1994 and continues to this day.

Why did *Clerks* resonate with viewers to the degree that it did? Even more so, why does it continue to resonate with viewers today, well beyond the Generation-X audience it was made for? Kevin Smith believes it's highly relatable. "I think I completely understand why *Clerks* not only connected then, but why people still talk about it today, even though it's an old-ass black-and-white movie that was made in the '90s," Smith told journalist Timothy McClelland. "It turns out, that movie can be appreciated by anybody who's ever had a shitty job, and that's literally everybody in the world. So for that reason, it's like one of the most identifiable flicks in the world."

So where did Smith go from there? After the whirlwind success he experienced with *Clerks*, he kicked around some ideas for follow-up films. Like most American Gen-Xers, Smith had spent a great deal of time goofing off at the mall as a kid. So, he thought, what if he made a film that was similar to *Clerks*—something people his age could relate to—only this time set inside a mall? He thought the idea had potential.

During this period, Smith was introduced to James Jacks, who had produced such notable pictures as *Raising Arizona*, *Dazed and Confused*, and *Tombstone*. Jacks lamented that he wished he'd picked up *Clerks* for Universal Pictures, but he still wanted to work with Smith. When Smith told him about his "*Clerks* at the mall" idea, the producer told him he'd like to help him make it. Jacks, his production partner Sean Daniel, and Smith then pitched the film—now titled *Mallrats*—to the powers that be at Universal. The studio said if Smith and company could sign Shannen Doherty, a young actress whose star was on the rise following her five-season run on TV's *Beverly Hills 90210*, they would agree to make it. Other popular actresses, including Reese Witherspoon, had expressed interest in the part, but it was the attachment of Doherty that convinced Universal to fund the picture.

As Smith and casting director Don Phillips were meeting with actors, Jacks informed Smith that he didn't want one of the actors he was auditioning to be cast. The actor's name was Ben Affleck. Jacks had worked with Affleck previously on *Dazed and Confused* and felt that the actor had interjected too many curse words into the film. Jacks asserted that Affleck had a "potty mouth." He said that the script for *Dazed and Confused* already had a lot of "fucks and curses" in it, but "Ben threw in like hundreds more." Smith reminded Jacks that his *Mallrats* script was already filled with plenty of f-words, but Jacks warned that if he cast Affleck, the actor would add even more. Interestingly, the day Affleck auditioned for Smith and Phillips was the same day it was announced that Affleck and Matt Damon had just sold their script for *Good Will Hunting* to Castle Rock Pictures. Smith watched Affleck's reading and knew immediately that he was the right guy for the role. After Smith cast him, Jacks unhappily reminded Smith that Affleck would "potty the movie up." Nevertheless, Affleck remained in the cast.

One performer who Phillips brought to Smith's attention was a former pro skateboarder named Jason Lee, who read for the role of TS, which ultimately went to Jeremy London. Smith and Mosier both knew right off the bat that Lee was wrong for the role, but they liked him, so they kept inviting him back for reads just so they could spend time with him. Although Lee wasn't right for the TS role, they wanted him in the movie because he was charismatic and, despite having no acting experience, immensely talented. In the end, they cast him in the role of Brodie. When Smith gave him the good news, Lee was in the middle of eating a sandwich. Smith told journalist Clark Collis, "[Lee] looks up for a brief second, and he goes, 'Yeah?' and he goes right back to eating his sandwich, looking back down. Eating was more exciting than being cast in his very first movie at that moment in time."

Smith again included *Clerks* characters Jay and Silent Bob in his *Mallrats* script. The only problem was, Universal didn't want him to cast Jason Mewes in the role that was actually based on him and that he'd originated because they didn't think he could act. The studio wanted either Breckin Meyer or Seth Green to essay the part of Jay. Humorously, neither Meyer nor Green really wanted the part because they were fans of Mewes's work in *Clerks*. Ultimately, Smith convinced the studio to give Mewes the opportunity to read and had Mewes read a scene that required very little heavy lifting. Mewes nailed the audition, and Smith was then given the go-ahead to cast him.

The ensemble was rounded out with Claire Forlani, Joey Lauren Adams, Ethan Supplee, and Michael Rooker, with a cameo by comic book pioneer Stan Lee. Familiar Smith cohorts Scott Mosier, Walt Flanagan, Bryan Johnson, and Brian O'Halloran also make appearances.

The film's mall location was Eden Prairie Center in Eden Prairie, Minnesota. Why Nowheresville, Minnesota, you ask? Because, like everything that happens in Hollywood, it was a financial decision. Smith had hoped to film at the Seaview Square Mall in Ocean Township, New Jersey, but at only $10,000, Eden Prairie Center wound up being the cheapest location the producers could find that would suit their needs. Smith and his crew also set up their production offices inside the mall, making it their primary base of operations.

The film's $6.1 million budget was far bigger than what Smith had to work with on *Clerks*. It was also a union picture, with a full-size crew of fifty or more people, which was a strange experience for Smith, who'd made *Clerks* with the barest of skeleton crews. "My first experience in making a film with a budget was like, there are far too many fucking people around here!" Smith said in 2005.

Similar to the experience of making *Clerks*, most of the cast and crew of *Mallrats* were about the same age and had a good chemistry. As a result, they spent their after-hours partying and hanging out in the hotel bar, lending the shoot a summer-camp feel.

The film initially screened at the San Diego Comicon, where the audience roared with laughter. Jacks later recalled, "When we walked out of there, you'd swear we'd made *Animal House*." But *Mallrats* deals with comic books to a large degree, so naturally a movie about comic book fans would resonate with real-life comic book fans. The big question was, Would that enthusiasm cross over to a more mainstream audience?

The answer, Smith and crew soon learned, was a resounding no. When *Mallrats* opened on October 20, 1995, it landed with a deafening thud. Smith later recalled a phone conversation he'd had with Jacks on the morning after the film was released. He asked the producer how much the film had made, and Jacks told him $400,000. Smith then asked, "On what screen?" When Jacks told him that was all *Mallrats* had made nationwide, Smith's heart sank. "The movie comes out, and the movie dies, and it was like, 'We're done,'" Smith said in "*Mallrats*: Erection of an Epic—The Making of *Mallrats*." "Not only are . . . our careers finished, but we humiliated ourselves. Nobody fuckin' went to the movie."

In his *Los Angeles Times* review, Kenneth Turan observed, "If the Sundance Institute or the American Film Institute ever offers a course advising directors of successful first films what to avoid the second time around, *Mallrats* could be at the heart of the curriculum." *Chicago Sun-Times* critic Roger Ebert leveled even sharper criticism, essentially accusing Smith of selling out to make a larger movie: "Before *Mallrats* was released, I chaired a panel that Smith participated in and Kevin Smith cheerfully said he'd be happy to do whatever the studios wanted, if they'd pay for his films. At the time, I thought he was joking."

Smith later said the problem was that he'd tried to force everything that had made *Clerks* work onto a film that was expected to be something bigger, and it just didn't work. The budget was bigger, the equipment was slicker, some of the cast were professional actors, and the film was in color. All of the charming little things that had given *Clerks* its feeling of sincerity and made it relatable were polished into something bigger, shinier, fancier, and prettier—adjectives that don't necessarily fit Kevin Smith's style. As time ultimately showed, *Mallrats* is a better film than it was initially given credit for, but it's still far from one of Smith's better efforts.

Another problem was that *Mallrats* had been aimed at an "incredibly small niche market" consisting of comic book readers who were old enough to go see an R-rated film. Smith later described the film as being "almost like a fantasy, a world where people knew all the comic books and everyone knew who Stan Lee was."

In the telephone call Jacks made to Smith the morning after *Mallrats'* release, he told Smith that he believed the movie was funny but that it had just been "too early." Jacks predicted the film would find its audience in time. As it turned out, the producer was correct in his assessment. In the years that followed, *Mallrats* became a cult film with a substantial following. In truth, pretty much everything Smith made would gain a massive following, with the popularity of the older films continuing to find new fans with the release of each new one. At the time, Smith had no way of knowing that *Mallrats* would catch on one day. All he knew was that he'd just made a misstep that could potentially jeopardize his career.

His personal life was no cakewalk either. Smith was dating Joey Lauren Adams, an actress whose then short list of credits included *Coneheads* and *Dazed and Confused*. Smith, like many young men—yes, it's mostly men—blew up the relationship because he couldn't stop focusing on (and judging) Adams's sex life before they'd met. Even though he knew he had no right to feel angry about her past, he did. "The guy who'd mused over myriad things sexual in his first flick (from sucking one's own dick to necrophilia) was undone by sex his significant other had had long before she knew he existed," Smith lamented in a 2000 Criterion essay. "And the day I saw disbelief, outrage, and hurt reflected in the eyes of the woman I loved as she realized I was insisting that she apologize for her life up until the moment we met, . . . well, that was the day it struck me that I wasn't quite as liberal as I fancied myself and instead came to grips with the fact that I was rather conservative." Smith said he could have gone to therapy to dive into all of this, but he instead chose to write a script about it, titled *Chasing Amy*. The plot isn't directly about Smith and Adams's relationship, but the pain, hurt, and confusion he'd felt is at the center of the story.

In *Chasing Amy*, the antagonist, Holden, and the girlfriend, Alyssa, face a far more difficult truth than their real-life counterparts: Alyssa is a lesbian, and Holden tries to make her love him despite this monumental hurdle. The idea for this switch that obscures the original real-life relationship between Smith and Adams came from producer Mosier having a crush on lesbian screenwriter Guinevere Turner. So although Smith is quick to point out that Holden is actually Smith in almost every way imaginable, *Chasing Amy* is ultimately a mashup of both Smith's and Mosier's private lives.

Early drafts of the screenplay were broader comedy like Smith's earlier films had been. In the beginning, Smith planned for the couple to be in high school rather than the adults they are in the final film. A subplot in which Holden's ex-girlfriend returns was excised, as was a storyline that found Jay and Silent Bob becoming real-life superheroes rather than simply inspiring the comic that Holden writes.

During the writing process, Smith dug up old scenes he'd cut from other scripts and integrated them into his new story. Dialogue in *Chasing Amy* in which the couple are contemplating love while playing a game of darts originally was written for *Clerks* and featured Dante and Randal (under obviously different circumstances). Another memorable and previously cut scene was one that Smith had written for *Mallrats* in which the characters pay homage to *Jaws* by comparing the scars they've obtained from cunnilingus gone wrong.

Smith, Mosier, and John Pierson pitched *Chasing Amy* to Harvey Weinstein over breakfast at Sundance, and Weinstein agreed to greenlight the film with a $2 million budget. Because Miramax had exclusive deals at the time with Jon Stewart, Drew Barrymore, and David Schwimmer, those were the performers

Weinstein wanted for the primary roles. However, Smith had written the roles specifically for Ben Affleck, Joey Lauren Adams, and Jason Lee. Having made way too many concessions on *Mallrats* and paying the price for it, Smith stood his ground. Because they made *Clerks* for $28,000, Smith and Mosier knew they could make *Chasing Amy* for a lot less, so Smith made Weinstein an offer he couldn't refuse: He would make *Chasing Amy* with a significantly smaller $250,000 budget but without studio interference. Then, if Weinstein liked the resulting picture, it would be his. If he didn't, they would shop it elsewhere. Weinstein agreed to these terms. Making a movie for less money in order to cast the actors he wanted set a precedent; this was a move Smith repeated multiple times in the future.

Smith and Mosier were in a unique position. As Smith later wrote in the DVD liner notes, "*Clerks* had been overpraised. *Mallrats* had been over-bashed. We'd been at both ends of the spectrum. The third time is always supposed to be the charm so we were able to approach *Chasing Amy* from a very liberated position: what better could they ever say about us than they did the first time, and what worse could they ever say about us than they did the second time?"

Smith and company spent a month rehearsing before filming. The shoot lasted twenty days, and by and large, it was a smooth shoot. This is not to suggest that there were no issues. Producer Mosier found himself in hot water when the crew was caught filming in a location where they didn't have permission to shoot. Because of the film's low budget, Mosier attempted to film the scene guerrilla style without permits.

In the scene in which Adams's character has an emotional breakdown, Smith shot sixteen takes. He found that Adams was good in each take but that she was becoming more and more emotional each time she said her lines, so by the sixteenth take, she was nearly hysterical. Smith's decision to keep filming proved to be wise because Adams is absolutely terrific in the film's most pivotal (and memorable) scene. Smith's monologue (as Silent Bob) took him thirteen takes, not because his performance was getting better and better like Adams's, but because he kept flubbing his lines.

When shooting was over, Smith and Mosier edited the film just as they had on *Clerks*, without anyone watching over their shoulders. Smith's gamble paid off—Weinstein loved the picture, and *Chasing Amy* was released by Miramax. And Weinstein wasn't the only viewer who loved the film. *Chasing Amy* screened first at Sundance on January 24, 1997, where it was a hit with viewers and critics alike. When the film was released theatrically the following April, that trend continued. The same critics who had bashed *Mallrats* were now falling over themselves to praise *Chasing Amy*. Audiences loved the film, too. It wound up making $12 million at the box office. That amount may not sound like much, but when you remember that the film was shot for $250,000, it's a substantial profit. Like Smith's other films, *Chasing Amy* continued (and continues) to find fans on video.

Chasing Amy is Smith's masterpiece. It is a far more mature project than Smith's previous films are. David Klein's static camerawork hadn't matured much beyond the earlier films, but there was really no need. No one was watching Kevin Smith

Ben Affleck in a publicity still from Chasing Amy. *Courtesy of Miramax Films/Photofest © Miramax Films*

films looking for visual aesthetics. In Kevin Smith's world, everything is about the writing, and the script for *Chasing Amy* is exceptional. The big question was, Now that Smith had made something this thoughtful, moving, and mature, would he continue to follow that trend?

Smith's fourth film was a project he'd conceived while attending film school in Vancouver, predating *Clerks*. At that time, Smith envisioned it as a film simply titled *God*. The project, poking fun at religion and its tenets while simultaneously giving true consideration to the subject, was the result of Smith's life in and struggles with Catholicism. Smith had written his first draft in the fall of 1994, and Miramax had agreed to finance the film, now titled *Dogma*, as Smith's follow-up to *Clerks*. However, the writer/director decided he wasn't ready to tackle such a large and controversial project and set it aside for later.

Early concepts for the story were radically different. In the beginning, Smith conceived the story as being about high school students. In his first official draft, Bethany, the last descendant of Christ, was a stripper instead of an employee at an abortion clinic. (It's not hard to imagine the giddy glee Smith must have felt when he had the *aha!* idea of putting Bethany to work inside the clinic.) In the stripper draft, Bethany was waiting for a prophet, eventually finding one by bedding him. In the draft Smith first gave Miramax, the Golgothan "shit demon" even had a full conversation's worth of dialogue.

Not only did Weinstein and the Miramax suits like the script for *Dogma*, but the actors Smith showed it to were enthusiastic, as well, particularly Affleck, who immediately knew he *had* to play the angel Bartleby. Where else would an actor get an opportunity to play a fallen angel quoting lyrics from a Run-D.M.C. song? Affleck then passed the script to his friend Matt Damon, who signed on to play Bartleby's no-good cohort Loki.

For a period, Holly Hunter was considered for the role of Bethany. Emma Thompson then signed on to play the role but ultimately backed out due to a pregnancy. Linda Fiorentino became the next and final actress to play the role. The rest of the cast consisted of Chris Rock, Bud Cort, George Carlin, Janeane Garofolo, Alan Rickman, Salma Hayek, Jason Lee, Ethan Suplee, and Alanis Morissette, who played God. Regular players Brian O'Halloran, Jeff Anderson, Jason Mewes, and of course Smith himself all returned for another round of mayhem. With *Dogma*, Smith had his biggest budget yet, at $10 million, and shot the film from March to June 1998.

Dogma was the first Kevin Smith film to feature extensive special effects and makeup effects. Not only were "realistic" demon horns and angel wings fashioned, but Smith and the effects team also decided what they should look like. Smith had strong ideas about what he wanted. He'd seen the angel wings John Travolta sported in the film *Michael*, and he'd hated them. What he wanted were wings that looked like the ones he'd seen in *Justice League of America* comics, so the effects team made animatronic wings that looked like the ones Smith envisioned. The wings weighed sixty pounds, which was a considerable amount of weight for the actors to carry. Affleck wore the wings with minimal discomfort, but they proved difficult for Rickman, who had back problems already. The Golgothan shit demon was another notable effects-team creation. The demon appeared to be made of feces but was actually made of a mixture that mostly consisted of oatmeal.

Smith and Mosier's first edit of *Dogma* came in at nearly three and a half hours long. Both of them liked the cut, but this wasn't *Lawrence of Arabia*; three hours was too long. The duo sequestered themselves and worked nonstop to trim the movie to a more acceptable length. When they were finished, the final cut came in at a tight two hours and eight minutes.

Before *Dogma* was released, it was attacked by outraged religious groups. The most vocal among the film's detractors, none of whom had even seen it yet, was the Catholic League for Religious and Civil Rights. The group, which consisted of about 350,000 people at the time and was fronted by a former sociology professor named Bill Donohue, seemed to exist solely for the purpose of targeting popular-culture entities they found offensive. Their previous targets included the Joan Osborne song "One of Us," the film *Priest*, and the short-lived ABC television series *Nothing Sacred*. "[Smith] doesn't get a free pass to make an anti-Catholic movie because he happens to be a Catholic," Catholic League media director Patrick Scully told *The Guardian*.

Dogma had its first screening at Cannes on May 21, 1999. The Catholic League and other like-minded individuals showed up to protest the premiere six months later, with similar protests popping up at screenings around the country. Smith himself showed up at one of the protests, pretending to be a protester. Proving that none of the protesters had seen the film, none of them recognized him. Despite the objections of its detractors, *Dogma* premiered with an $8.7 million opening weekend. It eventually raked in more than $30 million.

Reviews for the film were largely positive. Roger Ebert of the *Chicago Sun-Times* suggested that the Catholic God might actually enjoy *Dogma* if he were to watch it. He went on to assess that Kevin Smith was a "gifted comic writer who loves paradox, rhetoric and unexpected zingers from the blind side." *Austin Chronicle* critic Marjorie Baumgarten praised, "The film is funny, contentious, blasphemous, and surreal. With this fourth film, Smith again demonstrates that he is one of our ablest writers of smart movie dialogue. . . . *Dogma* is one of the most intelligent, engaging, and gut-bustingly funny revelations to come along in a while."

One writer who was not as fond of *Dogma* was *Entertainment Weekly*'s Bruce Frett, who proposed an eleventh commandment that would disallow Smith from directing more films. Humorously, *Entertainment Weekly*, the same publication that had published Frett's review, later declared *Dogma* to be one of the ten best films of 1999.

Smith was extremely proud of the completed film. "I'm a big fan of the film," he wrote in the introduction to the published screenplay.

> I loved it as a script, and I love it now that it's a finished flick. I know it's considered gauche to talk about how in love with your own material you are, but whenever I see or read *Dogma*, I wish it would never end. I'm usually an annoyingly modest or self-deprecating person, but I have to admit that I exempt *Dogma* from the usual self-derision I afford my other flicks, comics, etc. A lot of thought went into crafting it, a lot of heart, a lot of wit, and a lot of myself. And because of that, I feel it's my finest hour professionally.

Most of Smith's positive reviews focus on his writing, illuminating an inconvenient truth that Kevin Smith isn't nearly as good a director as he is a writer. I'm sure he himself would be the first to admit that. Another truth is that it doesn't matter because Smith's films are good. They are all that they need to be—adequate skins hanging on the strongest of bones, and those bones are Smith's screenplays. His writing is masterful, particularly his dialogue, which is sharper than a Ginsu knife. Smith is a writer who directs to protect his vision. The types of films he directed and the writing within them made him a standout in the pack of new filmmakers who emerged in the 1990s.

Kevin Smith has displayed an unwillingness to compromise his unique visions since the *Mallrats* debacle. His films focus on subjects that other filmmakers' films don't, he's continued to write and cast in ways that often go against conventional wisdom, and he's not afraid to occasionally step out of his comfort zone to direct something completely different, like *Red State*, *Tusk*, or *Cop Out*. Smith has his share of detractors, but he's a gifted scribe who continues to improve as a director. He makes and does whatever the hell he wants to, making him a maverick in the truest sense of the word.

9

The Deeply Personal Cinema of Noah Baumbach

Noah Baumbach was born and raised in Brooklyn, New York. His father, Jonathan Baumbach, was a writer of experimental fiction and a film critic for the *Partisan Review*. His mother, Georgia Brown, wrote fiction and was a film critic for *The Village Voice*. Being raised by two lovers of cinema, Baumbach saw a lot of movies at a young age. The 1974 Robert Bresson film *Lancelot du Lac* was the first movie he saw in a theater. "For pretty much as long as I can remember I [knew] that I was going to write and direct movies," Baumbach told the *Boston Phoenix*. He also created his own homegrown comic books. He recognized at an early age that his strength as a writer was crafting witty dialogue, and this understanding led him to screenwriting.

As a young man, Baumbach fell in love with the comedy films of guys like Bill Murray and Steve Martin, but his parents also exposed him to lots of American and European classic films. As a teen, he looked at life experiences like they were movies, always trying to work out how a filmmaker might best tell these stories. While at Vassar, he began to consider screenplay structure. He didn't have the equipment to make films, so he wrote plays instead.

After graduating college in 1991, he set to work writing a screenplay about a group of friends, several of whom had just finished college. With the project, Baumbach wanted to combine two separate ideas he'd had: The first idea was to create some sort of facsimile of his friendship with three of his childhood friends. The second idea was to explore the idea of people who graduate from college but don't leave. First, he and his longtime friend Bo Berkman sat down and reminisced about situations that could lend themselves to a good story. Baumbach then wrote the script alone, enjoying the quiet process.

While writing, he felt high on the power of creation. Baumbach wrote without abandon, giving no considerations to the marketplace or whether what he was writing could be sold. He wrote from the heart, crafting the story he wanted to tell. This was the first screenplay he'd ever written. Because there was no screenwriting software available at the time, he had to write it in Word. As a result, he experienced a number of formatting issues and was constantly having to reformat the script. Additionally, having only read published Woody Allen screenplays, he wasn't sure what the format of an actual shooting script was supposed to look like.

Discussing the just-after-college period his characters experience, Baumbach told journalist Charles Taylor,

> It's a time when you're discovering your possibilities but also your limitations, so it's a time when you're forced to compromise. It's a time when you have the luxury to try out a lot of different things. When I first graduated, the script was more about actually leaving college, because it was my instant experience. I think by the time I made it, it became more about leaving anywhere, moving on from one kind of long-term relationship or job or marriage. In this case, college is the first one. College was always the time people would try that hairstyle they'd always thought about. I think that what these characters are discovering is, "Well, which of those things is gonna stick?" A lot of the time, it's the things you don't want.

Although many would-be screenwriters believe that writing something commercial is the best way to gain entrance into the film industry, Baumbach believed then and believes now that the best path is to write something unique and personal, something that only that writer could create. The script Baumbach wrote—originally titled *Fifth Year*—fit that bill. Reflecting on the kinds of personal films that he wanted to make, Baumbach said

Every so often there are movies, not necessarily about a generation, but that capture a group of people. When I saw *Diner*, I was, like, ten years old, and I thought, "I am these people." These guys are all screwed up about sex, living in the '50s in Baltimore. I was ten years old, living in Brooklyn. My feeling is, when a filmmaker makes a movie—whatever it's about—and I respond to it, that's what I set out to do.

Baumbach had no connections in the film industry, so he started mailing out copies to anyone he believed "might know someone" or who had "sat next to someone on a plane." He later reflected to author Sara Caldwell, "When you're starting out, it's great to be both naïve and ambitious. . . . In the beginning, I didn't know what the risks were. I just had a script that I was submitting, with the confidence that I could direct it. Anything seemed possible."

Early on, Baumbach got comedy legend Steve Martin to read his script, and Martin wrote the young screenwriter a letter telling him how much he'd enjoyed it. Baumbach included a copy of Martin's letter with the script whenever he sent it out to potential readers. At the time, there was a lot of discussion about the newly named Generation X. Although Baumbach says he didn't really feel connected to Gen X, he included an article about Gen X with the script, hoping to form a connection between *Fifth Year* and Gen X in the minds of producers.

Eventually, Baumbach found his way onto the set of a movie called *Sleep with Me*. There he met producer Joe Kastelberg, who'd made a movie called *Bodies, Rest and Motion* that a friend (Roger Hedden) of Baumbach's brother had written. Baumbach used this opportunity to convince Kastelberg to read his script. Kastelberg liked *Fifth Year* and decided he would help Baumbach get his film made. Everything came together easily, at least initially, with Kastelberg convincing the financiers of his two previous features to put up the money. However, the financing fell through at the last minute, leading Kastelberg to put up a significant amount of the $2 million budget himself.

Eventually, Kastelberg found new financiers to help make the picture, but they would only fork over the money if

Baumbach cast actor Eric Stoltz in his film. This would have been great except for the fact that there were no roles in the script that fit Stoltz, who was older than the characters. According to Kastelberg, the producer sent a fax to Stoltz: "We have no part for you, but we will create one, and if you agree.... If you commit *right now* to do this movie—in a part that we don't know about yet—then I can get the money."

Stoltz accepted the producer's invitation, and Kastelberg asked Baumbach to create a new role for Stoltz. Baumbach later told author Sara Caldwell, "I had to write Eric Stoltz a part to get the movie made. Up until then, I'd felt the script was this precious document, but suddenly, I had to write in an entirely new character to get the money. I wrote the part in a way that I knew I could cut it out if it didn't work, but it ended up making the movie better."

Around this time, *Fifth Year* was retitled *Kicking and Screaming*, which was likely what Baumbach himself felt like doing because it had become such a chore to get the picture made. He later commented that he wished he'd kept the original title, even joking about the fact that Will Ferrell had starred in a wholly different movie titled *Kicking and Screaming* a few years later. It's not difficult to imagine the cringing expression on Baumbach's face and the pain in his stomach every time someone asks, "Hey, you directed that Will Ferrell movie about the kid's soccer team, right?" Nevertheless, with a new title, new financiers, a new actor, and a new version of his script, Baumbach's film was getting made.

Cinematographer Steven Bernstein believes that *Kicking and Screaming*'s true strength is Baumbach's writing. Bernstein said,

> What was interesting about Noah was, at that point, he was highly inexperienced. He hadn't really been on a professional film set. He had really good intuitions, for language most of all, the rhythms of language, the rhythms of the sub-culture that he was portraying, their vernacular. That kind of carried us. It was very much an ad hoc crew. It wasn't like they were A-list out of Warner Brothers. That's not to say that they didn't all go on to storied careers—we worked with a lot of good

people—but we didn't have the crew members who would [normally] be required for a film like that. Not everybody was the most experienced, and the equipment we had was kind of what we could find and put together. So that film, by its antecedence, should not have succeeded. There was no way that film should have been successful. And yet, because of these remarkable characters that he created, the way he used language, it sustained despite the production value not being what it ought to be.

Baumbach said that he felt like a bit of a fraud while directing the film's first scene. According to Bernstein, Baumbach's initial discomfort wasn't noticeable. The cinematographer believes Baumbach's smooth transition into the role of director came as the result of detailed planning and Baumbach trusting his collaborators. "Noah was very confident in some respects," Bernstein said.

> What he was confident in was his writing. He knew who his characters were. He knew what their dramatic arc was going to be. He wasn't necessarily familiar with the technical side of it. But he kind of left that to those of us who were comfortable with that. What was really good that I did with him on that film (and the subsequent films) is, we spent weeks planning. When we were on that film, we went day in and day out, going scene by scene, sequence by sequence, talking about visual references—some were from other films, some were from literature. We planned in great detail. So I think Noah was comfortable with the characters and where they were going, and for the technical side he relied on our prep so he felt comfortable and knew that as his chief technician or collaborator—he knew where I was going. He pre-planned so he wouldn't be figuring things out on the day [of shooting] on the technical side, where he had a lesser level of comfort.

One way Baumbach created the energy and familial feeling that he wanted to convey on the screen was by working to build bonds with the actors when the cameras weren't rolling. Getting believable performances from his actors was of the utmost importance to him. Bernstein added,

168 / Chapter 9

Director Noah Baumbach has become one of the most respected filmmakers to emerge in the '90s. Courtesy of American Empirical Pictures/Photofest © American Empirical Pictures, Photographer: James Hamilton

I think the most takes we ever did was the scene when Josh is deciding not to go on the plane to Paris. It was the key scene. The coda of the film. I think we maybe did eight takes. The problem is, we didn't have a lot of money or time, so we were cranking through this. Performances are so very important to Noah, so we would work very hard on getting it right, knowing that if we didn't, and if we did a lot of takes, we'd be punished by running out of time at the end of the day.

In early screenings, audience members were confused by the film's flashback scenes, which use resolves with a black-and-white sepia. Some audience members didn't know if these scenes were supposed to be flashbacks or contemporary scenes, so Trimark, the studio releasing the film, suggested that Baumbach re-edit the scenes so that they would transform through three stages to color and then to motion. Baumbach did this and later said he believed this improved the film.

Kicking and Screaming was accepted for competition by the Cannes Film Festival but only if Baumbach agreed to cut fifteen minutes. Baumbach refused to make the cuts, so Cannes refused to screen the picture. The film then premiered at the New York Film Festival in October 1995 and was released theatrically soon after, earning a disappointing $19,000 over its opening weekend and going on to earn a worldwide total of $718,000.

Critics largely appreciated the film. They weren't blown away by it, but they *liked* it and recognized Baumbach as a budding talent. *Chicago Sun-Times* critic Roger Ebert gave the picture three (out of a possible four) stars, congratulating Baumbach's movie for being smart rather than something aimed at the back row of the theater, like *Doom Generation*, which he saw on the same day and despised. Beyond that, Ebert observed, "*Kicking and Screaming* doesn't have much of a plot, but of course it wouldn't; this is a movie about characters waiting for their plots to begin. What it does have is a good idea and a terrific ear; the dialogue by writer-director Noah Baumbach is not simply accurate, which would be a bore, but a distillation of reality-elevating aimless brainy small-talk into a statement." *The New York Times'* Janet Maslin stated, "*Kicking and Screaming* occupies its postage-stamp size terrain with confident comic style." *Newsweek*'s David Ansen assessed it as a "witty movie—with a fine ear for the undertone of aimless chatter—that never raises its voice to make hollow Gen-X proclamations." Hal Hinson of the *Washington Post* wrote, "As a writer, Baumbach loves smart, glib talk, and he has a sharp ear for fast-paced, overlapping dialogue; as a director, though, he prefers long takes that allow his characters to work out their feelings."

Baumbach's second picture was based on an idea he'd had several years before. A jealous boyfriend becomes obsessed with his girlfriend's successful ex-boyfriend and then stalks him and ingratiates himself into his life. The second film, *Mr. Jealousy*, again was produced by Kastelberg and shot in New York City on a budget of "about $2 million." Baumbach saw the film as an homage to the French New Wave films of the 1960s, and he hoped to shoot in a style that was similar. Due to budgetary constraints, he also shot using available lighting and a minimal number of takes.

The location was extremely important to Baumbach. Because he and his mother both lived in the West Village and his father lived in Brooklyn, he set the picture in neighborhoods and locations that he knew personally. This, he believed, would give the film a more authentic, lived-in feeling. "I like to know the place when I'm writing," he told the BBC. "I like to have even visual ideas of the streets, the locations, if I can when I'm writing. Because I feel like it grounds me. It's the same reason I often use real names in my scripts, of people I know. Not because I'm writing about them at all—I would never do that—but because it's immediately a real person to me. I believe it."

Despite the fact that he'd had to shoehorn Eric Stoltz into *Kicking and Screaming*, Baumbach enjoyed working with the actor and felt they were simpatico, so this time out, he cast Stoltz as his lead. Stoltz was also given an executive producer role. One of the primary things, production-wise, that Stoltz brought to *Mr. Jealousy* was his popularity among his fellow actors. Because of this, he was able to introduce the filmmakers to a lot of actors during the casting process. Stoltz was dating Bridget Fonda, who was a big name at the time, and she was offered the role of Stoltz's character's girlfriend. Fonda read the script and loved it. Of course she wanted to be in the movie, she said. There was only one problem: She wanted to play the character Stoltz was playing! Baumbach refused to rewrite the script to change the gender of the character. He also wanted Stoltz to be his lead, so Fonda turned down the role of the girlfriend, but as a favor to Stoltz, she agreed to play a small role.

Stoltz had another idea for an actress who could play the girlfriend. Stoltz knew an up-and-coming actress named Jennifer Aniston. He showed Aniston the script, and she loved it and agreed to do it, so Kastelberg raised money for *Mr. Jealousy* by pitching it as an Eric Stoltz/Jennifer Aniston picture. A sales representative then sold the foreign rights to the film based on this scenario, as well, but just before filming was to begin,

Aniston changed her mind and dropped out of the picture. So it was back to the drawing board for Baumbach and company.

Stoltz had yet another idea. At the time, he was working on a horror picture called *Anaconda* with an attractive young actress named Jennifer Lopez. Would Baumbach and Kastelberg consider her? Sure. So they went to the set of *Anaconda* and met with her. Lopez liked the script and signed on, but again, as they neared filming, the actress's management decided they didn't want her to make the film, so she backed out.

What now? Thankfully, casting director Todd Thaler suggested an actress named Annabella Sciorra, who'd made a splash in such films as *Jungle Fever*, *The Hard Way*, and *The Hand That Rocks the Cradle*. Would Baumbach and Kastelberg take a look at her? Okay, sure. Sciorra liked the role and agreed to do the part.

Baumbach was a big fan of director Peter Bogdanovich's films, such as *The Last Picture Show* and *Paper Moon*. Because Stoltz had worked with the director on *Mask*, Baumbach threw caution to the wind and offered the role of the psychiatrist to Bogdanovich. Bogdanovich, who wasn't all that known for his acting at that point, accepted the role. Bogdanovich was so good in that role that he was later cast as a psychiatrist on the television series *The Sopranos*.

Baumbach cast Marianne Jean-Baptiste, an English actress who was at the time largely unknown in the United States. Interestingly, Jean-Baptiste was nominated for an Academy Award during the filming of *Mr. Jealousy*. Chris Eigeman, Carlos Jacott, and John Lehr had all been in *Kicking and Screaming*, and all of them returned for *Mr. Jealousy*. Brian Kerwin, another actor who was brought in by Stoltz, later said there was a familial atmosphere between all the actors and crew members who'd worked on the previous film. "They were a bunch of people who thought alike," he explained in "Revisiting Mr. Jealousy." He went on to say that "there was a lot of love on the set" and they were pretty much all on the same page most of the time.

During the shoot, Stoltz developed a real-life crush on Sciorra. "I became a little obsessed," he told IndieWire. "I had a little crush. I became a little curious about her exes and her life.

That's what we do. That's what I do. There's a point where you know this is a job and you don't bring it home. But basically one of our jobs is to fall in love with the person that we are falling in love with on film."

Although Bridget Fonda's role was small, she contributed a new aspect to her character. While Fonda could have played the character simply as an intelligent, attractive woman, as the role was written, she decided to give the character a speech impediment. This newly conceived trait works exceptionally well.

Much of *Mr. Jealousy*'s effectiveness comes from Baumbach's use and strategic placement of music. Because he'd wanted the picture to pay homage to the French New Wave films, he used Georges Delerue's theme music from the 1962 François Truffaut film *Jules et Jim*. He also got permission from Leonard Cohen to use his song "Hey, That's No Way to Say Goodbye" in the film. Baumbach wanted to use a rerecorded version of John Lennon's song "Jealous Guy," too, so he went to Lennon's widow, Yoko Ono, and convinced her to let him use the song. The version in the film was recorded by Dean Wareham's band Luna.

The film's cinematographer, Steven Bernstein, believed *Mr. Jealousy* is a "small masterpiece." Again, as with *Kicking and Screaming*, he credited Baumbach's writing as being the primary reason for this. However, he believed the screenwriter showed tremendous growth between his first and second films. Bernstein observed,

> By the time we got to *Mr. Jealousy*, he had evolved so that we could have characters that were even more complex and nuanced. I think they had even more depth than in *Kicking and Screaming*. Maybe not the same charm, but a great depth. So if you look and examine the film, it's a hugely satisfying insight into a shared human condition about the nature of jealousy and love and frailty. I just found it really very powerful, and the central conceit of having someone pretend to be someone else in therapy so that person could get therapy rather than going, that was absolutely brilliant.

After making the festival rounds, *Mr. Jealousy* opened theatrically on June 5, 1998. It ultimately earned a mere $302,000. The reviews for the film were positive, averaging somewhere in the B range. The *Los Angeles Times'* Kenneth Turan observed that the film's "easygoing and engaging quality masks how rare an accomplishment it is to create something achingly true as well as amusing, as wise about people as it is about the craft of film." Monica Eng of the *Chicago Tribune* wrote, "While the plot suffers from a few sitcom-ish aspects and some dumbly juvenile joking around between Lester and his buddies, the film gains strength from small, nutty scenes, dead-on reactions, and off-the-wall lines that almost seem improvised." In his three-star "a must-see" review, *Chicago Reader* critic Jonathan Rosenbaum first pointed out the similarities—all positive—between *Mr. Jealousy* and the films of Woody Allen. He then added, "Baumbach's best trait as a filmmaker [is] his handling of actors. . . . Like Renoir and Truffaut, he's often at his best dealing with the interactions of friends hanging out together and enjoying one another's company."

While *Mr. Jealousy* is a fairly conventional picture, Baumbach sought to make something more experimental, so before shooting had wrapped, he'd come up with the idea to shoot a very quick experimental film with the same actors immediately after finishing *Mr. Jealousy*. The film takes place entirely in one location—a Brooklyn apartment. Baumbach had long been a fan of improvisation and both *Saturday Night Live* and *SCTV*, so he wanted this film to be almost entirely improvised. There was a script, written by Baumbach and his friends Carlos Jacott and Christopher Reed, but it mostly served as a jumping-off point.

"Noah had decided to make a film this way long before we shot *Mr. Jealousy*," Kastelberg told *Independent Film and Video Monthly*. "He wanted to do something plain fun that the critics wouldn't particularly berate him for. This seemed like the perfect spirit to do it in." So, when *Mr. Jealousy* wrapped, Baumbach and his cast and crew took a week off. They then reunited for the new picture, *Highball*. There would be a one-week rehearsal, followed by a short seven-day shoot. At the time of shooting, the budget was reported to be $250,000. Years later, Kastelberg said that the budget was "about $100,000." Either way, it was cheaper than the average movie.

Highball was shot on 16 mm and mostly using a handheld camera. Most scenes were single takes. In addition to the cast of *Mr. Jealousy*, *Highball* featured Justine Bateman, Ally Sheedy, Rae Dawn Chong, and Baumbach himself. "It was a really amazing little thing we put together," Kastelberg recalled in "Revisiting Mr. Jealousy." "It was really done as a way to highlight the comic talent of all these young guys."

Just after finishing *Highball*, Baumbach explained his motives for making the film to journalist Eve Claxton:

> I always thought *Kicking and Screaming* would be made this way, with no money and with friends. In the end, we had over a million for the film, and then we doubled that budget on *Mr. Jealousy*, so I wanted to go back and fill in the gap. Also, my other films have had a strong melancholy streak, and I wanted to do something that was all-out funny, that an audience could just laugh at all the way through.

Ultimately, Baumbach wasn't pleased with the final product. He expressed unhappiness with *Highball*, calling it a "failed experiment," and wound up removing his name from the film, instead crediting a pseudonym, Ernie Fusco. As unlikely as it may be, *Highball* made more money for Lionsgate, the distributor of both pictures, than *Mr. Jealousy*.

In the decades following those three pictures, Baumbach has continued to create artistically triumphant, very personal films. His standout films as a director include *The Squid and the Whale*, *Margot at the Wedding*, and *Marriage Story*. His films are often compared to those of Woody Allen and Whit Stillman, but Baumbach dismisses comparisons to other filmmakers, presumably desiring to be seen and judged on his own merits.

Baumbach's characters are often artistic intellectuals living in New York City who discuss such highbrow topics as literature and philosophy. The characters' introspective dialogue often reveals their unhappiness with or disappointment regarding their lives. The loss of youth and the inevitability of aging plays a role in much of Baumbach's work. His films often examine crumbling relationships of different types, and these examinations can be raw and impactful because of Baumbach's unique talent of poking extremely sensitive and universally exposed nerves, making the characters and their struggles relatable. While much is made of the recurring subject of divorce in Baumbach's films, he has an equally frequent tendency to focus on flawed parents.

In addition to his work as director, Baumbach has also helped create some highly respected collaborative projects. He cowrote *The Life Aquatic with Steve Zissou* and *The Fantastic Mr. Fox* with Wes Anderson. Baumbach also cowrote the hit film *Barbie* with his wife, Greta Gerwig.

Baumbach has been nominated three times by the Academy of Motion Picture Arts and Sciences as a screenwriter (for *The Squid and the Whale*, *Marriage Story*, and *Barbie*). Additionally, *Marriage Story* was nominated for Best Picture. These nominations have failed to yield any Oscars, but the fact that he's been nominated four times (to date) says almost as much as his characters do.

10

The Whimsical World of Wes Anderson

Wes Anderson grew up in Houston, Texas, the product of divorced parents. The second of three sons, he was a creative child who dreamed of growing up to be an author. As a child, he made Super 8 movies with his friends, but his real passion was storytelling, and he usually had his nose in a novel of some sort. He attended St. John's School in Houston, where he produced his own plays. "I was having a problem with self-discipline," Anderson told the *San Francisco Chronicle* in 1999. "So this teacher who knew I liked to write plays made this deal that every two weeks that went by that I didn't have this self-discipline problem, I got to put on another play." These high school plays were based on such television series and movies as *Starsky and Hutch* and the Kenny Rogers telefilm *The Gambler*.

Schoolmates Mike Maggart later recalled, "Wes was always writing stories. We took creative writing together at St. John's. Wes had this poem and he showed it to me. I thought it was the funniest thing I'd ever read." Anderson, who became known for writing quirky comedies that sometimes perplexed audience members, had this unique sense of humor even then. Maggart explained, "I said, 'You need to read this [poem] to the class, man.' So he raised his hand and read it to the class. No response."

After graduating high school, Anderson attended the University of Texas at Austin, where he studied playwriting. It was there that he met a classmate named Owen Wilson. Anderson produced another of his plays, and he asked Wilson to appear in the production. Wilson had never acted before but agreed to take the role. Anderson and Wilson hit it off, finding they had much in common, including a love of films by Robert Altman, Martin Scorsese, and Sam Peckinpah. Soon they became roommates and writing partners. When the two staged a break-in into their own apartment in order to get their landlord's attention and convince him to fix a window that wouldn't close, they considered why a person might actually rob his own house. This inadvertently created the seed that grew into the script for a short film about bumbling rich-kid robbers titled *Bottle Rocket*.

Before making *Bottle Rocket*, Anderson made a film about their elderly German landlord. This, he hoped, would get them into his good graces. In the film, the landlord shared anecdotes about his life, including a story he told Anderson about a pet snake he'd once seized from a tenant who hadn't paid his rent. The landlord wept as he told him that he'd come to love the serpent, who eventually got sick and died in his arms. In the end, the landlord even paid Anderson $600 for filming his story.

That's when Anderson made *Bottle Rocket*. It was shot on 16 mm black-and-white film. Although the first incarnation of *Bottle Rocket* was an eight-minute short, this wasn't their original intention. Anderson later said, "We started working on *Bottle Rocket* as a feature script. We wanted to write a movie script, and that was the script we came up with. We started trying to film it as a feature with some money from our fathers—we each borrowed $2,000—and we ran out of money, and it became a short."

Wilson showed the short to *Texas Chainsaw Massacre 2* scribe and family friend L. M. Kit Carson, who appreciated it. Comprised of the first scenes of the full-length script, the short was certainly unique. Carson convinced Wilson and Anderson to shoot some more footage and expand it. When they got it to thirteen minutes, Carson submitted it to the Sundance Film Festival, where it was well received, but no one came forward to purchase it. Carson then sent the full-length script to a producer he knew named Barbara Boyle. Boyle, who had produced *Eight Men Out*, among other films, liked the script and took it to *The Last Picture Show* producer Polly Platt. Platt also liked what she saw, so she took it to James L. Brooks, the Academy

Award–winning director of such films as *Terms of Endearment* and *Broadcast News*. When Brooks screened the thirteen-minute short, he told Platt, "We have to make a deal with these guys!"

Brooks had a deal set up with Columbia Pictures, so he took the short to them, convincing the studio to bankroll the feature-length version of *Bottle Rocket* with a $5 million budget. Remembering this surreal event, Wilson told the *Dallas Observer*, "It was a scary feeling. I'd think, 'Man, are we really gonna do this? Does something like this come from when me and Wes used to sit around during college making up funny stuff? Is this what it was all leading up to?"

Platt and Brooks produced the film and helped Anderson and Wilson tighten up the script. Anderson directed, and the producers wanted the majority of the actors who'd appeared in the short film to return for the feature. This included Wilson and his brother Luke, who both went on to sizable acting careers.

Under Brooks's supervision, Anderson and Wilson performed a number of rewrites. They weren't always happy with the suggestions, but they continued moving forward, trying to walk a tightrope that made the script something that pleased the producers without compromising too much and sacrificing things they felt were necessary. Changes included new scenes, rewriting old scenes, character development, and cutting some scenes. "The first thing was to cut the script," Platt explained in the 2008 *Making of Bottle Rocket* featurette.

> There were scenes in it. . . . For instance, the three lost boys are traveling around Dallas and they hit the back of a car, and they have a really bad accident and get into a fistfight with the driver of the car. Then you never see those people again. There was a character called Little Richard who comes in and fights with them, and you never see him again. There were all these strange scenes that had to go.

Anderson later admitted that most of the changes were necessary: "I think the movie we originally made probably didn't work. There was a renovation process that took place. Making that movie, and in particular working with Jim Brooks, was a

Owen and Luke Wilson in Wes Anderson's Bottle Rocket. *Courtesy of Columbia Pictures/Photofest © Columbia Pictures*

bit of a film-school experience for me and Owen, both when we were writing the movie and . . . in the editing room. We spent a lot of time trying to get the movie to work properly."

The producers wanted a known actor to play the small but pivotal role of Mr. Henry. Anderson and Wilson initially wanted Donald Sutherland, but then they learned that veteran actor James Caan was interested in the part. Despite his initial reaction to the film's title, asking, "What kind of fuckin' title is this?" he was intrigued. And how could you turn down the actor who had essayed Sonny Corleone in *The Godfather*? So they agreed to meet with him.

When Caan arrived, he was wearing an oversized T-shirt, faded jeans, and cowboy boots. "When he came in the office, everybody was trying to put him at ease and make him feel comfortable," Wilson told the *Dallas Observer*. "It turned out the thing he felt most comfortable talking about was karate and kicking people's asses." Caan wanted to talk about his karate training instead of the movie. Then he decided he would give them a display of the techniques he'd mastered, so he used some moves on Wilson and Brooks. Wanting to please the actor so he would do their film, they exaggerated their responses to his attacks. Then Caan dislocated Wilson's shoulder.

Anderson later told AMC that the Mr. Henry character resonated with Caan. "He liked the character. He's that kind of guy. I mean, he's totally into karate, and he kind of liked the idea of being someone who everyone on the set would look up to. For one thing, he's really scary; he's a violent person."

The feature-length version of *Bottle Rocket* began shooting on May 19, 1992. Anderson soon concluded that many of the methods he'd used in his short films were outside the norm: "I began to realize, 'I think the way we're doing things is not quite right, because some of our techniques seem to be getting sort of a puzzled reaction." The actor who was the most confused by Anderson's methods was Caan, who asked him, "Why is this happening?" Caan failed to grasp that the film they were making was a comedy until he was midway through the shoot. Additionally, he expressed unhappiness with Anderson's decision to shoot with a 27 mm lens. Even then, it was apparent that Anderson was a maverick who saw things differently from other filmmakers.

Anderson wanted to use the theme music from the animated *Peanuts* specials in *Bottle Rocket*, so he wrote a number of letters to creator Charles M. Schulz, but his attempts to contact him were blocked by television producer Lee Mendelson. This led to several angry exchanges. In the end, Mendelson expressed that he didn't want the music to appear in a film containing curse words.

Anderson hired Mark Mothersbaugh to score *Bottle Rocket*. He was a founding member of Devo who, like Anderson, was known for creating art that was unique, and he, also like Anderson, had a reputation for doing things his own way. Anderson kept Mothersbaugh in the loop throughout the shoot, even allowing him to visit the set.

Producer Brooks, however, wanted something different than what Mothersbaugh was creating. Just as he'd attempted to get Anderson to make *Bottle Rocket* more mainstream and accessible, Brooks tried to convince Mothersbaugh to make the score more traditional. Mothersbaugh told journalist Ryan Leas,

> James Brooks would show up at the different playbacks when I'd write music for Wes. Wes would be there. Every time James would show up, he'd leave and his office would send me another copy of [the movie] *Big*, like "Listen to this, this is what your music should sound like." I said, "Wes, I have a stack of *Big* VHS tapes, what should I do?" He said, "Just ignore him. Don't worry, you and me are going to work this out."

After the shoot, Anderson spent six days a week locked in an editing room with editor David Moritz. Anderson wanted to make *Bottle Rocket* the very best it could be, and he made a number of cuts, but he was never quite sure the film was right. He'd been working on *Bottle Rocket* for so long that he'd lost the ability to see it with an objective eye. Making matters worse, Columbia was genuinely confused by the picture and never understood it. The film (and Anderson's perspective) are so radically different from what the studio execs had known previously that they weren't sure what to make of it. But one thing the studio did understand was that they wanted the film's running time cut down.

After the film was finished, audience test screenings were a disaster. According to Platt, the picture received the lowest test-screening scores on record. At the film's first screening in Santa Monica, Anderson watched in horror as audience members walked out en masse. Comment cards filled out by the audience gave such unhelpful commentary as "Sucked" and "This is shit." Anderson told Noah Baumbach in 2009 that he'd never felt more confident than he had while making *Bottle Rocket* and had never felt less confident than he had at the test screenings.

The studio started talking about more recuts and shooting new footage, but Anderson wasn't having it. He'd worked damn hard on the film, and he wasn't going to change it just because simple minds couldn't understand what he was doing. One day, he was summoned to the studio for a meeting to discuss the film. When he got there, he told them in no uncertain terms that he was not going to change anything in *Bottle Rocket*, and somehow, some way, the studio heads understood and let it stand.

Anderson and the film's producers had a plan to generate enthusiasm for *Bottle Rocket* before its release. Brooks later explained this to documentarian Barry Braverman: "Our whole idea was to submit it to Sundance, where their short had been. And that would [give this] small-budget picture . . . some attention there. Do that circuit, which so many people do. And Sundance turned it down." Although Anderson later pooh-poohed the Sundance snub, he was understandably devastated at the time.

When *Bottle Rocket* was released theatrically in February 1996, it did disappointing business, earning $560,069 during its short run. Nevertheless, it was generally well received by the critics. Andy Klein of the *Dallas Observer* observed that it had "elements of Jim Jarmusch and the Coen brothers but without Jarmusch's self-conscious artiness or the Coens' hip snottiness. While the characters are clearly portrayed as barely functional, there is never even a trace of condescension; the filmmakers really like, even admire, these guys—and so do we." *The Hollywood Reporter*'s David Hunter praised, "A marvelous debut film for its director, writer, and lead actors, *Bottle Rocket* is propelled by a fresh approach to the caper genre." *Variety* noted that the film was "full of surprising warmth and charm, unexpected plot turns, and droll characters that bounce off each other in refreshing ways." *Los Angeles Times* critic Kenneth Turan's review not only praised Anderson and the film but also scolded the Sundance festival for dismissing it.

Bottle Rocket is less stylized than Anderson's later pictures, but it contains many of the traits and techniques he became known for. These include his exquisite use of needle drops; slow motion; warm colors; and soft, naturalistic lighting.

While the film may not have garnered any Academy Award attention, Anderson was given the MTV Movie Award for Best New Filmmaker. Hopefully that made Anderson feel a little bit better, but if that didn't do the trick, the great Martin Scorsese later called *Bottle Rocket* one of his favorite movies of the 1990s. On another occasion, Scorsese praised Anderson's ability to "convey the simple joys and interactions between people so well and with such richness." *Bottle Rocket* may not have made the splash at the box office that Anderson hoped for, but it earned Scorsese's praise. What more could a filmmaker ask for?

Anderson and Wilson had started working on the script that became the director's second film years before. It was a project they'd referred to as the "school movie." It ultimately became *Rushmore*, and it was a story about an eccentric boy's experiences in high school. With the script, Anderson and Wilson wanted to create a "slightly heightened reality, like a Roald Dahl children's book." Discussing the story later, cinematographer Robert Yeoman told journalist Andrew Dansby, "[*Rushmore*'s protagonist, Max, is] not always a likeable character. But in the end, you're rooting for him. That's because of Wes and Owen. . . . Wes' parents went through a divorce. Owen had some struggles growing up. They're expressing that through writing."

Anderson hadn't planned to make *Rushmore* autobiographical, although in many respects it is. "Max is like me," he said in 1999, "except he's not shy." Anderson's intention was to craft a film that appealed to his younger high-school-aged self rather than reflect him. Anderson later told Charlie Rose, "If I had seen this movie when I was fifteen years old, that would have been my movie." It was difficult to miss the similarities between Max and Anderson because the character is an eccentric, precocious teen who writes and produces plays based on television shows. Instead of *Starsky and Hutch*, however, Max writes his play based on the Sidney Lumet film *Serpico*.

This isn't to say that the real-life elements that inspired the character were entirely Anderson's. Max also had similarities to Owen Wilson. For instance, Wilson, like Max, had been expelled from an elite preparatory school. Another instance is the speech Herman Blume gives about privilege at the beginning of the film, which Wilson's father had given him previously. And Wilson, like Max, had been aimless in high school and had had a strong crush on an older woman. Like the younger characters in many of Anderson's films, Max acts with a maturity that is beyond his age. One aspect of the picture that appealed to Anderson and Wilson was the idea of teenage Max becoming close friends with a fifty-year-old man.

Rushmore was originally set up to be made at New Line Cinema, but this fell apart because New Line refused to give Anderson the budget to make the film properly. After that, producer Barry Mendel held an auction for the film rights. Walt Disney Studios chairman Joe Roth won by offering Anderson a $10 million budget.

Anderson and Wilson had written the part of Herman Blume with comic actor Bill Murray in mind, but neither of them believed they could actually land him. When Anderson and the producers reached out to Murray's agent, the agent read the script with appreciation and took it to Murray, who *loved* the screenplay. In fact, Murray loved it so much that he considered appearing in it for free. In the end, he appeared in *Rushmore* for scale (which amounted to approximately $9,000).

Casting lead character Max proved to be much more difficult. Anderson searched high and low trying to find the right actor, auditioning more than a thousand actors, but no one seemed right. The search seemed like it would never end and started driving everyone crazy. Anderson told Mendel that he didn't want to make *Rushmore* if he couldn't find the right actor to play the role. At one point, Mendel and the other producers considered canceling the film entirely. But fate then took a hand when casting director Davia Nelson mentioned the film to Sofia Coppola. Actor Jason Schwartzman later explained,

> Davia was talking to my cousin, Sofia, and she said, "I'm casting for this movie called *Rushmore* and we are looking for a fifteen-year-old teenager who is a playwright and in love with this older woman." Just the summer before, I had written a play and directed it and I was in love with my nanny, like deeply. And Sofia said, "Oh, that's funny. That sounds like my cousin, Jason." She pointed to me and I'm wearing a tuxedo and tails. It was just a fortuitous type of weird lucky moment.

Schwartzman then auditioned for the part, and he and Anderson spent half of the session discussing their admiration for one another's sneakers and their shared love of the band Weezer. Anderson originally envisioned Max looking like a fifteen-year-old Mick Jagger, but he decided Schwartzman was the right actor for the role. The rest of the cast included Olivia Williams, Brian Cox, and Seymour Cassel. Wilson didn't act in *Rushmore*, but he appeared in a nonacting cameo as the dead husband of Mrs. Cross in a photograph.

While writing *Rushmore*, Anderson envisioned St. John's as the setting, although the fictional version of the school is the Rushmore Academy. But Anderson had never intended to shoot the film at St. John's. He hadn't even intended for the story to take place in Houston, but things eventually changed. After Anderson and Mendel scouted several East Coast locations, Anderson's mother suggested that he shoot the film at St. John's. The director considered this and realized that it made sense. As far as changing the location to Houston, Anderson had to rewrite a single scene in the script depicting characters ice fishing. *Rushmore* began filming in November 1997 and continued into the following January.

Anderson asked for permission to paint a room inside the high school to match the color palette he wanted. The school allowed the crew to paint the room as long as they agreed to repaint it the original color. After Anderson filmed the scene, however, school officials liked the new color and decided to keep it.

Because Schwartzman was hairy and appeared older than the character, some minor alterations had to be done. First Schwartzman's body was shaved, and then his hands and chest were waxed. He was also given braces to give him the appearance of someone younger.

Bill Murray joked around and had a good time with the film's cast and crew members. He gave many of them nicknames, and he took some of them with him to Houston Rockets games, where they sat courtside. He also gave younger cast members money to purchase expensive acne medicine.

Murray's character drives a Bentley in the film, but the producers had a difficult time securing the car and wound up making a deal with a local to use his car in the film. The only catch was that they had to find a part for the car owner's daughter in the film. Because the vehicle was borrowed, the producers freaked out when Murray decided it would be funny to peel out in the car, driving in circles and leaving skid marks on the pavement.

Anderson once again tapped Mark Mothersbaugh to score the picture. Anderson originally envisioned that *Rushmore* would feature a soundtrack consisting entirely of songs by the Kinks, because he believed that music matched Max's angry disposition. In the end, Anderson rethought this and included only one Kinks song ("Nothin' in the World Can Stop Me Worryin' 'bout That Girl"). The rest of the film's soundtrack is filled with 1960s pop songs by British artists, including Cat Stevens, Donovan, and the Rolling Stones. After having no luck securing the *Peanuts* theme music for *Bottle Rocket*, Anderson included "Hark the Herald Angels Sing" from *A Charlie Brown Christmas* in the film.

Remembering how difficult the test-screening process for *Bottle Rocket* was, Anderson had to be nervous. But things would be different this time, right? Sadly, no. Producer Mendel stated that *Rushmore* had the single worst test screening he'd been involved with in his (then) thirty-year career. When the audience cards came back, the comments were scathing once again. But then something incredible happened. As Mendel told the *Houston Chronicle*, "Joe Roth, head of the studio, said, 'You know what, guys? We know how great our movie is. Let's not change a frame.' That's something I've heard no studio head say or do. We were forever grateful for that."

Rushmore premiered at the Toronto International Film Festival on September 17, 1998. It was released theatrically two months later. This time out, Anderson's film fared much better. It earned approximately $19 million against a $10 million budget. While this doesn't make it a huge hit, it was a good amount for such a unique film that so many people didn't get. Critics were generally positive. *Fort Worth Star-Telegram* critic Elvis Mitchell wrote, "*Rushmore* has the gentle, insulated feel of a film by the Scottish director Bill Forsyth. And like Forsyth's best works, it has a lovely mesmerizing peculiarity that draws you into it immediately." Frank Scheck of *The Hollywood Reporter* observed, "*Rushmore* has far more imagination and wit that most major studio efforts." He continued, "Anderson and Owen Wilson's concise screenplay deftly avoids sentimentality but somehow manages to be touching anyway. The former's astute direction displays an excellent knack for visual as well as verbal gags, and Robert Yeoman's widescreen lensing is unusually beautiful and textured for a comedy."

Anderson was happy to receive all this praise, but the critic's opinion he was the most interested in was Pauline Kael's. Anderson had long been a fan of the writer's work and had once written a letter to her saying, "Your thoughts and writing about the movies [have] been a very important source of inspiration for me." Because Kael had retired in 1991, he begged her to screen *Rushmore*, so Kael relented and watched the film. When it was over, she told Anderson, "I genuinely don't know what to make of this movie." The legendary critic, like so many other viewers, was perplexed by Anderson's work. This is, again, because it is radically different from everything that preceded it, which is a testament to Anderson's maverick sensibilities. He is as unique an artist as you are likely to encounter.

In the decades that have followed, Anderson has continued to craft quirky, unique, highly creative pictures that divide audiences; either you get them, or you don't. No one seems to fall in between.

Anderson's films are, by and large, immediately recognizable. In terms of his screenplays, Anderson's films often feature flawed, clumsy, eccentric antiheroes who are usually gifted. When he writes about children, which he does with some frequency, those characters are precocious. He often writes about melancholic characters who are lonely and who often meet and connect with unlikely people.

His visual aesthetic has changed somewhat. In the two 1990s efforts discussed in this chapter, he used fairly muted colors.

But with his 2002 film *The Royal Tenenbaums*, he used a distinct color palette of uncommonly, unrealistically, highly saturated, bright basic colors. Equally noticeable is his unusual predilection for symmetrical compositions. Other stylistic choices he's known for are flat-space camera movements; slow-motion walking shots; rapid, shaky zooms on his characters, and the use of miniatures.

For a long time, Anderson publicly questioned with genuine curiosity why his films caused so much division; why did some viewers love his work and herald each project as a masterpiece while others hated, hated, hated them and took every opportunity to criticize them? Finally, in a 2013 interview with Terry Gross, Anderson explained that he had come to grips with the uniqueness to his filmmaking approach. "I have a way of filming things and staging them and designing sets," Anderson said. "There were times when I thought I should change my approach, but in fact, this is what I like to do. It's sort of like my handwriting as a movie director. And somewhere along the way, I think I've made the decision: I'm going to write in my own handwriting. That's just sort of my way."

Anderson's post-'90s filmography includes such films as *The Life Aquatic with Steve Zissou*, *Moonrise Kingdom*, *The Grand Budapest Hotel*, and *Asteroid City*. Additionally, he has crafted the stop-motion animation films *The Fantastic Mr. Fox* and *Isle of Dogs*.

11

Paul Thomas Anderson
Born to Make Movies

Paul Thomas Anderson grew up in San Fernando Valley. He started making crude films before he became a teenager, never having a desire to do anything else. While other kids were imagining their adult selves fighting fires or playing outfield for the New York Yankees, Anderson was planning to be a filmmaker. *Planning*. There was never a doubt, never a backup plan. One of his high school teachers later recalled Anderson telling her that one day he would be a "famous director" who was going to "win an Academy Award." Another high school teacher told *Esquire* that the young Anderson was "not a rule follower"; this is key in sharing his story.

While still in high school, Anderson saw the film *Midnight Run*. The Martin Brest–directed picture starred Robert De Niro and Charles Grodin, but those actors were of no concern to the young would-be filmmaker. When Anderson saw the film, his attention was fixed on character actor Philip Baker Hall. He only had a few scenes in the picture and wasn't the focus of any of them, but something about Baker and his character, Sidney, resonated. Soon after, Anderson began making short crime films of all stripes—gangster films, cop films, heist films, and private-eye films. These weren't the only films he churned out; there were also parodies of *Young Guns* and *Terminator*. Anderson also started talking about a potential film he called *Sydney*.

While still a seventeen-year-old high school student, Anderson began work on a mockumentary in the vein of *This Is Spinal*

Tap about a fictitious John Holmes–like porn star named Dirk Diggler, titled *The Dirk Diggler Story*. Anderson shot some of it inside a seedy motel room on Ventura Boulevard. His dad even provided narration for the thirty-two-minute film. Humorously, Anderson's senior year high yearbook quote was attributed to the fictional porn star: "All I ever wanted was a cool '78 Vette and a house in the country."

After talking his way into the premiere for *The Commitments*, Anderson passed a tape of *The Dirk Diggler Story* to director Alan Parker. Parker viewed the tape and called Anderson to tell him that his film was brilliant. This motivated Anderson to work even harder to get his work seen. Soon after that, Anderson got a job as a production assistant on a PBS telefilm about a campus uprising. One of the actors on the project was Philip Baker Hall, the actor he'd fallen in love with while watching *Midnight Run*.

The would-be director approached his idol and arrogantly blurted, "I'm gonna make you a star." Anderson convinced Hall to appear in a short film he'd written called *Cigarettes and Coffee*, which ambitiously features multiple storylines connected by a twenty-dollar bill changing hands. Hall later recalled his first impression of Anderson's script, telling journalist John H. Richardson, "I was wondering, who was the first actor in the seventeenth century to see a Shakespeare script, and did he know what he was reading? I certainly knew what I had in my hand." Anderson also managed to land a handful of other professional actors, including Miguel Ferrer.

Anderson borrowed a Panaflex camera that usually rented for $6,000 a weekend and shot the short film in Las Vegas on a budget of $10,000, which Anderson had scraped together using credit cards and money his father had saved for him to go to college. The shoot was supposed to take only a weekend but ended up going intermittently over a span of three weeks. *Cigarettes and Coffee* ultimately became a tight, terrific calling card that screened at the Sundance Film Festival in January 1993.

During this period, Anderson was working on another script, a full-length feature about a character written specifically for Hall named Sydney, like the character the actor had essayed in *Midnight Run* only with a different spelling, and another named John written specifically for John C. Reilly. Was the Sydney character intended to be the same character from *Midnight Run*? That has long been the word around the campfire, and while Anderson doesn't give credence to the idea, he doesn't dispel it either. He has, however, said that he saw the character as being someone akin to the character James Cagney played in *White Heat*, alive decades later and trying to repent. Both Cagney's Cody Jarrett and Hall's Sidney (from *Midnight Run*) are gangsters, and even if their places in the mob hierarchy are different, the idea of the character being an old gangster trying to make up for past sins still applies.

When he started writing the script, Anderson didn't know what exactly his film was going to be about. He decided that if he put two interesting characters together in a coffee shop and let them chat, the plot would reveal itself. Even as he was getting deeper into the script, he still wasn't entirely sure where the story and characters were going. While most screenwriters outline their plots ahead of time, he chose not to because he "thought it would be more fun" to write blindly. Anderson wrote for two weeks and—voila!—he had a finished script.

It took Anderson almost two years to secure financing for *Sydney*. Rysher Entertainment agreed to give the young director a $3 million budget to make the film. Along the way, Rysher changed the film's title to *Hard Eight*, which Anderson *hated*. He bitched and moaned some but eventually let it go. After all, what could he do? Rysher was holding all the cards.

Before filming began, the director took his script to the Sundance Lab to tighten it up. While there, he worked with actors and ran a dress rehearsal for some of the scenes under the supervision of *The Bridges of Madison County* scribe Richard LaGravenese. Anderson was initially hesitant to work at the lab but ultimately found it helpful: "I was very fortunate to have the actors who were going to be in the movie—Philip Baker Hall and John C. Reilly—with me. I mean, I met all these directors that I admired, like Michael Caton-Jones and John Schlesinger, and that was really quite a big deal. I remember Jeremy Kagan saying, 'You're here to fuck up, and then fuck up better the next day.'"

One important suggestion LaGravenese made that improved the film was that Anderson should move some of the conversations out of the coffee shop. In a scene where Sydney explains a casino scam to John, LaGravenese convinced Anderson to move the conversation into the casino itself, showing the scam in action rather than simply explaining it. An eighteen-minute revelatory motel room scene was also studied, discussed, and tightened at the lab.

By the time the cameras started rolling, *Hard Eight* had a magnificent cast that included Hall, Reilly, Gwyneth Paltrow, Samuel L. Jackson, and a talented young actor named Philip Seymour Hoffman. As he'd done previously with Philip Baker Hall in *Midnight Run*, Anderson discovered and fell in love with Hoffman in a different Martin Brest–directed film, *Scent of a Woman*.

Because Anderson was just as much in love with his words as everyone else was, he tried to keep the actors on script, but he found that he had to change his unofficial policy when it came to Hoffman. Philip Baker Hall later told *Rolling Stone* about Hoffman, "When we filmed *Hard Eight*, I was shocked by his ability to improvise his way through. He . . . had such a sense for timing. At that point, I was older and he was very young. I was like, 'Who is this kid?' He was so aware of everything and had the instinct of an older trooper. . . . He was a genius and operating at a different level than the rest of us." Anderson himself later estimated that Hoffman had improvised 80 percent of his lines in the film.

While the screenwriter/director had his ideas of who Sydney was and who he was or wasn't modeled after, Hall had his own ideas. In crafting his performance and embodying the character, he modeled Sydney after a restaurateur/gambler named Jack whom he'd worked for as a teen. Hall had no idea whether Jack had ever killed anyone or ordered others to hurt or kill, but the way he carried himself implied the distinct possibility.

The actors in *Hard Eight* discovered that Anderson's method of direction was different from most others'. While most filmmakers watch the actors perform their scenes on a monitor, Anderson stood just a few feet away, remaining at eye level, occasionally even locking eyes with the performers. In doing this, Anderson became a sort of active participant in the proceedings. Hall later credited that for pushing his and the other actors' performances. "Many directors don't even watch the box, they stand off to the side somewhere," Hall explained on the DVD commentary.

> I don't know what they're looking at. But Paul gets right down in there so that it's very intimate. And it could be disconcerting.... There's something about the hard focus and his physical presence ... inches away, that gives a kind of a dynamic to the performance that I'm not sure you can achieve in quite the same way. Or any other way. It's unusual. There are other directors who do this, I've seen this a couple of times, but Paul does it on virtually every shot. It's almost like he is helping to will the appropriate performance from you.

Anderson discovered that the actor who was best able to deliver the lines he'd written with the rhythm and cadence he'd envisioned while writing it was Hall. He learned that other performers, particularly Reilly, delivered their lines differently. Reilly, he found, didn't pay attention to the punctuation in the script, instead adding his own pauses, so Anderson had to allow him to be looser with his recitations.

Anderson showed a penchant for experimentation. He mixed up tones, moving easily from one to another with great ease. In *Hard Eight*, the smallest details mattered and had meaning. Beats, moments of silence, shots of characters walking, and even the characters' postures told their own stories, sometimes conveying as much or more than dialogue could. One interesting aspect of the film is its timeless quality. Author Adam Nayman observed, "Although unmistakably set in the mid-nineties present tense of its production, the film still has the vague feeling of a period piece, of a story slightly unstuck in time."

During the shoot, Anderson argued with the film's producers and even barred them from the set. He refused to let them have their way with his film. The shoot lasted twenty-eight days, and editing took three weeks. At some point, Anderson was fired and then rehired. After that, he refused to include the

John C. Reilly and Philip Baker Hall in Hard Eight. *Courtesy of MGM/Photofest © MGM*

producers in the editing process. When one of the producers (allegedly) figured out they could piss Anderson off by forcing him to include a credit sequence, due to a contractual clause, things became even nastier.

After the film screened at Sundance and then Cannes in early 1996, squabbles with Rysher delayed its release. And retitling the film wasn't all the studio did. "They were altering the performances," Anderson said. "They were butchering it. Rescoring it, reformatting it. I shot the film widescreen and they reformatted it 1:1.85. I mean, that's fucking insane—it's a very conscientiously framed movie—and every shot changed. Literally every composition."

On February 28, 1997, at long last, *Hard Eight* was unceremoniously dumped into a handful of theaters with little to no fanfare. As a result, it made a mere $222,000 at the box office. While a few critics expressed disapproval of the film's final act, most reviewers were impressed. The *Los Angeles Times'* John Anderson wrote, "[Paul Thomas] Anderson, who makes as impressive a directing debut as has been seen in some time, creates a perfectly modulated mystery that doesn't even feel like one." The *Chicago Tribune*'s Michael Wilmington assessed, "*Hard Eight* [is] an admirable debut film by young writer/director Paul Thomas Anderson. . . . Anderson's script is smart and engrossing throughout. And, as a director, he has a quiet, somber eloquence that keeps us floating along in the story's darkness." *Variety*'s review read, "Four excellent lead performances, vividly evoked ambiance and a masterfully sustained mood of quiet desperation mark pic as an impressive piece of work."

Of his experiences on the film, Anderson explained to podcaster Marc Maron, "It was emotionally a huge mind-fuck. It was a fuck in every way. It was my baptism of fire getting into Hollywood. It was crazy to go through that, and I didn't know how to deal with that [because] I was too young."

Anderson had already finished shooting his second film, *Boogie Nights*, by the time *Hard Eight* was released. *Boogie Nights*, like *Hard Eight*, is an offshoot of a concept Anderson had toyed with in high school. This time the film is based on the Dirk Diggler character he'd created for his mockumentary, however it is a much more somber affair than *The Dirk Diggler Story* had been.

The script for *Boogie Nights* was 185 pages. While shopping the script that his agent, John Lesher, declared to be the "best script I've ever read," Anderson was laying down ground rules. He felt he'd been screwed over on *Hard Eight*, and the experience had left him feeling bitter and distrusting. So going into negotiations, he insisted that *Boogie Nights* had to be three hours long and rated NC-17.

Mike DeLuca, a hotshot exec at New Line Cinema who was searching for qualitative, edgy projects, fell in love with the script. "It was easier for us to take chances with new people than compete for the already-established top-five directors in town," DeLuca told Grantland. "We tried to zig when the majors zagged." Despite Anderson's initial unwillingness to compromise, DeLuca convinced him to agree to make *Boogie Nights*' running time less than three hours and make it a film that could be rated R. It was also agreed that Anderson would not have the final cut, but he would get a $15 million budget to play with.

The first draft of *Boogie Nights* to circulate around Hollywood was much racier than the film we know today. Actor William H. Macy has said that it was beyond even an NC-17 rating.

Interestingly, Anderson's script was a complete blueprint of how the film should look, from set descriptions to the lighting and camera movements.

A number of actors were considered for the role of Dirk Diggler, including Christian Bale, Joaquin Phoenix, and Ethan Hawke, to name a few. For a brief period, Leonardo DiCaprio was attached, but he eventually backed out so he could make *Titanic*. Anderson and casting director Christine Sheaks then approached DiCaprio's *Basketball Diaries* costar Mark Wahlberg. At that time, Wahlberg was mostly known for making crappy rap albums (as Marky Mark) and modeling underwear. Wahlberg was apprehensive about making the film because of its subject matter, but everyone in Hollywood was talking about the script. Also, it was a project that was generating interest from high-profile actors; Sean Penn and Robert De Niro were circling the film. Wahlberg read thirty pages of the script and was impressed, so he called Anderson. The director later reflected on that call to Charlie Rose:

> He said "Listen, I love these thirty pages, and I know I'm going to love the rest of it, but I want to make sure before I really fall in love with this and want to do it, that you don't want me because I'm the guy who will get in his underwear . . ." I said, "I don't know anything about that. I want you because I saw you in *The Basketball Diaries* and I want to hear what you think about the script."

Pleased with the director's response, Wahlberg signed on.

DeLuca was dating actress Julianne Moore at the time. He showed the script to her, and she loved it, leading to her being cast as Amber Waves. The names of several well-known actresses were bandied about for the role of Skater Girl, including Drew Barrymore and Tatum O'Neal. But stars or not, they didn't stand a chance; when newcomer Heather Graham rolled in and read, it was instantly apparent that she *was* Skater Girl.

Another key role in the film was that of porn mogul Jack Horner. Warren Beatty came to Anderson and told him he wanted to play the role, or so Anderson thought. It eventually came to light that Beatty actually wanted to play Diggler, who was way, way younger than Beatty was, so Beatty's dream casting didn't happen, and Anderson still had to find his Jack Horner. He approached a plethora of well-known actors to play Horner, including Bill Murray, Harvey Keitel, Albert Brooks, and Sydney Pollack. In the end, Burt Reynolds landed the role and, like everyone else in *Boogie Nights*, is an example of perfect casting.

John C. Reilly, Philip Baker Hall, and Philip Seymour Hoffman all returned for Anderson's second feature. The rest of the impressive ensemble included such talented and respected performers as Luis Guzmán, Don Cheadle, William H. Macy, Alfred Molina, Thomas Jane, Ricky Jay, Melora Walters, and director Robert Downey Sr. A number of actual porn stars, including Nina Hartley and Veronica Hart, were also cast.

Anderson, who had watched his first porno at age nine, worked hard to get every detail exactly right. He encouraged members of the cast and crew to watch and study vintage porn films, as well as read porn-related books. The filmmaker also interviewed and spent time with porn stars and directors, picking their brains about everything he could think of regarding the adult-film industry. Some of the actors even watched the filming of porn films. Porn legend and eventual convict Ron Jeremy served as a consultant.

The role of Rahad Jackson was still vacant when Anderson began filming. It had been offered to John Turturro, who passed. It was then offered to Alfred Molina, a theater actor who made his debut in 1982 when he'd screwed over Indiana Jones in the opening scene of *Raiders of the Lost Ark*. Since then, Molina had appeared in such films as *Maverick* and Jim Jarmusch's weird (but terrific) western *Dead Man*. Molina, like the rest of the cast, loved the script, so he took the part.

Anderson allowed the actors more leeway on his second film than he had on *Hard Eight*. While speaking to a crowd at the New Beverly Theater, Thomas Jane explained, "One thing that's notable about the way Paul Thomas Anderson works is the freedom he gives his actors.... We did have lines to say and stuff, but if you had an idea at the moment or a line to throw in or if something happens by mistake, he always encouraged that spontaneity and that freedom."

Unfortunately, Burt Reynolds and Anderson struggled to get along. Reynolds was a cinematic legend, and here was this punk kid telling him what to do. That didn't sit well with him at all. Things became more and more heated. Reynolds believed he was being treated disrespectfully, which was more than his ego could handle. He also accused Anderson of not allowing him to improvise the way he did with other actors. Finally, after multiple episodes of arguing and screaming, the sixty-year-old actor erupted and attempted to physically attack the twenty-six-year-old director.

Despite all this, Reynolds continued to give his all for the film, although he believed he'd been suckered into making some kind of big-budget porno. Many members of the cast later commented that Reynolds looked like he could explode at any moment throughout the shoot. At one point, he shoved Thomas Jane. Maybe it was Reynolds redirecting his anger and resentment, maybe it was Anderson's direction, or maybe it was a bit of both, but Reynolds wound up giving one of—if not *the*—finest performances of his career.

Dylan Tichenor, who had previously edited *Hard Eight* under Anderson's supervision, cut *Boogie Nights*. Anderson, Tichenor, and the producers had numerous disagreements during postproduction. Anderson's first cut was just over three hours long and, by some accounts, unfocused. The final cut is two hours and thirty-five minutes. Naturally, a lot of edits were made to appease the Motion Picture Association of America's ratings board. In all, Anderson and New Line submitted a stunning eighteen cuts, an MPAA record. About forty seconds of the film was ultimately excised to obtain an R rating.

The studio knew upfront that *Boogie Nights* wasn't going to be a movie for everyone, and the test screenings bore that out. In the first screening, fifty people stood up and walked out. The film scored low, with many of the remaining audience members expressing disdain for it. It screened at the New York Film Festival and the Toronto International Film Festival in September 1997, before being released theatrically on October 10. Because

Rysher had taken so long to release Anderson's debut, the director ended up having two films released in 1997. Anderson's father died that same year, so it was a period of extreme highs and lows.

Boogie Nights opened to rave reviews. Roger Ebert wrote in the *Chicago Sun-Times*,

> The sweep and variety of the characters have brought the movie comparisons to Robert Altman's *Nashville* and *The Player*. There is also some of the same appeal as *Pulp Fiction* in scenes that balance precariously between comedy and violence. . . . Anderson's screenplay centers on the human qualities of the players. . . . *Boogie Nights* has the quality of many great films, in that it always seems alive.

The *San Francisco Chronicle*'s Mick LaSalle praised, "Paul Thomas Anderson . . . has pulled off a wonderful, sprawling, sophisticated film." Peter Travers of *Rolling Stone* called the film a "chunk of movie dynamite," and the *Chicago Tribune*'s Gene Siskel hailed it as "beautifully made."

The film earned $43 million during its theatrical run, roughly three times its budget. Additionally, *Boogie Nights* received three Academy Award nominations, which isn't too shabby for an edgy movie about the porn industry. These nods went to Anderson for Best Original Screenplay, Reynolds for Best Supporting Actor, and Julianne Moore for Best Supporting Actress. However, these nominations failed to yield Oscar gold. Wahlberg later said he regretted making the film, and Reynolds, depending on which day someone was interviewing him, either loved or hated it.

While promoting the film, Anderson started to think about his next film. He had the title in his mind right upfront: *Magnolia*. He started making random notes about seemingly unrelated characters and situations he conceived. He later said that the project began with a vision he had of actress Melora Walters. As he continued to write, he started considering different actors and actresses he wanted to work with and then writing roles with them in mind. This future film was still in its conceptual infancy when New Line Cinema gave Anderson a once-in-a-lifetime offer: They agreed to fully finance his next film, sight and concept completely unseen, also giving him the final cut. Having faced meddling on *Hard Eight*, he was fully aware how precious the final cut was. He accepted.

Over time, the project expanded in scope. Anderson originally planned to write something small and personal that he could shoot in a month. But with New Line having given him full rein, he decided that *Magnolia* would be something epic. "It came from a much smaller place," Anderson told *The Guardian*.

> I wanted to make something that was intimate and small-scale, and I thought that I would do it very, very quickly. The point was that I wanted to shed myself of everything that was happening around *Boogie Nights*. And I started to write and well, it kept blossoming. And I got to the point where still it's a very intimate movie, but I realized I had so many actors I wanted to write for that the form started to come more from them. Then I thought it would be really interesting to put this epic spin on topics that don't necessarily get the epic treatment, which is usually reserved for war movies or political topics. But the things that I know as big and emotional are these real intimate everyday moments, like losing your car keys, for example. You could start with something like that and go anywhere.

As he wrote, he listened to his friend Aimee Mann's music on loop. Not only did Mann's songs serve as the soundtrack to his writing, but they also served as the soundtrack to the actual film. (Mann wrote two new songs expressly for the film and allowed Anderson to use another seven she had already been working on.)

Anderson told some of the actors he planned to cast that he was writing roles for them very early in the process, however it took him two years to complete his script. Interestingly, he later said that most of the writing took place in the final two weeks of those two years while he was staying alone in a remote cabin owned by William H. Macy. Whenever Anderson attempted to leave the cabin, he saw a large snake outside the door. He was afraid of the snake, so he fled back into the cabin, where the writer/director was basically trapped inside with nothing to do but write. In an interview with *The Montreal Gazette*, Anderson later said that he structured the film similarly to the Beatles song "A Day in the Life" in that it "kind of builds up, note by note, then drops or recedes, then builds again."

Magnolia is about nine characters—nine *lead* characters, as Anderson saw it. His idea was that the stories of these characters intersect in San Fernando Valley. While creating them, Anderson looked to the actors for inspiration; he wrote to their strengths and, in some cases, the kinds of characters they desired to play. Anderson and John C. Reilly had become close friends, and Reilly told Anderson that he was tired of playing the same kinds of characters and wanted to play something more relatable. He said he'd like to play someone in love. For a couple years, just for fun, Reilly had been developing a dimwitted cop character. "John Reilly came up with most of his character . . . after he grew a moustache for fun," Anderson said later. "He started to work up this not very smart cop character and we did a sort of take off on *Cops* with me chasing him around the streets with a video camera." Reilly's *Magnolia* character, Jim Kurring, grew from that. Anderson even incorporated lines Reilly had spoken in their just-for-fun *Cops* parodies into the script.

Anderson had spent time working as a production assistant on a game show called *Quiz Kid Challenge*. Drawing from this experience, he fashioned a similar fictional game show called *What Do Kids Know?* He decided that his frequent collaborator Philip Baker Hall would play the show's host, Jimmy Gator. (The name *Jimmy Gator* is mentioned in passing in *Hard Eight*. Anderson liked the sound of the name and recycled it here.) Hall himself modeled the public persona of his character largely on *The Price Is Right* host Bob Barker.

William H. Macy had once told Anderson that he believed actors shouldn't cry, so the screenwriter/director decided to push Macy's talents by writing him a character with emotional scenes.

After having already decided on the title *Magnolia*, Anderson studied magnolia flowers and trees. Because his father had recently succumbed to cancer, the revelation that some people believed that eating the bark of magnolia trees could cure the disease was particularly meaningful. He then incorporated a storyline about cancer into the script. Research also played a role in Anderson's decision to write the film's most memorable scene; after reading about real-life (and biblical) occurrences of frogs falling from the sky, the writer/director wrote a frog storm into the script.

While most of the primary cast members—Reilly, Hall, Hoffman, Macy, Moore, and Walters—had worked with Anderson previously, there were others in the film who had not. After learning that Tom Cruise was a fan of his work, Anderson met with the actor. Following this meeting, he wrote the part of self-help guru Frank "T. J." Mackey specifically for him. Cruise initially had reservations about playing such a brash, potty-mouthed, sexist pig. He knew there wasn't a woman alive who was going to like the character. But he also knew it was a loud, obnoxious, showy character he could sink his teeth into; it was the kind of role every actor wanted to play and the kind that often drew the attention of Academy voters. Awards weren't everything, and they certainly weren't the reason professionals like Cruise made movies, but they didn't hurt their careers either. So Cruise signed on to play Frank Mackey, which—spoiler alert—eventually got him an Oscar nomination.

Anderson had written the role of cancer-ridden Earl Partridge for Jason Robards. However, Robards was terribly ill and in the hospital, fighting for his life, so he had to decline. The role was then offered to another veteran performer, George C. Scott, who also passed. But Robards soon recovered, and his daughter convinced him to take the role by pointing out the similarities to the character's experiences and Robards' real-life near-death experience.

In 2015, Burt Reynolds told Hannah Ellis-Petersen that Anderson had offered him a role in *Magnolia*, which he declined. This was one of the instances where Reynolds said he "hated" *Boogie Nights*, even going so far as to claim he'd never even watched it. Of his *Magnolia* job offer, Reynolds said, "I'd done my picture with Paul Thomas Anderson. That was enough for me."

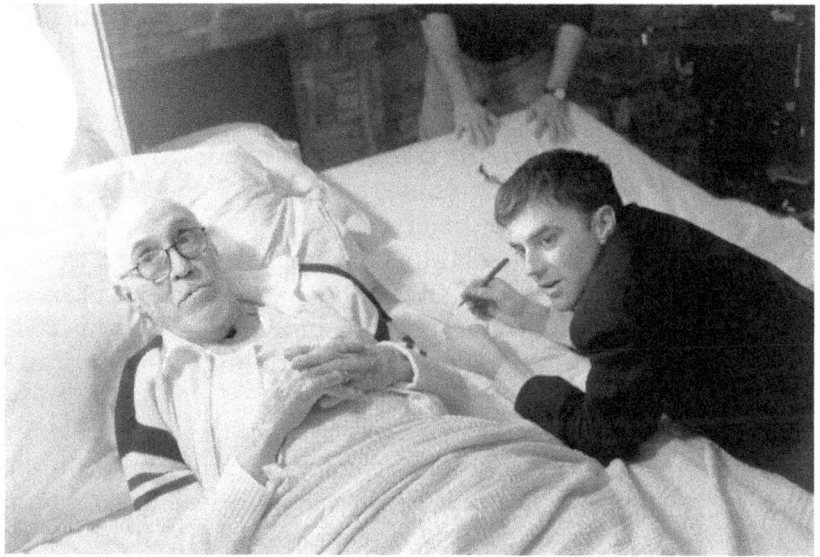

Paul Thomas Anderson gives direction to Jason Robards on the set of Magnolia. *Courtesy of New Line Cinema/Photofest © New Line Cinema*

Before filming, Anderson screened *Network* for the crew to illuminate some of the aesthetics he wanted to imitate. Cameras began rolling on *Magnolia* on January 12, 1999. The shoot was scheduled to last seventy-nine days, however the film went over time and budget. It ended up taking ninety days to shoot, with an additional ten days of second-unit filming.

In one scene, each of the main characters sings along dreamily with Mann's song "Wise Up." It is one of the film's most poetic and moving scenes. Several actors expressed concerns about singing in the film because they were not singers. Mostly they were just nervous. Because Julianne Moore is game for anything, Anderson turned to her to sing first and set the pace for her costars. He believed that once the other performers saw her do it, they would want to jump in and try to compete with her without showing signs of nervousness. It turned out that Anderson was correct, and each of the actors gave him a spot-on performance.

Magnolia had a limited release that began on December 17, 1999. It was then released wide on January 7, 2000, earning $5.7 million in its opening weekend. Reviews for Anderson's most ambitious film to that point were largely positive. Lou Lumenick of the *New York Post* called *Magnolia* "hands down the best movie of the year." *Chicago Sun-Times* critic Roger Ebert gave the picture four out of four stars, raving, "*Magnolia* is the kind of film I instinctively respond to. Leave logic at the door. Do not expect subdued taste and restraint, but instead a kind of operatic ecstasy." A decade later, Ebert included the film in his 2008 "Great Movies" list, saying, "As an act of filmmaking, it draws us in and doesn't let go." *USA Today* called *Magnolia* the "most imperfect of the year's best movies." And while *Chicago Reader* critic Jonathan Rosenbaum had some minor problems with the picture, he assessed it as being a "quantum leap in ambition from *Hard Eight* and *Boogie Nights* and is, to my mind, much more interesting."

Magnolia earned $48.5 million at the box office. Ingmar Bergman later cited the film as proof of the remaining strength of American cinema. In 2008, *Empire* magazine ranked *Magnolia* as the eighty-ninth-greatest film of all time on their list of the five hundred greatest films ever made.

Throughout his career, which now includes such notable films as *Punch-Drunk Love*, *There Will Be Blood*, and *Phantom Thread*, Anderson has continued to hone his craft. In his films, he explores flawed, desperate characters. The themes of alienation, regret, redemption, family conflict, and depression frequently pop up. Despite a recurrence of themes, no two of his films are alike; each is its own unique thing, and Anderson consistently achieves a level of high art despite moving between subjects and genres.

Like many of the talented filmmakers discussed here, a great deal of Anderson's strength comes from his writing. But while his vision begins on the page, his cinematic command goes well beyond that. Anderson is perhaps *the* master of composition among his contemporaries, with onscreen figures framed in doorways, hallways, and other natural frames. He is recognized for his use of long, unbroken shots that sometimes last as long as four minutes. He masterfully uses every artistic tool at his disposal, including manipulation and/or the fine-tuning of colors, lighting, sound, and music. Another of Anderson's many strengths is his ability to assist actors in achieving the very best performances they're capable of—often resulting in the finest turns of their careers. With a notable exception of Burt Reynolds, most of the actors Anderson collaborates with love him and gladly return to work with him.

The features Paul Thomas Anderson has crafted beyond his first, *Hard Eight*, are his visions and his alone. A Paul Thomas Anderson picture is unique. They are examples of art at its purest. He is one of the greatest directors to emerge from the '90s wave of mavericks, and arguments for his being *the* strongest filmmaker of his generation are worthy of consideration.

12

Christopher Nolan
American Master

Christopher Nolan was born on July 30, 1970, in Westminster, London. As a kid, like most future filmmakers of his generation, he watched *Star Wars* incessantly. He also fell in love with *Blade Runner*, which became his lifelong favorite film. At age seven, he borrowed his dad's Super 8 camera and started making his own films, crafting stop-motion pictures and movies starring his *Star Wars* action figures. At the age of eleven, Nolan decided on his career path: He wanted to become a professional filmmaker. As a teen, he collaborated with another future filmmaker, Roko Belic, on a handful of Super 8 films. One of them, *Tarantella*, aired on a Public Broadcasting Service program called *Image Union*.

"I just carried on making films as I grew up," Nolan later told *Vice*. "Over the years they got bigger. Hopefully better. But more elaborate. There never really was a period in my life where I completely stopped doing them, although I was always moving up, from Super 8 to 16 mm film."

Nolan attended University College London. His major was English lit, but his real reason for attending the school was so he could use its filmmaking equipment. There Nolan was president of the Union's Film Society, where he screened 35 mm movies throughout the school year. He then used the money he'd earned from the screenings to finance the making of his own 16 mm films in the summer.

After graduation, Nolan began working on industrial films. Like the making of his own films, he saw the production of industrial films as a kind of DIY film school. "I actually learned a lot doing that kind of video camerawork," Nolan said in 2014.

> I learned a lot about going into an environment, using a couple of lights, setting up very fast, and then having to do something on a very rigorous schedule. Because you'd be interviewing the chairman of some huge corporation. He'd come in for ten minutes and expect you to just run in and then walk out. . . . And you'd figure out how to do something that looked good fairly quickly.

In 1996, he wrote, shot, and edited an eight-minute film titled *Larceny*, shot in black-and-white and filmed in a single weekend with equipment borrowed from the Film Society. It was screened at the Cambridge Film Festival, where it received great acclaim. After that, he and producer/frequent collaborator (and future wife) Emma Thomas crafted a three-minute Kafkaesque short called *Doodlebug*, about a man trying to smash a troublesome insect only to wind up getting smashed himself. When the short was later released as an extra feature on *Following*, a number of critics writing for such publications as *Esquire*, *The Daily Telegraph*, and the *Independent*, gave the film high marks while (all) conceding that Nolan wasn't quite there yet; this is proof that he hadn't emerged from the womb fully formed as a filmmaker and was still learning his craft.

Nolan tried to make his first feature-length project—something called *Larry Mahoney*—in the midnineties but wound up scrapping it after finding himself unable to secure sufficient funding. He then set about trying to make another feature, called *Following*. The idea for the film, about a man who follows strangers around the streets, eventually getting himself in hot water, came from Nolan's living in a crowded neighborhood. Nolan told an audience at the IFC Center, "You'd go out of your flat and you'd be surrounded by people. I became interested in the idea of looking at individuals and saying, 'What's that person's story?'" According to the writer/director, the criminal aspects of the storyline were inspired by someone breaking into his apartment and robbing him.

Nolan planned to make *Following* with a nonlinear structure from the beginning, but he first wrote the screenplay in chronological order to make sure all the pieces fit together. He later said that doing this taught him a lot of things that would eventually help him script his second feature, *Memento*, which is also nonlinear.

Following was shot on 16 mm, using black-and-white film to accomplish three things: Nolan didn't have to worry about matching color between shots; it gave the film a stylish, expressionistic appearance; and perhaps most importantly, it was relatively inexpensive. "When you have absolutely no money and absolutely no resources, [trying] to achieve color cinematography is extremely difficult," Nolan explained in 2012. "[With black-and-white,] it's much more possible to get some kind of level of style to the thing—quickly and easily throwing in some lights and shadow going with that."

The film was made for about $6,000 and was mostly shot with a handheld camera. Because the cast and crew worked full-time jobs, *Following* was shot each week on Saturdays. Craft services? Nolan's mother made sandwiches for everyone. To ensure that he'd get useable versions of scenes in only one or two takes, he orchestrated extensive rehearsals for six months prior to filming. Between the rehearsal time and filming, *Following* took a year to complete. Nolan viewed *Following* as a series of short films edited together because he was, in essence, filming two- or three-minute chunks of the film each weekend. Wanting to make the picture as economically as possible, he primarily used natural light. This is why, as he's pointed out, most of the scenes take place near windows.

Just as he'd done on his short films, the director doubled as director of photography. Nolan purchased the black-and-white film out of his own pocket, so anytime he ran out, he had to dig a little deeper. Although a single camera was used to shoot each scene, Nolan used two cameras in the making of the film; indoor shots were filmed using an Arriflex 16BL camera, and street scenes were shot with a Bolex 16 mm wind-up camera.

As he'd done on his short films, Nolan (along with Gareth Heal) edited *Following*. While he'd appreciated cutting on film,

Nolan had come to understand that it was problematic because it was hard to raise the funds needed to cut the negative and print it. As such, he cut *Following* on tape, using two Umatic recorders and working tape to tape. Nolan also began cross-cutting to protect himself in case he missed anything or the film was somehow damaged, which he continued to do on his future films. Nolan later stated that *Following* represented the peak of what he could do by himself without a real budget, better equipment, and proper actors.

Once the film was complete, it made the rounds on the festival circuit, where it won a few awards and garnered Nolan some praise and attention. The San Francisco International Film Festival awarded *Following* the Best First Feature prize. Additionally, it received top honors at the International Film Festival Rotterdam's, taking home the Tiger Award Prize. It was also nominated for the Grand Jury Prize at the Slamdance Film Festival. But *Following*'s biggest festival honor was Zeitgeist Films' decision to distribute it following the San Francisco Film Festival screening.

Bruce Diones of *The New Yorker* likened the film to Alfred Hitchcock's best pictures but said *Following* was "leaner and meaner." Kevin Thomas of the *Los Angeles Times* raved that *Following* was a "taut and ingenious neo-noir" and that "Nolan relishes the nastiness he keeps stirred up, unabated for seventy minutes." Not every critic loved *Following*, but the film clearly identified Nolan as a burgeoning talent worth watching.

While Robert Rodriguez's *El Mariachi* has gotten most of the ink and credit in discussions regarding low-budget, DIY, career-establishing features, *Following* is at least as good, if not better. But for whatever reason, *Following* has never gotten the love and credit it deserves. Nevertheless, Nolan's stock was on the rise. If the world hadn't paid close enough attention to the young director with his first feature, they would soon have no choice but to take notice.

The story of Nolan's second feature, *Memento*, started during a July 1997 road trip on which Nolan and his brother Jonathan drove from Chicago to Los Angeles. Jonathan was working on a short story titled "Memento Mori" about a man suffering from anterograde amnesia who is trying to find out who killed his wife. The story was eventually published in *Esquire* magazine in March 2001. At the time of their road trip, Jonathan was trying to work out the story's format. He knew what the story was, but he wasn't completely sure how best to present it. After Jonathan told Nolan about his story, Nolan asked him for permission to adapt it into a screenplay. Jonathan agreed. They both knew from the beginning that the best way to tell the story was to tell it in first person from the protagonist's point of view.

While writing the script, which he titled *Memento*, Nolan decided to tell the story backward, starting at the end and working his way to the beginning. This way the audience would remain as confused and in the dark as the protagonist. Nolan was inspired to tell the story in a nonlinear style by novels, where the practice is much more commonplace. He later said, "To me it really is a question of finding the most suitable order for releasing information to the audience and not feeling any responsibility to do it chronologically, just like we don't in real life."

Nolan explained his intent to *Creative Screenwriting*:

> I was interested in taking this extreme situation and using it as a filter or prism through which to view some familiar tropes of film noir, because . . . it's very difficult to write a fresh thriller these days. Combinations had been done, but I felt that we had a situation here that would allow us to freshen up and re-awaken some of the neuroses behind the familiar elements. You know, the betrayal, the double-cross, the femme fatale—all of these things function very powerfully in the way they were intended in the old film noir by exaggerating our fears and insecurities. I felt that by taking this particular approach and filtering it through this concept, we would be able to reawaken some of the confusion and uncertainty and ambiguity that those types of character reversals used to have, but lost because we've come to expect these kinds of surprises.

Nolan's working draft was 170 pages long, but he has never considered this an actual first draft because he always knew that it was too long and would have to be cut. He showed these 170 pages to close friend Aaron Ryder, who worked at Newmarket Films, and asked, "What are your thoughts on this?" Ryder then gave him feedback on the pages, which Nolan called "fantastic notes," saying they helped him understand how to make the story "shorter and simpler." Nolan then trimmed and tightened his script, reducing it to a workable 127 pages.

The screenplay was shown to a number of producers, making its way around Hollywood. A lot of producers liked the script but were afraid to make it. Ultimately, it was Newmarket who optioned the script at the same time *Following* was screening at the San Francisco Film Festival in 1998. After that, he performed more rewrites of his script, trying to simplify it. For instance, the protagonist stays in three different motels in the first draft. In Nolan's final draft, he stays in just one room (although he is duped into paying for two).

Nolan considered a number of actors for the lead role of Leonard Shelby, including Thomas Jane, Alec Baldwin, Aaron Eckhart, Charlie Sheen, and Brad Pitt. Although Pitt didn't end up making the film, the news that he'd been in talks to make it drew attention to the previously obscure project. Guy Pearce was an up-and-coming actor at the time, fresh off *Hollywood Confidential*. Pearce, who was not as big a star as the others Nolan considered, read the script and badly wanted the part. Nolan ended up casting him, in part because Pearce strongly connected with the material and in part because Nolan believed casting a lesser-known actor would make it easier for audiences to see the character as a real person rather than the star playing him.

Memento was filmed in twenty-five days with a budget of $9 million. That must have seemed like $100 million to Nolan, whose previous film had cost just $6,000. One thing it taught him was to allow actors to have an extra take if they feel they need it. Nolan told *DGA Quarterly*,

> I was shooting a very important scene with Guy Pearce in which his character is extremely upset, and it's the lead-in to where Carrie-Anne Moss' character takes Pearce's shirt off and sees all the tattoos on his chest. That day, the financier of the film just happened to be visiting the set and was literally

Guy Pearce in a scene from Christopher Nolan's Memento. *Courtesy of ICF Films/ Photofest © ICF Films, Photographer Danny Rothenberg*

standing right behind me. We did a take that I thought was very good, and I knew we were out of time. So I asked Guy if he felt he'd gotten it, and he said, "No, we should do it again." I remember having a "What do I do?" moment. Do I let him do it and risk running over? Or do I insist that we move on, which Guy would have done, because he's flexible and professional? But I let him do another take, and that's the one used in the film. It was very special, beyond what he had done previously, and way beyond what I had imagined was even possible for the scene.

After *Memento* screened in Venice, Nolan happily told reporters how he'd intended the film's ambiguous ending to be interpreted. His brother Jonathan took him aside and said, "You can't do that. Your interpretation isn't any more valid than anyone else's. Those are the terms of storytelling that you've put out there, because it's a subjectively told story and Leonard can't know with total certainty." After considering this, Nolan agreed. After all, the message he'd intended to convey with the film is that people are at the mercy of their perceptions.

Nolan said he crafted the picture to be told specifically in the backward order it's presented in. Otherwise, it doesn't work. "To me, the structure and the story are one and the same," he explained.

> They are totally inseparable. People are often saying to me, "Can you reorder the film and view it in a chronological sense?" And my answer is, you can, logically it holds up. I felt that was important because you're inviting all kinds of logical scrutiny by adopting this unconventional structure. But it's a completely different story. I mean, the narrative is entirely different. Your perception of the character is entirely different and to me that was very important. That's why I wrote the script the way it appears on the screen.

With *Memento*, Nolan sought to create a film that audiences would be compelled to view multiple times. He wasn't simply interested in making something coherent that still entertains after multiple viewings but rather something that offers new insights and revelations upon second, third, and fourth viewings. One of the things that most interested him about the project was its episodic nature, which allowed him to continually change the context of each statement, scenario, and character as Leonard (and the audience) makes new discoveries.

As stated earlier, *Memento* bowed at the Venice Film Festival in September 2000. There, it received a standing ovation and was nominated for the festival's Lion of the Year Award. It played a few more festivals, including the Catalonian International Film Festival, the Toronto Film Festival, the Deauville Film Festival, and Sundance, winning one award after another. Then finally, on March 16, 2001, the film opened theatrically in the United States. It was a success, earning $40 million worldwide.

By and large, critics swooned. Even now, it enjoys a 93 percent Rotten Tomatoes score (based on nearly two hundred reviews). Roger Ebert of the *Chicago Sun-Times* gave the picture three (out of four) stars, writing that he loved it. He wrote, "*Memento* is a diabolical and absorbing experience." Peter Travers of *Rolling Stone* wrote, "Like the best filmmakers at Sundance 2001, Nolan leaps into the wild blue and dares us to leap with him. Go for it." The *New York Daily News'* Jack Mathews called it "one of the most original and ultimately confounding mind games to reach the screen since *The Usual Suspects*."

Nolan and his brother received an Academy Award nomination for Best Original Screenplay. Dody Dorn also received a nomination for Best Film Editing. Sadly, the *Memento* crew left the ceremony empty handed. But the film has since been included on many, many greatest films lists.

In the years since *Memento*, Nolan has continued to make impressive films, one after the other. His post-'90s filmography includes such notable films as *The Prestige, Inception, Dunkirk,* and *Oppenheimer*, as well as the Batman pictures *Batman Begins, The Dark Knight,* and *The Dark Knight Rises*. While all of Nolan's films are impressive, *The Dark Knight, Dunkirk,* and *Oppenheimer* are widely recognized as masterworks. Additionally, Nolan's *Batman Begins* has been called the first "prestige" superhero movie. With his three Batman films, Nolan demonstrated how a comic book superhero movie (and a blockbuster film in general) can be made with intelligence and without sacrificing artistry.

Nolan is a consummate professional who has studied every aspect of the filmmaking process so he can ensure that all facets of his work are as close to perfection as possible. He's a master storyteller who has a unique ability to craft intelligent and thought-provoking films that are also commercially successful. His films are visually striking, and the craft and execution behind them are as close to perfection as humanly possible. Nolan is also a staunch advocate of sustaining celluloid film at a time when much of the industry has moved to digital.

Simply put, Christopher Nolan is a visionary and one of the most gifted artists in the history of medium.

13

Darren Aronofsky
"The Ripsnorting Bull of American Cinema"

Darren Aronofsky grew up in Brooklyn, the child of two educators. He was a fan of such films as *E.T.*, *Raiders of the Lost Ark*, and *Star Wars*, but he had no childhood aspirations of becoming a filmmaker. He attended Edward R. Murrow High School. As a teen, he traveled to Kenya and then to Alaska to study field biology. While in the United States, the young Aronofsky occasionally attended plays with his older brother, which would eventually have a significant impact on his own art.

After graduation, he attended Harvard, where he majored first in sociology. Unsure what he wanted to do with his life, Aronofsky changed his major to social anthropology, but that didn't stick either. By this time, he had developed an interest in the arts. Still unsure of his path, Aronofsky applied for sculpture and filmmaking classes but was only accepted to the filmmaking program. His senior thesis was a short film titled *Supermarket Sweep* that was a finalist in the 1991 Student Academy Awards. After leaving Harvard, he attended the American Film Institute (AFI) Conservatory, where he dove deeper into filmmaking. He received an MFA in directing from AFI and was awarded the Franklin J. Schaffner Alumni Medal.

After he left the AFI, Aronofsky believed he was ready to make a feature film. He later stated that with that film, *Pi*, he set out to make the first cyberpunk movie. The story Aronofsky conceived was about a mathematician who becomes obsessed with the idea that mathematics can be used to reveal and understand a connecting pattern that runs throughout everything in the universe. This obsession becomes so intense and overwhelming that he starts to unravel, slowly descending into madness.

Before he started writing, Aronofsky imposed six rules for himself:

1. Always move forward. If you have a problem, type through it.
2. Only take a break after something good happens on the page or you accomplish a goal. No breaks for confusion—type through it.
3. Ten pages a day minimum.
4. Only go back to add something. Do not remove contradictions; just make a note.
5. Do it. Suffer, live, cry, struggle for one week. You'll feel like a million bucks [when you're done].
6. Have fun.

He wrote the first draft of *Pi* in April 1996. After he'd completed this draft, Aronofsky collaborated closely with Eric Watson (producer) and Sean Gullette (lead actor) to workshop and fine-tune the shooting script. During these sessions, the three men (along with director of photography Matthew Libatique) reorganized the structure of the film and worked on the performances, camera angles, and variations of the scenarios they envisioned in ways that were cost effective.

The screenplay brought together many seemingly different ideas. Aronofsky said,

> It's strange when you start with all these different ideas, and they seem totally foreign and different, and then you start to push them together, and slowly but surely, they start to fit together in a way that you never expected. It's almost like [the character] Max, the way he sees patterns everywhere. You're always looking for a unifying pattern for all these different themes in your movie, and as you start to work on them more and more, they start to come together.

The filmmaker later told Peter Chattaway, "It's sort of a scrapbook of experiences I've had, stories I've heard, things I've read. I sort of had a deck full of stuff and shuffled them and out came *Pi*." In a Q&A for the film, Aronofsky elaborated even further, saying the ideas the three collaborators incorporated were "some things kind of floating around in the ether for us." Inspirations for the script included a public-access program that focused on a paranoid man speaking directly to the camera and the writings of Philip K. Dick.

Once there was a completed screenplay, Aronofsky and Watson went to everyone they knew, hat in hand, asking for money to make the picture. Aronofsky described this as "early crowd sourcing." The plan, conceived by associate producer Scott Franklin, was to convince each person to pitch in $100. Not everyone they pitched the idea to spoke to the filmmakers in person. Some people received a form letter that started by saying, "This is a form letter, but it's not because we don't love you." The idea was that, if the film made a profit, each investor would be paid $150. And if the film didn't make any money, said investor would still have a film credit to their name. Eventually, the filmmakers wound up with $60,000 to make the film. That amount was nothing in Hollywood; craft services for a couple of days on a major motion picture probably costs that and more. But $60,000 was enough for Aronofsky and Watson, who vowed to cut every corner they could to keep costs down.

The *Pi* shoot began on October 14, 1996, and lasted twenty-eight days. The hours were long, and the majority of the shoot occurred at night. Crew members were paid $200 a day, and the actors received $75 per day. The film was shot on 16 mm black-and-white reversal film stock, which immediately produces a positive image, foregoing the costly processing of the negative. Two cameras were used to make *Pi*. The static scenes, which comprise most of the film, were shot with an Aaton XTR Prod camera. The film's handheld scenes were shot with a Bolex H16 camera. Aronofsky wanted high-contrast shots to give the film a raw documentary-like feel. Additionally, the grainy black-and-white film covered filming and editorial blunders, making it easier to match shots.

According to Gullette, Aronofsky and his crew weren't sure what they were making was good. Gullette wasn't allowed to view the dailies, but he said, "I remember their faces when they came out of the dailies screening. They all looked like they'd just watched someone get shot. They were not having a good time watching that stuff screened on a sheet. They thought they'd screwed up big time. But, of course, the opposite was true. They had really captured the sparkle of the ideas with that high-contrast reversal film."

To save money, the actors wore their own clothes. Occasionally, clothes were purchased for particular scenes at a nearby thrift shop. Also, shots and scenes taking place in public were "stolen," meaning they were filmed without shooting permits. The father of associate producer Scott Franklin owned an empty warehouse that he allowed the filmmakers to use. The protagonist's homemade super-computer, Euclid, was assembled on a soundstage inside the warehouse using discarded computer parts the crew dug out of the dumpsters behind computer stores and colleges around New York City. While the crew was

Sean Gullette and Ben Shenkman in Darren Aronofsky's Pi. *Courtesy of Live Entertainment/Photofest © Live Entertainment*

allowed to use the warehouse free of charge, they were later asked to pay for the electric bill accrued during the shoot.

Gullette later spoke about the exceedingly high level of dedication and talent the crew possessed. They remained mostly positive, doing their very best to make the film as good as it could possibly be. According to Gullette, "When you're on the set, and you're looking around at the people who are there and they're not getting paid, why are they there? They're there because they read the pitch and they meet the people, and they're like, 'This seems fucking cool.'" The *Pi* team was a tightknit group, and they were careful about adding new people to the production team in order to avoid questionable attitudes and work ethics.

Aronofsky had a natural talent for working with actors. He understood how to motivate, manipulate, and support actors in order to get the performances he needed. An example of this was the scene in which Gullette was supposed to go crazy and demolish a cow brain. Gullette told Aronofsky that he refused to touch the brain because it had been sitting in a van for several days and was "fucking ripe." Because Aronofsky and Gullette were good friends, the director knew exactly what buttons to push to provoke and enrage the actor. One of the things Aronofsky whispered to Gullette was, "I remember when you used to be tough." Gullette said this "went straight to the heart of [his] male ego." He recalled, "He forced me to prove him wrong. I just kind of screamed at everybody, and I called 'roll camera' myself, and said 'fuck it.' I cursed and spit and roared through the whole scene, smashing the shit out of it. Matty and Darren had trash bags over their heads to avoid getting splattered with shrapnel from the cow brain."

Although the *Pi* crew never got into trouble while shooting without permits, there was one near-miss. Aronofsky explained,

> We were shooting that sequence with the brains on the steps in a subway in Brooklyn, and there was blood everywhere, and every time a train would pull in, we'd have to stop production and cover the brain and ask people to watch out for the blood. . . . And we had lookouts and everything, and we really tried to be [cautious]. And finally I'm off thinking about

a shot, and my first AD Laura comes up to me, she's like, "Darren, how many stops to Coney Island?" And I'm like, "Laura, we're not going to Coney Island until tomorrow." And she's like, "No, how many more stops to Coney Island?" And she's pointing, and it's a cop, New York City's finest, staring at the brain, and I'm like, "Fuck!" The cop just nods and walks away, and I'm like, "New York City's finest is so great, so awesome!"

Aronofsky later learned that Martin Scorsese was shooting a film across the street at Prospect Park, so he concluded that the officer likely believed they were shooting second unit for the Scorsese picture. (Aronofsky has also said that Woody Allen was the one filming across the street, but of the two explanations, Scorsese is the more likely of the two men to make a film featuring splattered brains.)

While making *Pi*, Aronofsky was introduced to musician Clint Mansell. Mansell had been the lead vocalist and guitarist for alt-rock band Pop Will Eat Itself, who had recorded for RCA and was briefly signed to Trent Reznor's Nothing Records. Aronofsky and Mansell bonded over a fondness for hip-hop music and a strong dislike for contemporary music scores, so Aronofsky invited Mansell to score *Pi*. Mansell's breakbeat-heavy electro-grunge music is distinctive and, accompanying the images onscreen, maddening. Mansell and Aronofsky collaborated again on other pictures, including *Requiem for a Dream*, *Black Swan*, and *The Wrestler*.

Aronofsky cut the film on Avid. He later said that his editing on the picture was inspired by the hip-hop culture of his youth. "I've always wanted to introduce hip-hop filmmaking to film," he told *Combustible Celluloid*.

> So I've been thinking of ways of doing that for a long time. There's hip-hop art—graffiti, there's hip-hop dance—breakdancing. There's hip-hop music—rap, but there really isn't hip-hop film. So for a long time, I was trying to do that—to introduce some ideas. I think it's partly an attitude. I think this film is sort of hip-hop in the fact that we were shooting in subways late at night for ten or twenty-eight days. Also, I think it needs to be anti-establishment. It's a hip-hop cyberpunk film.

Pi made its debut at the 1998 Sundance Film Festival, where it garnered praise and received attention. The picture was nominated for the Grand Jury Prize, and Aronofsky took home the award for director. But that wasn't the only thing he won at Sundance: During the festival, Artisan Entertainment stepped forward and picked up the $60,000 film for a cool $1 million. *Pi* also did well at the Independent Spirit Awards, where it was nominated for Best First Feature and Best Cinematography and won for Best Screenplay. The film was given a limited theatrical release, during which it earned more than $3 million. It sold well on video and became the first motion picture to be sold by download on the internet.

The film's critical response was overwhelmingly positive. In his three-and-a-half-star (out of four) review, Roger Ebert of the *Chicago Sun-Times* wrote, "*Pi* is a thriller. I am not very thrilled these days by whether the bad guys will get shot or the chase scene will end one way instead of another. You have to make a movie like that pretty skillfully before I care. But I am thrilled when a man risks his mind in the pursuit of a dangerous obsession." David Edelstein of *Slate* wrote, "This is very much a first feature, with all the hyperbolic, sometimes indiscriminate cinematic energy of a student film. But it's also sensational, a febrile mediation on the mathematics of existence." *San Francisco Examiner* critic Barbara Shulgasser wrote, "*Pi* will not be for everyone, but for those who are fed up with the mainstream idiocy that gets dumped into theaters each summer, this movie will be like a great big palate-clearing taste of sorbet." Marc Savlov of *The Austin Chronicle* raved, "Brilliant, surreal, and emotionally draining, this first feature from American Film Institute grad Aronofsky recalls such low-budget sci-fi epics as *Tetsuo: The Iron Man* and more traditional paranoiac suspense films (Adrian Lyne's *Jacob's Ladder* in particular, but also Polanski's *Rosemary's Baby*) and yet manages to be a wholly original animal."

Aronofsky's follow-up to *Pi* was supposed to be a science fiction/horror film for Dimension Films set during World War II. Aronofsky promised that the film, *Proteus*, would be the most frightening film that had been made in at least a decade. But alas, *Proteus* wasn't meant to be. In the end, Aronofsky's terrifying horror pic, like so many proposed Hollywood films, fell apart. So, what now?

Aronofsy had been a fan of author Hubert Selby Jr. since accidentally stumbling across his novel *Last Exit to Brooklyn* during college, when Selby became his literary idol. Why was this? As Aronofsky explained to the BBC's James Mottram, "Anyone that reads Selby's work can see how intense his world is. He writes the most discordant, angry words that tickle the air with some sweet music around it. It's an unbelievable experience to read his books." Aronofsky had met and befriended Selby while he was still in film school, when he'd made a short film based on one of the author's stories, "Fortune Cookie."

After the success of *Pi*, everyone and their mother were telling Aronofsky and Watson that they could essentially make anything they wanted. Watson convinced Aronofsky to option the film rights to Hubert Selby Jr.'s bleak 1978 novel *Requiem for a Dream* so they could adapt it as their next film. They paid $1,000 for the film rights, and Aronofsky learned that Selby had written an unproduced screenplay based on his novel years before. Nevertheless, he wrote his own script, taking cues from both Selby and his unproduced script. The two men never worked together in the same room, but their words blended together seamlessly.

Aronofsky wanted the film to be about different kinds of addiction. Aronofsky explained to *Salon*,

> *Requiem for a Dream* is not about heroin or drugs. . . . The Harry-Tyrone-Marion story is a very traditional heroin story. But putting it side by side with the Sara story, we suddenly say, "Oh, my God, what *is* a drug?" The idea that the same inner monologue goes through a person's head when they're trying to quit drugs, as with cigarettes, as when they're trying to not eat food so they can lose twenty pounds, was really fascinating to me. I thought it was an idea that we hadn't seen on film and I wanted to bring it up on the screen.

Aronofsky initially wanted to make the film with younger characters than those Selby had written about, but the producers talked him out of it; they worried that making the characters high school students could make the film even more unsettling and bring about unwanted criticism. One change Aronofsky made from the novel was relocating the action from Selby's beloved Brooklyn to the Bronx. Although several studios were frightened by the project, Artisan agreed to finance it.

Aronofsky and his casting directors auditioned, considered, and approached many performers for the film. Faye Dunaway turned down the role of Sara. Aronofsky told *Vulture*, "There were a lot of great actors that said, 'No fucking way.' I had offered it to Anne Bancroft, and I had a beautiful conversation with her, and she told me that it's the first role she passed on that she had to talk to her shrink about." Ellen Burstyn also passed on the role, saying the material was too dark. However, Burstyn was eventually persuaded to make the film by her manager, who had asked her to watch *Pi*.

Giovanni Ribisi and Tobey McGuire were approached to play the role of Harry. Both declined. Jared Leto then stepped into the role after having auditioned multiple times and "begging" for it.

Jennifer Connelly was cast in the role of Marion after Neve Campbell passed when she learned she would have a nude scene. Aronofsky later recalled that at one of Connelly's auditions, the actress "just destroyed the room," violently kicking a chair. According to Aronofsky, he and Leto, who was also present for the rehearsal, just looked at one another and knew Connelly was the right actress for the role.

Dave Chappelle was offered the role of Tyrone but declined the offer. Marlon Wayans auditioned six times for the part. "I slept in the same clothes, literally, for ten days," Wayans later recalled of his audition(s). "I barely washed. I would talk like the character. My boys would come over to the house—Omar Epps was concerned, like, 'Are you okay?'" To prepare himself for his auditions, Wayans read Selby's novel multiple times. Eventually, Aronofsky cast Wayans.

Early in his career, Leto was known as a Method actor who submerged himself in whatever role he was playing. For this particular role, he starved himself, losing twenty-eight pounds. Because Leto was already skinny, the effect is both frightening and effective. But looking like a heroin addict wasn't enough;

Leto wanted to make his performance as authentic as possible, so he spent time living on the streets, hanging out with real-life drug addicts. He later told *Rolling Stone* that he injected himself with water so he could simulate the heroin injection.

Aronofsky instructed Leto and Wayans to remain free of sex and sugar for the duration of the shoot in order to make their characters' cravings feel more realistic because they themselves would be battling their own cravings. The director also had Wayans walk around the streets of New York during the winter without a shirt so he could experience some of what his character would experience.

Connelly immersed herself in her role by moving into the apartment building where her character lived and trying to emulate Marion's life as she envisioned it. She spent time with real-life addicts and attended Narcotics Anonymous meetings with a recovering addict. Connelly also made her own clothes for the film.

There were eight weeks of rehearsals before the cameras began rolling. Filming began on April 19, 1999, and wrapped on June 16. The film's budget was $4.5 million. Most of the picture was shot on a soundstage in Red Hook, Brooklyn, the same neighborhood where the 1989 adaptation of Selby's *The Last Exit to Brooklyn* had been filmed. Cinematographer Libatique, who had previously shot *Pi*, returned to lens *Requiem for a Dream*.

Burstyn wore two different fat suits of different weights so the film could depict her character's dramatic weight loss in a believable fashion. Additionally, Burstyn lost ten pounds of her own by undergoing an all-cabbage-soup diet for ten days. She wore nine wigs and four different necks showing different stages of her being overweight and then emaciated. Application of the prosthetic makeup took four hours each day. Burstyn later said that the role was the most challenging of her career. In the time-lapse scene (shot with a motion-controlled camera) where Sara is cleaning, cleaning, cleaning her house, Burstyn hurt her back. The scene, in real time, took forty minutes to film, but Burstyn wasn't happy with her performance in the scene and, despite her back hurting like hell, asked to do the whole thing over again.

In 2020, Burstyn recalled,

> We were very aware of our interplay with Matty [Libatique], and how much the actors and the camera and the special effects and the lighting—It was all part of it, you know. The refrigerator moving and, you know, when the world fell apart, it was terrifying, somehow. It was very real on the set. And it felt like teamwork. All the various departments were involved and engaging and giving their all, and it had a high-intensity degree of creativity at its most fertile and vital and tough and hard and exciting and terrifying. It was quite an experience.

In one scene, Connelly's character, Marion, participates in lewd group sex to obtain cash for drugs, which required the actress to appear nude. Connelly didn't feel wholly comfortable with this, but she'd known about the scene from the start, and she understood its importance to the film. Strippers were hired to play the other women in the scene because they were comfortable showing their bodies.

There are a couple of notable cameos in the film by men who'd made memorable impressions on Aronofsky. The first is author Hubert Selby Jr., as a police officer overseeing Tyrone's incarceration. Selby visited the set several times during the shoot, occasionally reading passages from his novel to inspire the cast and crew. The second notable cameo is Aronofsky's father, Abraham Aronofsky, as the man on the subway who yells, "You're whacked!" at Sara.

The film's editing is a key part of the film's success. Obviously, that's true with any film, but it's even more so with *Requiem*. There are scenes that use a technique Aronofsky and editor Jay Rabinowitz call "hip-hop montage." In these scenes, there are many extremely brief shots rapidly intercut. As a result, the film used far more shots than most films. The average film has roughly six hundred cuts; *Requiem for a Dream* has more than two thousand. These rapid montages show the viewer the addicts' feelings of loss of control. Aronofsky and Rabinowitz also employed such filmmaking devices as split-screen and extremely tight close-ups. By making the length of the scenes shorter and shorter as the film progresses, they continually escalate the tension and dread in the film, sending audiences hurtling toward the picture's disturbing climax. Aronofsky also used a rig that strapped a camera to the actors' bodies; this camera, known as a SnorriCam, faced the actor directly from the front, providing a unique perspective.

Music plays an important role in the film. In the beginning, Aronofsky asked Clint Mansell to create bombastic hip-hop-influenced pieces of music. One of the songs Aronofsky used to show the composer what kind of sound he wanted was Public Enemy's "She Watch Channel Zero?!" But when the songs that Mansell made in this style were edited into the film, they didn't work, so Mansell created new music. When one piece of music that he'd made called "Lux Aeterna" was placed under a scene in which Marion leaves her psychiatrist's apartment after sleeping with him, the connection between the music and the action onscreen blew Mansell and Aronofsky away. This extraordinary musical marriage worked far more effectively than either of them had imagined possible.

Requiem for a Dream made the festival rounds, and it was nominated for just about every award it could have been nominated for, winning a great many. *Requiem* was nominated for Best Picture at just about every festival and by just about every critical group. Aronofsky and his cast were pretty much all nominated and honored, but most of the attention went to Burstyn for her stunning performance. The following year, Burstyn received a Best Actress Academy Award nomination for her work.

When *Requiem for a Dream* was submitted to the Motion Picture Association of America, it was slapped with the dreaded NC-17 rating. The primary reason for this is the film's explicit group sex scene. Artisan appealed the decision, but the MPAA would not budge. Rather than demand Aronofsky cut scenes from the film, which they recognized as a masterwork, Artisan decided to release the film without a rating. Because of this, many theaters refused to show it, and at those that did, no one under the age of seventeen was allowed to view it. This obviously resulted in the film making far less money than it would have otherwise. Still, in the end, it made $7.4 million.

Requiem for a Dream was a critical wet dream. In his three-and-a-half star (out of four) review, *Chicago Sun-Times* critic Roger Ebert wrote, "What is fascinating about *Requiem for a Dream* . . . is how well [Aronofsky] portrays the mental states of his addicts. When they use, a window opens briefly into a world where everything is right. Then it slides shut, and life reduces itself to a search for the money and drugs to open it again." In *The New York Times*, Elvis Mitchell wrote, "After the young director's phenomenal debut with the barely budgeted *Pi*, which was like watching a middleweight boxer win a fight purely on reflexes, he comes back with a picture that shows maturation." *Rolling Stone*'s Peter Travers wrote, "No one interested in the power and magic of movies should miss it." Owen Gleiberman of *Entertainment Weekly* posited that *Requiem* "may be the first movie to fully capture the way drugs dislocate us from ourselves." He also observed, "The movie, a full-throttle mind-bender, is hypnotically harrowing and intense, a visual and spiritual plunge into the seduction and terror of drug addiction."

For Aronofsky, none of the reviews or awards could have compared to seeing Selby, his spiritual mentor, weep after watching the film for the first time. Aronofsky had gotten it right. Who cares if Desson Howe of the *Washington Post* or William Arnold of the *Seattle Post-Intelligencer* hadn't gotten it? How could their words of dissent and disapproval possibly matter after Aronofsky had learned that he'd pleased Hubert Selby Jr. and done justice to the work?

In the decades that have followed, Aronofsky has continued to craft intelligent films that succeed in terms of artistry and execution. His post-'90s filmography includes such gems as *The Wrestler*, *Black Swan*, *The Whale*, and *Mother!* While Aronofsky excels in every aspect of filmmaking, he has displayed a unique talent for crafting artful films that cause audiences to squirm in discomfort. "Some directors dazzle and some seduce," Xan Brooks observed in *The Guardian*. "Aronofsky simply tramples you in your seat. His is the ripsnorting bull of American cinema, flanks matted with sweat, hooves kicking up clods; meaning to shock and awe; and possibly impregnate us as well."

Aronofsky just wants audiences to feel *something*. And he wants them to feel it *strongly*. He once told his father, "All I want in my life is for people to either cheer or boo. I just don't want anything in the middle." In a 2011 interview with *Time* magazine, Aronofsky expounded, "I definitely want to make them feel something. I'm inspired by the Cyclone roller coaster at Coney Island, where I grew up. It is the greatest ride in the world. I've always tried to construct my films with the same structure; intense, on the edge of your seat."

14

Sofia Coppola
Cinema of Isolation

Sofia Coppola came into the world on May 14, 1971, the youngest child of documentary filmmaker Eleanor Coppola and legendary director Francis Ford Coppola. Francis was in the process of directing *The Godfather*, the film that established him as one of the greatest filmmakers in the history of cinema. Coppola wasted no time before going to work in film; she made her first film appearance in *The Godfather*, playing, of course, a baby. It is rare that an actor begins their film career as a newborn, and it's ever rarer to begin that career as a newborn in what is arguably the greatest American film ever produced. But Sofia Coppola is something special.

As a child, Coppola was a constant presence on her father's film sets. Her mother, Eleanor, later recalled Coppola's experiences on the Lake Tahoe set of *The Godfather Part II*, saying, "Sofia, our daughter, was a toddler, so she would run around among the crew. She was like the pet monkey, and they would give her candy." Aside from playing monkey to the crew, Coppola was again cast in the film. In the previous *Godfather* film, she had played baby Michael in the baptism scene. In the second installment, she played a young boy. Father Francis also stuck Coppola's older brother Roman in both films.

As a young girl, Coppola and her playmates, Jilian and Jenny Gersten, the daughters of theater producer Bernard Gersten, sang and danced for everyone who would watch. Around age seven or eight, the three girls established their own dancing group, which they dubbed the Dingbats. Within a couple years, Coppola and her friends were publishing a summer newspaper they called *The Dingbat News*. The three girls hung out around her father's office and sets, trying to assist wherever they could. Despite this desire to help out, there weren't a lot of film-production jobs suited to ten-year-olds, so they occasionally got underfoot, driving Francis's secretaries crazy. This reaction was understandable, but doting father Francis fired some of the secretaries at Astoria Studios who he believed had it in for Coppola and her friends.

Coppola appeared in several more of her father's films as a child, including *The Outsiders*, *Rumble Fish*, *The Cotton Club*, *Peggy Sue Got Married*, and *Tucker: The Man and His Dream*. At the age of thirteen, she made her first appearance in a film not directed by her father, in Tim Burton's *Frankenweenie*. In 1988, at the age of seventeen, she helped her dad write the vignette "Life without Zoe" for the anthology film *New York Stories*. The elder Coppola described the segment, which focuses on a character loosely based on Sofia, as being about "one of the rich kids you see in New York who have their own credit cards and have lunch at the Russian Tea Room."

In 1990, Coppola appeared in her largest role yet; when Winona Ryder backed out of *The Godfather Part III*, Francis asked Coppola to step into the role of Mary Corleone. This was Coppola's third role in the trilogy. Reviews for the film were far more critical than those of the previous *Godfather* films, and many writers took exception with the director's decision to cast his own daughter. The general consensus was that Coppola was, as the *Washington Post*'s Hal Hinson described her, "hopelessly amateurish."

After being critically bombarded the way she was for *Godfather Part III*, a lot of actors would have hung up their jerseys and gone home, but not Coppola. She popped up in music videos by Madonna, the Black Crowes, and Sonic Youth. In 1992, she appeared alongside Patricia Arquette and Sandra Bernhard in the largely unseen comedy *Inside Monkey Zetterland*. In 1994, she cocreated and starred in a television series with another child of famous parents, Zoe Cassavetes. (Zoe's parents are actor/

director John Cassavetes and actress Gena Rowland. Additionally, Zoe's brother Nick helmed *The Notebook*.) The sketch series, *Hi Octane*, aired on Comedy Central and lasted a mere three episodes (although four were filmed). Coppola and Cassavetes called in favors from seemingly everyone they knew, landing appearances by such noted celebs as Martin Scorsese, the Beastie Boys, Gus Van Sant, Keanu Reeves, and Coppola's cousin Nicolas Cage.

A few years later, Coppola read in the trades that one of her favorite novels was being made into a film. Because that novel, Jeffrey Eugenides's *The Virgin Suicides*, had developed a reputation as being something that could not be adapted to film, Coppola became worried. How would they approach the material? What would the film's tone be? Would they do Eugenides's book justice? After much consideration, Coppola decided that she wanted to make the film to ensure that it would be done correctly. "That book made me want to become a filmmaker," she later explained. "Because I wasn't planning on becoming a director, but I loved that book so much that when I heard they were making a movie I just thought, out of protectiveness for that book, 'Well, I hope they don't mess it up when they make the movie.' I heard a man was directing it and it was supposed to be very dark."

She asked her father to purchase the screen rights for her. Like a good dad, Francis went to work trying to make this happen but to no avail; even a Hollywood player as powerful as he is can't do everything. "Don't break your heart," he advised her. "You're not going to be able to do anything with it, because you don't own the book."

Nevertheless, she persisted. Coppola had never tried her hand at screenwriting before, but she was excited about the prospect of getting to know the characters better and also to learn more about the screenwriting process. Years later, after she'd written many more scripts, she said that writing original screenplays was more difficult for her than adapting because when adapting an existing work, there is a road map to aid her in her journey. She also said she believed writing an adaptation was like putting a puzzle together and trying to figure out how the pieces fit together to best serve the film. While writing and fleshing out the characters, she fell in love with them. Interestingly, she saw them in her mind's eye as people she knew in real-life as she wrote.

Once she had finished her first draft of *The Virgin Suicides*, Coppola asked her father to read it so she could ascertain whether it was any good. Had she written a decent script? Or would hers be like the countless stacks of forgettable and mediocre scripts that comprise the slush piles found in every producer's office? If Francis was even the slightest bit hesitant to read his daughter's script, he quickly found those fears unfounded. He was legitimately impressed by what he read. His daughter, it turned out, had real talent as a writer. He later remarked that it was one of the best scripts he'd ever read.

Coppola then managed to meet with the producers who owned the rights to the novel so she could show them her script and tell them about her vision for the film. At the time, the producer, Chris Hanley, and his wife, Roberta, with whom he co-owned the rights to the novel, were working with writer/director Nick Gomez, who had previously made a splash with *The Laws of Gravity* and *New Jersey Drive*. Gomez had taken a pass at the screenplay, but the Hanleys were dissatisfied with it, so Coppola unknowingly came into the picture at precisely the right moment.

When the Hanleys read her script, they, like everyone else who read it, were blown away. Somehow, Coppola wrote and then talked her way into a job directing *The Virgin Suicides*. While the fact that her father was one of the greatest filmmakers in the history of film may have played a slight role in the producers' decision, there was no doubt that Coppola's script was impressive. Novelist Ernest Hemingway once observed that the goal of any storyteller is to make the audience or reader remember the story as if they themselves had lived it. That, as it turned out, was exactly what Coppola had done with her first screenplay.

While author Jeffrey Eugenides admitted that Coppola's vision and his own were somewhat different—the novel focuses more on the neighborhood boys who are in love with the Lisbon sisters than the sisters themselves—he thought the screenplay was solid. Of the twenty-seven-year-old Coppola, he said, "She seems to me to be completely un-ruined by her upbringing and by the sort of notoriety that's descended on her just by being born."

The first actor to come onboard was Kathleen Turner, who signed on to play the role of the matriarch, Mrs. Lisbon. Turner expressed that she was extremely impressed with Coppola's script. Another veteran actor, James Woods, came onboard soon after to essay the role of Mr. Lisbon. Woods, too, was blown

Sofia Coppola has established herself as a genuine talent. Courtesy of Photofest

away by what Coppola had written. He later said, "The script was wonderful, and I thought if Sofia could write this, . . . if she can direct half as well as she writes, then we might really have a shot. And she turned out to not only be half the director she is a writer, but twice the director she is a writer, which is really saying a lot."

Another experienced actor, Scott Glenn, signed on to appear as the family priest. Glenn had worked with Coppola's father on *Apocalypse Now* and had first met her when she was five years old. Glenn gushed in *Making of 'The Virgin Suicides'*, "She's got the touch. She knows what she wants and reminds you of pieces of the reality of the scene that escape me, and I like to pride myself in [the fact that] not a whole lot escapes me. And yet she leaves you alone to find your own rhythm."

When it came to casting the daughters, Coppola saw Kirsten Dunst in the role of the much-loved and lusted-over Lux Lisbon. She had seen the actress in such films as *Interview with the Vampire: The Vampire Chronicles* and *Little Women* and had been impressed. Coppola traveled to Toronto, where Dunst was working on another picture, to talk to her about *The Virgin Suicides*. Dunst was initially apprehensive due to some of the character's actions in the film but recognized quickly while talking with Coppola that the film "would be something special." Coppola told *Vanity Fair* in 2017, "I loved working with Kirsten. I mean, obviously, I guess. That's when we met and had our first connection. We just clicked right away, and she knew what I had in mind. . . . She was really there for me." Coppola and Dunst became friends off-screen and collaborated so well together that they reunited for the films *Marie Antoinette*, *The Bling Ring*, and *The Beguiled*.

Because most of the actresses playing the titular "virgin" Lisbon daughters were young and inexperienced, Coppola hired acting coach Chris Neil to help them with their performances. Although her father proudly sat on the sidelines of the set while Coppola made *The Virgin Suicides*, he stayed out of her way and allowed her to make her own directorial decisions. His primary piece of advice to his daughter was that she needed to "find [her] team." While Coppola ultimately compiled a core team of collaborators that includes editor Sarah Flack, production designer Anne Ross, costume designer Stacey Battat, and of course Dunst, she found most of them on subsequent projects.

Coppola chose not to use storyboards because she wanted to make the actors feel comfortable and have the impression that the staging was more natural than something planned out. Making the actors feel comfortable is (and was) one of the most important aspects of filmmaking for Coppola. In fact, she wanted to make the set have a party atmosphere to keep everyone relaxed. Actor Josh Hartnett, who called *The Virgin Suicides* his favorite filming experience, observed that shooting the film felt like going to camp. In fact, veteran actor James Woods said that Coppola's film was the only project he'd ever made where he didn't want to leave once the shoot was over. Actress A. J. Cook, who played the role of Mary Lisbon, said she's spent the decades since trying in vain to duplicate that experience on every film she's made.

One way Coppola made the actors feel relaxed was to organize a group laser-tag outing before the actual shoot began. By all accounts, the performers had a good time on the outing, although Woods apparently took things too seriously and shot actress Cook ad nauseam. The outing helped create bonds and chemistry between the cast, and actress Leslie Hayman, who played Therese Lisbon, said that the actresses playing the siblings became so close that they actually felt like sisters by the time filming was finished.

Coppola also maintained a loose atmosphere on the set by encouraging physical improvisation whenever she felt that the scripted actions or movements by the actors were unnatural. The cast and crew also celebrated the performers' birthdays on the set, including Hartnett, who turned twenty during the shoot.

Because she'd studied photography, Coppola used (and continues to use) photographs as visual references to convey to her collaborators the look and atmosphere she seeks. Many of these photos were shot by Bill Owens, who was known for his photographs of suburban domestic scenes. Coppola also uses scenes and shots from other films as references.

A publicity photo from Sofia Coppola's film The Virgin Suicides. *Courtesy of Paramount Classics/Photofest © Paramount Classics*

The young director shot most of *The Virgin Suicides* on location and mostly in chronological order, which isn't employed much in Hollywood due to cost restrictions. Coppola preferred that method and continues to shoot this way whenever possible. Her brother Roman shot some second unit on the film, including a shot of the horse made up to look like a unicorn.

Because Hartnett was still a fairly inexperienced actor, Woods gave him pointers and coached him throughout the shoot. To achieve the hair Coppola envisioned for Hartnett's character, Hartnett had to wear a wig in the film, which he described as being a "huge pain in the ass." Coppola first tried to use extensions, but the glue was visible because Hartnett's hair was too short. During some scenes, such as the intimate kissing scene with Dunst's character, the wig fell off over and over again.

Coppola later admitted that, although she had some great memories of the shoot, she'd felt unsure of herself while she made *The Virgin Suicides*. But no one watching the film would ever guess that. Additionally, it's doubtful that anyone would guess that it was made by a first-time director.

The Virgin Suicides bowed at the Sundance Film Festival in January 2000 and then received its full theatrical release the following April. The film was appreciated by both critics and general audiences. *Chicago Sun-Times* critic Roger Ebert complimented Coppola's handling of the story about teenage girls who commit suicide: "She has the courage to play it in a minor key. She doesn't hammer home ideas and interpretations. She is content with the air of mystery and loss that hangs in the air like bitter poignancy." Peter Stack of the *San Francisco Chronicle* wrote, "Coppola infuses her movie with a dreamy poetic tone, and deftly translates the essential metaphors of youth, sexuality, and death without sacrificing an earthy humor." *New York Times* scribe A. O. Scott wrote,

> *The Virgin Suicides* should quiet the buzz of skepticism that has preceded this film. Yes, Ms. Coppola is the daughter of one famous director and the wife of another [her first husband, Spike Jonze], but she is also an assured filmmaker in her own right. Her instincts clearly tell her that film is not only a visual medium but also an emotional one, and she is eager to confront the pain, frustration, and grief that simmer beneath the tranquil affluence of her enchanted suburb.

Coppola won an MTV Movie Award for Best New Filmmaker for her efforts.

Coppola continues to make exciting, refreshing artistic films today, more than twenty years later. *The Virgin Suicides* helped set the tone for the rest of her career in terms of the style and types of films she would make. Her feature debut, like most of her films that have followed, is a character study about loneliness and isolation, characters detached from the world. Coppola's introspective characters desperately desire to connect with others and often attach themselves to unexpected characters. Almost every decision Coppola makes in crafting her films, from the color palette to the selection of clothing and production design, is done in service of creating a believable sense of detachment. Most of her films are about self-discovery and feature characters who are lost and find themselves in transition.

Aside from their similar motifs, Coppola's films generally feature some degree of autobiographical elements. They're also known for their striking visuals. The films are almost always sad and downbeat, to varying degrees. Coppola uses less editorial cuts than most directors because she believes it makes the scenes feel more like real life and less like a movie. Coppola also pays close attention to the music she uses in her films, and one of her chief concerns is attempting to make the music and the visuals mesh together perfectly.

Sofia Coppola is an immensely talented writer/director whose post–*Virgin Suicides* filmography includes such notable works as *Lost in Translation, Marie Antoinette,* and *Priscilla.*

References

Author Interviews

Steven Bernstein
Bill Borden
Guillermo Del Toro
Troy Duffy
Gary Fleder
Carlos Gallardo
Chris Gore

Sean Gullette
Monte Hellman
John Herzfeld
Richard Linklater
Guillermo Navarro
Peter O'Fallon
Vincent Pereira

Scott Rosenberg
Tom Savini
Darin Scott
Kevin Smith
CM Talkington
Quentin Tarantino

Books

Aronofsky, Darren. *Pi: The Screenplay and the Guerilla Diaries: 1996–1998*. Faber & Faber, 1999.

Bailey, Jason. *Pulp Fiction: The Complete Story of Quentin Tarantino's Masterpiece*. Voyageur Press, 2013.

Barboza, Craigh, ed. *John Singleton: Interviews*. University Press of Mississippi, 2009.

Berg, Charles Ramirez, *Latino Images in Film: Subversion and Resistance."* University of Texas Press, 2002.

Bernard, Jami, *Quentin Tarantino: The Man and His Movies*. Dey Street Books, 1995.

Berra, John, ed. *Directory of World Cinema: American Independent 3*. University of Chicago Press, 2016.
Bogosian, Eric. *SubUrbia*. St. Martin's Griffin, 1997.
Caldwell, Sara C., and Marie-Eve S. Kielson. *So You Want to Be a Screenwriter: How to Face the Fears and Take the Risks*. Allworth Press, 2000.
Cowie, Peter. *The Godfather Book*. Faber & Faber, 1997.
Dawson, Jeff. *Quentin Tarantino: The Cinema of Cool*. Applause Books, 2000.
Falsetto, Mario. *Personal Visions: Conversations with Independent Filmmakers*. Constable, 1999.
Hanson, Peter. *The Cinema of Generation X: A Critical Study of Films and Directors*. McFarland, 2002.
Ingle, Zachary, ed. *Robert Rodriguez: Interviews*. University Press of Mississippi, 2012.
Knapp, Laurence F., ed. *David Fincher: Interviews*. University Press of Mississippi, 2014.
Lowenstein, Stephen, ed. *My First Movie, Take Two: Ten Celebrated Directors Talk About Their First Film: Richard Linklater, Richard Kelly, Alejandro González, Iñárritu, Takeshi Kitano, Shekhar Kapur, Emir Kusturica, Agnès Jaoui, Lukas Moodysson, Terry Gilliam, Sam Mendes*. Pantheon Books, 2008.
Macor, Alison. *Chainsaws, Slackers, and Spy Kids: Thirty Years of Filmmaking in Austin, Texas*. University of Texas Press, 2010.
Maerz, Melissa. *Alright, Alright, Alright: The Oral History of Richard Linklater's* Dazed and Confused. Harper, 2020.
Mottram, James. *The Sundance Kids: How the Mavericks Took Back Hollywood*. Faber & Faber, 2006.
Muir, John Kenneth. *An Askew View: The Films of Kevin Smith*. Applause, 2002.
Nayman, Adam. *David Fincher: Mind Games*. Abrams, 2021.
Nayman, Adam. *Paul Thomas Anderson: Masterworks*. Abrams, 2020.
Page, Edwin. *Quintessential Tarantino*. Marion Boyars, 2005.
Peary, Gerald, ed. *Quentin Tarantino: Interviews*. University Press of Mississippi, 1998.
Phillips, Gene D., and Rodney Hill, eds. *Francis Ford Coppola: Interviews*. University of Mississippi Press, 2004.
Pierson, John. *Spike, Mike, Slackers and Dykes: A Guided Tour across a Decade of American Independent Cinema*. Hyperion, 1995.
Raftery, Brian. *Best. Movie. Year. Ever. How 1999 Blew Up the Big Screen*. Simon & Schuster, 2019.

Rausch, Andrew J. *Conversations on Quentin Tarantino.* Edited by Chris Watson. Bear Manor Media, 2016.

Rausch, Andrew J. *Fifty Filmmakers: Conversations with Directors from Roger Avary to Steven Zaillian.* Edited by Michael Dequina. McFarland, 2008.

Rodriguez, Robert. *Rebel without a Crew, or, How a 23-Year-Old Filmmaker with $7,000 Became a Hollywood Player.* Dutton, 1995.

Rubin, Rick. *The Creative Act: A Way of Being.* With Neil Strauss. Penguin Press, 2023.

Sherman, Dale. *Quentin Tarantino FAQ: Everything Left to Know about the Original Reservoir Dog.* Applause Books, 2015.

Singer, Michael. *A Cut Above: 50 Film Directors Talk about Their Craft.* Lone Eagle, 1998.

Singleton, John, and Veronica Chambers. *Poetic Justice: Filmmaking South Central Style.* Delta, 1993.

Smith, Jim. *Tarantino.* Virgin Books, 2005.

Smith, Kevin. *Dogma: A Screenplay.* Grove Press, 1999.

Smith, Kevin. *Silent Bob Speaks: The Collected Writings of Kevin Smith.* Miramax Books, 2005.

Smith, Kevin. *Tough Sh*t: Life Advice from a Fat, Lazy Slob Who Did Good.* Gotham Books, 2012.

Stanush, Claude, *The Newton Boys: Portrait of an Outlaw Gang.* State House Press, 1994.

Toles, George. *Paul Thomas Anderson.* University of Illinois Press, 2016.

Voisin, Scott. *Character Kings: Hollywood's Familiar Faces Discuss the Art and Business of Acting.* Bear Manor Media, 2016.

Waxman, Sharon. *Rebels on the Backlot: Six Maverick Directors and How They Conquered the Hollywood Studio System.* HarperEntertainment, 2005.

Periodicals and Online Magazines

Anderson, Jeffrey M. "Interview with Darren Aronofsky: Easy as 3.14 . . ." *Combustible Celluloid*, June 25, 1998. https://www.combustiblecelluloid.com/daint.shtml.

Ansen, David, "Kicking and Screaming," *Newsweek*, October 9, 1995.

Ariano, Ryan. "The Untold Truth of Dazed and Confused." *Looper*, updated September 8, 2022. https://www.looper.com/998097/the-untold-truth-of-dazed-and-confused/.

Arnold, William, "'Requiem' is overdose of junkie slice of life," *Seattle Post-Intelligencer*, November 3, 2000. https://web.archive.org/web/20010622063243/http:/seattlep-i.nwsource.com/movies/dreamq4.shtml.

Aronofsky, Darren. "10 Questions for Darren Aronofsky." *Time*, January 17, 2011. https://time.com/archive/6595132/10-questions-for-darren-aronofsky/.

Author unknown, "New Faces of 1996," *Newsweek*, January 14, 1996.

Author unknown, "The Alien Scents Ripley," *Empire*, September 2023. https://www.avpgalaxy.net/2023/10/09/its-powerful-david-fincher-talks-iconic-alien-3-imagery/.

Author unknown, "Empire Magazine's 500 Greatest Movies Ever Made," *Empire*, October 23, 2012. https://web.archive.org/web/20121023202400/http://www.empireonline.com/500/72.asp.

Aylmer, Olivia, "How the Virgin Suicides Brought Sofia Coppola and Kirsten Dunst Together," *Vanity Fair*, April 20, 2018. https://www.vanityfair.com/hollywood/2018/04/sofia-coppola-virgin-suicides-kirsten-dunst-criterion-collection.

Balderston, Michael. "From Dusk till Dawn: 9 Behind-the-Scenes Facts About the Rodriguez-Tarantino Movie." *CinemaBlend*, January 7, 2021. https://www.cinemablend.com/news/2560812/from-dusk-till-dawn-behind-the-scenes-facts-about-the-rodriguez-tarantino-movie.

Barbot, Matt. "Q&A: THE Danny Trejo." *Remezcla*, February 3, 2011. https://remezcla.com/film/danny-trejo-machete-brisk-interview/.

Barrios, Gregg. "Up and Coming: Robert Rodriguez; A Borrowed Camera, $7,000, and a Dream." *New York Times*, February 21, 1993. https://www.nytimes.com/1993/02/21/archives/up-and-coming-robert-rodriguez-a-borrowed-camera-7000-and-a-dream.html.

Bartle, Trisha. "'The Faculty' (1998): 24 Facts and Trivia About the Teen Horror Cult Classic." *Creepy Catalog*, updated June 17, 2022. https://creepycatalog.com/the-faculty-movie-trivia/.

Bates, Karen Grigsby. "They Gotta Have Us." *New York Times Magazine*, July 14, 1991. https://www.nytimes.com/1991/07/14/magazine/theyve-gotta-have-us.html.

Baumgarten, Marjorie, "Dogma," *Austin Chronicle*, November 12, 1999. https://www.austinchronicle.com/events/film/1999-11-12/140214/.

Baumgarten, Marjorie. "Subdividing subUrbia: Richard Linklater Discusses His New Movie." *Austin Chronicle*, February 21, 1997. https://www.austinchronicle.com/screens/1997-02-21/527433/.

Bedard, Mark. "The Wes Anderson Color Palette: Bright Colors Meet Dark Subjects." *StudioBinder*. September 6, 2020. https://www.studiobinder.com/blog/wes-anderson-color-palette/.

Beeler, Michael. "Salma Hayek, Vampire Queen." *Femme Fatales* 4, no. 6 (March 1996): 50–55, 60.

Beyl, Cameron. "David Fincher: The Ultimate Guide to His Films and Directing Style." *Indie Film Hustle*, October 7, 2022. https://indiefilmhustle.com/david-fincher/.

Black, Louis, "Roadracers," *Austin Chronicle*, July 22, 1994. https://www.austinchronicle.com/events/film/1994-07-22/138532/.

Blair, Iain. "David Fincher Interview." *Film and Video* (October 1997): 15–18.

Bland, Simon, "Richard Linklater on Before Sunrise's Enduring Legacy," Huck, September 28, 2020. https://www.huckmag.com/article/richard-linklater-on-before-sunrises-enduring-legacy.

Brooks, Xan. "Darren Aronofsky on Mother!—'Jennifer Lawrence Was Hyperventilating Because of the Emotion.'" *Guardian*, September 7, 2017. https://www.theguardian.com/film/2017/sep/07/darren-aronofsky-on-mother-jennifer-lawrence-was-hyperventilating-because-of-the-emotion.

Campbell, Duncan. "Catholics Vilify Dogma." *Guardian*, November 12, 1999. https://www.theguardian.com/film/1999/nov/13/world.news.

Carr, Jay, "Seven," *Boston Globe*, September 22, 1995. https://www.newspapers.com/article/the-boston-globe-seven/144218696/.

Carr, Jay. "John Singleton Searches for Justice in Rosewood." *Boston Globe*, February 16, 1997.

Chattaway, Peter T. "Interview with Darren Aronofsky." *Two Chairs*, August 7, 1998.

Chavoya, Rebecca. "Still Livin': Dazed and Confused." *Austin Monthly*, September 2013. https://www.austinmonthly.com/still-livin-dazed-and-confused/.

Cheshire, Godfrey, "A Pointed Comedy of Aimless Youth," *Variety*, October 14, 1996. https://variety.com/1996/film/reviews/a-pointed-comedy-of-aimless-youth-1200447368/.

Ciment, Michel, and Niogret, Hubert,"Quentin Tarantino," *Positif*, May 23, 1994. https://hibarr.substack.com/p/tarantino-1994.

Claxton, Eve. "Mr. Economy: Noah Baumbach's Two-for-One Trick with *Highball* and *Mr. Jealousy*." *Independent Film and Video Monthly*, December 1997, 30–33.

Collins, Cat. "Christopher Nolan Reveals the Truth Behind the Brad Pitt Memento Rumors." *Yahoo! Movies UK*, January 19, 2014. https://uk.movies.yahoo.com/movies/christopher-nolan-reveals-the-truth-behind-the-brad-pitt-memento-rumours-153202005.html.

Collis, Clark. "The Rise and Fall of Kevin Smith's *Mallrats*." *Entertainment Weekly*, October 12, 2020. https://ew.com/movies/mallrats-oral-history-kevin-smith/.

Corliss, Richard, "A Toke of Our Esteem," *Time*, October 11, 1993. https://time.com/archive/6723983/a-toke-of-our-esteem/.

Cormier, Roger. "14 Running Facts About Chasing Amy." *Mental Floss*, April 4, 2017. https://www.mentalfloss.com/article/84437/14-running-facts-about-chasing-amy.

Crockford, C. M. "The Alternate Ending to Guillermo Del Toro's Mimic That We Never Got to See." *Looper*, January 20, 2023. https://www.looper.com/406098/the-alternate-ending-to-guillermo-del-toros-mimic-that-we-never-got-to-see/.

Crouch, Stanley, "Film: A Lost Generation and Its Exploiters," *New York Times*, August 6, 2001. https://www.nytimes.com/2001/08/26/movies/film-a-lost-generation-and-its-exploiters.html.

Dansby, Andrew. "The Untold Story Behind Wes Anderson's 'Rushmore,' a Cult Classic with Houston Roots." *Houston Chronicle*, updated November 15, 2023. https://www.houstonchronicle.com/projects/2023/wes-anderson-rushmore-behind-the-scenes-houston/.

Dargis, Manohla, "Seven," *LA Weekly*, October 5, 1995. https://www.newspapers.com/article/la-weekly-seven/144219123/.

Dargis, Manohla. "Quentin Tarantino on *Pulp Fiction*." *Sight and Sound* 4, no. 11 (May 1994): 16–19.

Dauphin, Gary. "Ashes and Embers." *Village Voice*, May 21, 1996.

Dee, Jake. "10 Behind-the-Scenes Facts About the Making of Requiem for a Dream." *Screen Rant*, August 26, 2020. https://screenrant.com/requiem-dream-bts-darren-aronofsky-trivia-facts/.

Denson, Thom. "Stories from the Set: Requiem for a Dream." *One Room with a View*, September 14, 2017. https://oneroomwithaview.com/2017/09/14/stories-set-requiem-dream/#google_vignette.

Diones, Bruce, "Following," *The New Yorker*, April 19, 1999.

Doupe, Tyler. "Why Quentin Tarantino Says of Director David Fincher: 'He's Not in the Same Category as Me." *Dread Central*, May 21, 2004.

Ducker, Eric. "Dismantling the Myth of David Fincher." *Ringer*, September 21, 2020. https://www.theringer.com/movies/2020/9/21/21446089/david-fincher-profile-director-set-stories.

Dunaway, Michael. "Honoring Richard Linklater: A Slacker Turns Twenty." *Paste,* October 19, 2011. https://www.pastemagazine.com/movies/richard-linklater/honoring-richard-linklater-a-slacker-turns-twenty.

Ebert Roger, "Higher Learning," *Chicago Sun-Times,* January 11, 1995. https://www.rogerebert.com/reviews/higher-learning-1995.

Ebert, Roger, "Boyz n the Hood," *Chicago Sun-Times,* July 12, 1991. https://www.rogerebert.com/reviews/boyz-n-the-hood-1991.

Ebert, Roger, "Dogma," *Chicago Sun-Times,* November 12, 1999. https://www.rogerebert.com/reviews/dogma-1999.

Ebert, Roger, "Fight Club," *Chicago Sun-Times,* October 15, 1999. https://www.rogerebert.com/reviews/fight-club-1999.

Ebert, Roger, "Four Rooms," *Chicago Sun-Times,* December 25, 1995. https://www.rogerebert.com/reviews/four-rooms-1995.

Ebert, Roger, "From Dusk Till Dawn," *Chicago Sun-Times,* January 19, 1996. https://www.rogerebert.com/reviews/from-dusk-till-dawn-1996.

Ebert, Roger, "Kicking and Screaming," *Chicago Sun-Times,* November 10, 1995. https://www.rogerebert.com/reviews/kicking-and-screaming-1995.

Ebert, Roger, "Mallrats," *Chicago Sun-Times,* October 20, 1995. https://www.rogerebert.com/reviews/mallrats-1995.

Ebert, Roger, "Memento," *Chicago Sun-Times,* April 13, 2001. https://www.rogerebert.com/reviews/memento-2001.

Ebert, Roger, "Mimic," *Chicago Sun-Times,* August 22, 1997. https://www.rogerebert.com/reviews/mimic-1997.

Ebert, Roger, "Pi," *Chicago Sun-Times,* July 24, 1998. https://www.rogerebert.com/reviews/pi-1998.

Ebert, Roger, "Poetic Justice," *Chicago Sun-Times,* July 23, 1993. https://www.rogerebert.com/reviews/poetic-justice-1993.

Ebert, Roger, "Pulp Fiction," *Chicago Sun-Times,* October 14, 1994. https://www.rogerebert.com/reviews/pulp-fiction-1994.

Ebert, Roger, "Requiem for a Dream," *Chicago Sun-Times,* November 3, 2000. https://www.rogerebert.com/reviews/requiem-for-a-dream-2000.

Ebert, Roger, "Rosewood," *Chicago Sun-Times,* February 27, 1997. https://www.rogerebert.com/reviews/rosewood-1997.

Ebert, Roger, "Seven," *Chicago Sun-Times,* September 22, 1995. https://www.rogerebert.com/reviews/seven-1995.

Ebert, Roger, "The Newton Boys," *Chicago-Sun Times,* March 27, 1998. https://www.rogerebert.com/reviews/the-newton-boys-1998.

Ebert, Roger, "The Virgin Suicides," *Chicago Sun-Times*, May 5, 2000. https://www.rogerebert.com/reviews/the-virgin-suicides-2000.

Ebiri, Bilge. "Slackers, Stoners and Scanners: Richard Linklater's Films, Ranked." *Rolling Stone*, July 9, 2014. https://www.rollingstone.com/tv-movies/tv-movie-lists/slackers-stoners-and-scanners-richard-linklaters-films-ranked-26475/.

Edelstein, David, "Moral Characters," *Slate*, August 16, 1998. https://slate.com/culture/1998/08/moral-characters.html.

Ellis-Petersen, Hannah. "Burt Reynolds: 'I Regret Turning Down Greta Garbo.'" *Guardian*, December 3, 2015. https://www.theguardian.com/film/2015/dec/03/burt-reynolds-guardian-live-interview-hate-paul-thomas-anderson.

Eng, Monica, "Amusing Mr. Jealousy Explores Some Self-Absorbed Whiners," *Chicago Tribune*, June 19, 1998. https://www.chicagotribune.com/1998/06/19/amusing-mr-jealousy-explores-some-self-absorbed-whiners/.

Erbland, Kate. "Noah Baumbach Tells All: 7 Things We Learned About His Craft During a Candid Tribeca Talk." *IndieWire*, April 25, 2017. https://www.indiewire.com/features/general/noah-baumbach-tribeca-talk-dustin-hoffman-the-meyerowitz-stories-1201808876/.

Far Out, "The hardest part of give up," November 7, 2024. https://faroutmagazine.co.uk/samuel-l-jackson-role-quentin-tarantino-wrote-for-himself/.

Feinberg, Hugh. "Boogie Nights: A 25th Anniversary Oral History." *Cinema Scholars*, June 2, 2022. https://cinemascholars.com/boogie-nights-a-25th-anniversary-oral-history/.

Ferrier, Aimee. "The Sad Origins of Richard Linklater's 'Before' Trilogy." *Far Out*, November 10, 2022. https://faroutmagazine.co.uk/the-sad-origins-of-richard-linklaters-before-trilogy/.

Ferrier, Aimee. "The Story of How Sofia Coppola 'Empowered' Kirsten Dunst." *Far Out*, October 31, 2023. https://faroutmagazine.co.uk/the-story-of-how-sofia-coppola-empowered-kirsten-dunst/.

Filmsite, "50 Greatest Independent Films by Empire Magazine," https://www.filmsite.org/independentfilms3.html.

French, Alex, and Howie Kahn. "Livin' Thing: An Oral History of 'Boogie Nights.'" *Grantland*, accessed November 22, 2024. https://grantland.com/features/boogie-nights/.

Fretts, Bruce, "Why Kevin Smith shouldn't direct again," *Entertainment Weekly*, December 1, 1999. https://ew.com/article/1999/12/01/why-kevin-smith-shouldnt-direct-again/.

Gaspard, John. "Eric Bogosian on Writing 'subUrbia.'" LinkedIn. May 13, 2019. https://www.linkedin.com/pulse/eric-bogosian-writing-suburbia-john-gaspard/.

Gaughan, Liam. "The Antonio Banderas Neo-Western That Cut Dangerous Corners on Stunt Work." *Collider*, December 30, 2023. https://collider.com/antonio-banderas-desperado-budget-cuts/.

Gelbart, Bryn. "The Untold Truth of Wes Anderson." *Looper*, August 4, 2022. https://www.looper.com/952028/the-untold-truth-of-wes-anderson/.

Gilbert, Emily. "The Untold Truth of Clerks." *Looper*, July 12, 2022. https://www.looper.com/925483/the-untold-truth-of-clerks/.

Gilbey, Ryan. "Film: Precocious Prankster Who Gets a Thrill from Tripping People Up." *Independent*, October 9, 1997. https://www.independent.co.uk/life-style/film-precocious-prankster-who-gets-a-thrill-from-tripping-people-up-1234916.html.

Gleiberman, Owen, "No Looking Back," *Entertainment Weekly*, April 3, 1998. https://ew.com/article/1998/04/03/no-looking-back/.

Gleiberman, Owen, "Pulp Fiction," *Entertainment Weekly*, October 15, 2007. https://ew.com/article/1994/10/14/movie-review-pulp-fiction/.

Gleiberman, Owen, "Requiem for a Dream," *Entertainment Weekly*, October 13, 2000. https://ew.com/article/2000/10/13/movie-review-requiem-dream/.

Gleiberman, Owen, "Slacker: EW Review," *Entertainment Weekly*, August 2, 1991. https://ew.com/article/1991/08/02/slacker-3/.

Gleriberman, Owen, "Rosewood," *Entertainment Weekly*, March 7, 1997. https://ew.com/article/1997/03/07/rosewood-2/.

Goldberg, Matt. "'Se7en' Revisited: The Films of David Fincher." *Collider*, September 22, 2020. https://collider.com/se7en-review/.

Goldberg, Matt. "How 'Following' Laid the Groundwork of Christopher Nolan's Filmography." *Collider*, July 23, 2023. https://collider.com/christopher-nolan-following-movie-explained/.

Goldstein, Patrick. "His New 'Hood Is Hollywood: Fresh Out of Film School, John Singleton Has Become a Hot Property with 'Boyz n the Hood,' a Movie About His Old Neighborhood." *Los Angeles Times*, July 7, 1991. https://www.latimes.com/archives/la-xpm-1991-07-07-ca-2857-story.html.

Golianopolous, Thomas. "How John Singleton Made 'Boyz n the Hood.'" *Ringer*, May 1, 2019. https://www.theringer.com/movies/2019/5/1/18525191/john-singleton-boyz-n-the-hood-oral-history-ice-cube.

252 / References

Gordon, Michael, "The Samuel L. Jackson role Quentin Tarantino wrote for himself:

Gray, Gabran. "The Untold Truth of Darren Aronofsky." *Looper*, September 21, 2022. https://www.looper.com/1019444/the-untold-truth-of-darren-aronofsky/.

Green, David, "The Fight Club Debate: What Is the Message Here?" *Los Angeles Times*, November 1, 1999. https://www.latimes.com/archives/la-xpm-1999-nov-01-ca-28514-story.html.

Guardian. "Magnolia Maniac." March 9, 2000. https://www.theguardian.com/film/2000/mar/10/culture.features.

Haile, Michael, "From Rags to Riches," *BoxOffice*, August 1995.

Harris, Aisha. "Meet the Filmmaker Quentin Tarantino Calls His 'Favorite Imitator.'" *Slate*, October 23, 2015. https://slate.com/culture/2015/10/director-c-m-carty-talkington-talks-quentin-tarantinos-praise-for-love-and-a-45-oliver-stone-and-being-blacklisted-by-hollywood.html.

Harvey, Chris, "'Movies are the only thing I do': The Control and Chaos of Wes Anderson," *Independent*, February 23, 2021. https://www.independent.co.uk/arts-entertainment/films/features/wes-anderson-bottle-rocket-anniversary-b1806255.html.

Harvey, Dennis, "The Faculty," *Variety*, December 28, 1998. https://variety.com/1998/film/reviews/the-faculty-3-1200456169/.

Hellman, Monte. "On *It's Impossible to Learn to Plow by Reading Books*." *Criterion*, September 13, 2004. https://www.criterion.com/current/posts/1061-on-it-s-impossible-to-learn-to-plowby-reading-books?srsltid=AfmBOopmw9ONw25CRVzle-Ru-JLSnnIEfWOyrxvUsi0RuoKaFZg4_xdQ.

Hiatt, Brian, "Jared Leto: The Unlikely Triumphs of a Rock-Movie Super Star," *Rolling Stone*, July 27, 2016. https://www.rollingstone.com/tv-movies/tv-movie-features/jared-leto-the-unlikely-triumphs-of-a-rock-star-movie-star-250359/.

Hinson, Hal, "Godfather Part III," *Washington Post*, December 25, 1990. https://www.washingtonpost.com/wp-srv/style/longterm/movies/videos/thegodfatherpartiiirhinson_a0a9c5.htm.

Hinson, Hal, "Kicking and Screaming," *Washington Post*, November 17, 1995. https://www.washingtonpost.com/wp-srv/style/longterm/movies/videos/kickingandscreamingrhinson_c0379b.htm.

Hinson, Hal, "Slacker," *Washington Post*, August 23, 1991. https://www.washingtonpost.com/wp-srv/style/longterm/movies/videos/slackerrhinson_a0a6ff.htm.

Hoad, Phil. "Julie Delpy and Ethan Hawke: How We Made the Before Sunrise Trilogy." *Guardian*, November 4, 2019. https://www.theguardian.com/film/2019/nov/04/julie-delpy-ethan-hawke-how-we-made-before-sunrise-trilogy-sunset-midnight.

Holden, Stephen, "His Blood Is Colder Than Ice," *New York Times*, September 27, 1996. https://www.nytimes.com/1996/09/27/movies/his-blood-is-colder-than-ice.html.

Hornaday, Ann, "The First Gangster," *Los Angeles Times*, June 29, 1997. https://www.latimes.com/archives/la-xpm-1997-06-29-ca-7913-story.html.

Hornaday, Ann. "The First Gangster." *Los Angeles Times*, June 29, 1997. https://www.latimes.com/archives/la-xpm-1997-06-29-ca-7913-story.html.

Howe, Desson, "A Hopeless Dream," *Washington Post*, November 3, 2000. https://www.washingtonpost.com/archive/lifestyle/2000/11/03/a-hopeless-dream/cc3b4711-fbf0-4fd6-8cc9-6fed3e1c79fa/.

Howe, Desson, "The Game: Absurdly Inspired," *Washington Post*, September 12, 1997. https://www.washingtonpost.com/wp-srv/style/longterm/movies/review97/gamehowe.htm.

Howe, Desson, "Truth Is: Pulp Fiction Rules," *Washington Post*, October 13, 1994. https://www.washingtonpost.com/archive/lifestyle/1994/10/14/truth-is-pulp-fiction-rules/a0ac7d19-aacf-417f-8e38-4e0d95b3b567/.

Hunter, David, "Bottle Rocket," *Hollywood Reporter*, February 21, 1996. https://www.hollywoodreporter.com/news/general-news/bottle-rocket-review-1996-movie-1086888/.

Hunter, David, "From Dusk Till Dawn," *Hollywood Reporter*, January 19, 1996. https://www.hollywoodreporter.com/movies/movie-news/dusk-dawn-review-1996-movie-1076015/.

Hyden, Steven. "The Most Essential Quentin Tarantino Rip-Offs from the '90s." *Uproxx*, July 25, 2019. https://uproxx.com/movies/tarantino-rip-offs-the-90s/.

Irwin, Corey, "How From Dusk Till Dawn Went from 'Unsellable' to Cult Classic," Classic Rock & Culture, January 17, 2021. https://ultimateclassicrock.com/from-dusk-till-dawn-movie/.

Irwin, Corey. "How 'From Dusk 'till Dawn' Went from 'Unsellable' to Cult Classic." *Ultimate Classic Rock*, January 17, 2021. https://ultimateclassicrock.com/from-dusk-till-dawn-movie/.

Kaminsky, James. "Mr. Fincher's Neighborhood." *Advertising Age*, November 1, 1993.

Kaufman, Anthony. "Interview: No Mimic; Guillermo del Toro Declares His Independence with 'Devil's Backbone.'" *IndieWire*, November 27, 2001. https://www.indiewire.com/features/general/interview-no-mimic-guillermo-del-toro-declares-his-independence-with-devils-backbone-80646/.

Keegan, Rebecca, "James Cameron on Titanic's Legacy and the Impact of a Fox Studio Sale," *Vanity Fair*, November 26, 2017. https://www.vanityfair.com/hollywood/2017/11/james-cameron-titanic-20th-anniversary-avatar-terminator-fox-studios-sale.

Kelley, Seth, "Robert Rodriguez Recalls His Entrée to Hollywood with Student Film 'El Mariachi'," *Variety*, July 31, 2015. https://variety.com/2015/film/features/robert-rodriguez-on-el-mariachi-1201553791/.

Kimble, Julian. "Once upon a Time in L.A.: Revisiting the Ridiculous Fear of 'Boyz n the Hood.'" *Ringer*, July 10, 2020. https://www.theringer.com/movies/2020/7/10/21319691/boyz-n-the-hood-theater-violence-opening-weekend.

Klein, Andy, "Independents Day," *Dallas Observer*, January 2, 1997. https://www.dallasobserver.com/film/independents-day-6403094.

Koehler, Sezin. "The Untold Truth of Fight Club." *Looper*, updated August 16, 2023. https://www.looper.com/207639/the-untold-truth-of-fight-club/.

Konow, David. "Interview: Creative Screenwriting." *Cigarettes and Red Vines* (blog), January 23, 2000. https://cigsandredvines.blogspot.com/2000/01/interview-creative-screenwriting.html.

Konow, David. "The Untold Truth of Memento." *Looper*, August 9, 2022. https://www.looper.com/958576/the-untold-truth-of-memento/.

Koresky, Michael, and Jeff Reichert. "A Conversation with Richard Linklater." *Reverse Shot*, July 2, 2004. https://reverseshot.org/interviews/entry/204/richard-linklater.

Korman, Kenneth. "Mr. Mariachi." *Video Magazine*, December 1993.

Lambie, Ryan. "Guillermo del Toro Interview: The Director's Cut of Mimic, HP Lovecraft and More." *Den of Geek*, October 22, 2011. https://www.denofgeek.com/movies/guillermo-del-toro-interview-the-directors-cut-of-mimic-hp-lovecraft-and-more-2/.

Lane, Anthony, "Before Sunrise," *New Yorker*, July 15. 2022. https://www.newyorker.com/goings-on-about-town/movies/before-sunrise.

LaSalle, Mick, "2 Days a Funny, Only-in-LA Crime Story," *San Francisco Chronicle*, September 27, 1996. https://www.sfgate.com/movies/article/FILM-REVIEW-2-Days-a-Funny-Only-in-L-A-2965009.php.

LaSalle, Mick, "An Extraordinary Day Dawns Before Sunrise," *San Francisco Chronicle*, January 27, 1995. https://www.sfgate.com/movies/article/An-Extraordinary-Day-Dawns-Before-Sunrise-3334882.php.

Leas, Ryan. "We've Got a File on You: Mark Mothersbaugh." *Stereogum*, April 14, 2022. https://www.stereogum.com/2183004/mark-mothersbaugh-devo-neil-young-rugrats-wes-anderson-thor/interviews/weve-got-a-file-on-you/.

Levin, Jordan. "Dredging in the Deep South." *Los Angeles Times*, June 30, 1996. https://www.latimes.com/archives/la-xpm-1996-06-30-ca-19793-story.html.

Light, Alan. "John Singleton: Not Just One of the Boyz." *Rolling Stone*, September 5, 1991. https://www.rollingstone.com/music/music-news/john-singleton-not-just-one-of-the-boyz-201600/.

Lindsey, Craig D. "*Rushmore* Introduced the World to Wes Anderson (and Reintroduced Bill Murray)." *Paste*, December 11, 2023. https://www.pastemagazine.com/movies/wes-anderson/rushmore-wes-anderson-jason-schwartzman-bill-murray.

Linklater, Richard, "From the Archives: Linklater on Linklater," *Austin Chronicle*, July 24, 2020. https://www.austinchronicle.com/screens/2020-07-24/from-the-archives-linklater-on-linklater/.

Linklater, Richard, "New Again: Before Sunrise." *Interview*, May 14, 2013. https://www.interviewmagazine.com/film/new-again-before-sunrise.

Linklater, Richard. "From the Archives: Linklater on Linklater." *Austin Chronicle*, July 24, 2020. https://www.austinchronicle.com/screens/2020-07-24/from-the-archives-linklater-on-linklater/.

Locker, Melissa. "Harmony Korine on Kids: 'It Would Be Impossible to Make That Film Now.'" *Guardian*, June 22, 2015. https://www.theguardian.com/film/2015/jun/22/harmony-korine-kids-20th-anniversary.

Macnab, Geoffrey. "Guillermo del Toro Interview: 'I Think Adversity Is Good—That Is Very Catholic of Me.'" *Independent*, February 7, 2018. https://www.the-independent.com/arts-entertainment/films/features/guillermo-del-toro-interview-the-shape-of-water-oscars-mimic-weinstein-miramax-pans-labyrinth-harvey-a8197751.html.

Maslin, Janet, "Enough Blood to Feed The Thirstiest Vampires," *New York Times*, January 19, 1996. https://www.nytimes.com/1996/01/19/movies/film-review-enough-blood-to-feed-the-thirstiest-vampires.html.

Maslin, Janet, "Fight Club: Such a Very Long Way from Duvets to Danger," *New York Times*, October 15, 1999.

Maslin, Janet, "Graduates Whose Hero Could Be Peter Pan," *New York Times*, October 4, 1995. https://www.nytimes.com/1995/10/04/movies/film-festival-review-graduates-whose-hero-could-be-peter-pan.html.

Maslin, Janet, "Mired in the Land of Malls, and Searching for Meanings," *New York Times*, October 11, 1996. https://www.nytimes.com/1996/10/11/movies/mired-in-the-land-of-malls-and-itching-for-meanings.html.

Maslin, Janet, "Strangers on a Train and Soulmates for a Night," *New York Times*, January 27, 1995, https://www.nytimes.com/1995/01/27/movies/film-review-strangers-on-a-train-and-soul-mates-for-a-night.html.

Maslin, Janet, "Terrifying Tricks That Make a Big Man Little," *New York Times*, September 12, 1997.

Mathews, Jack, "Forget About Grasping 'Memento'," *New York Daily News*, March 16, 2001. https://www.nydailynews.com/2001/03/16/forget-about-grasping-memento/.

McCabe, Bob, "Desperado," *Empire*, original date unknown. https://web.archive.org/web/20150204145234/http:/www.empireonline.com/reviews/reviewcomplete.asp?FID=763.

McCarthy, Erin. "Christopher Nolan Discusses Making His First Film, Following." *Mental Floss*, November 28, 2012. https://www.mentalfloss.com/article/31628/director-christopher-nolan-discusses-making-his-first-film-following.

McCarthy, Todd, "From Dusk Till Dawn," *Variety*, January 17, 1996. https://variety.com/1996/film/reviews/from-dusk-till-dawn-2-1117904845/.

McClelland, Timothy. "Kevin Smith Reveals Why He Thinks Clerks Is Still Popular 30 Years Later." *Screen Rant*, July 8, 2022. https://screenrant.com/clerks-original-movie-legacy-popularity-kevin-smith-comments/.

McGranaghan, Mike. "Behind-the-Scenes Stories from 'Fight Club.'" *Ranker*, updated October 15, 2024. https://www.ranker.com/list/fight-club-behind-the-scenes/mike-mcgranaghan.

McGranaghan, Mike. "Behind-the-Scenes Stories from the Making of 'Se7en.'" *Ranker*, updated December 12, 2023. https://www.ranker.com/list/se7en-behind-the-scenes/mike-mcgranaghan.

McKenna, Kristine. "Larry Clark's Pictures of Survival: A Troubled Upbringing Inspired His Early Photographs of a Violent Drug

Culture and His Current Work About Victimized Adolescents." *Los Angeles Times*, November 9, 1990. https://www.latimes.com/archives/la-xpm-1990-11-04-ca-5341-story.html.

Medved, Michael, "Seven," *New York Post*, September 22, 1995. https://archive.org/details/isbn_0891981497/page/1252/mode/1up?view=theater.

Meyer, Andrea. "Jealous Guys Noah Baumbach and Eric Stoltz." *IndieWire*, June 4, 1998. https://www.indiewire.com/features/general/jealous-guys-noah-baumbach-and-eric-stoltz-82806/.

Mitchell, Elvis, "Addicted to Drugs and Drug Rituals," *New York Times*, October 6, 2000. https://www.nytimes.com/2000/10/06/movies/film-review-addicted-to-drugs-and-drug-rituals.html.

Mitchell, Elvis, "Murray shines quietly in moody, mesmerizing 'Rushmore'," *Fort Worth Telegram*, October 24, 1998. https://www.newspapers.com/article/fort-worth-star-telegram/136470292/.

Moore, Gary, "The Rosewood Massacre," *St. Petersburg Times*, July 25, 1982. https://www.tampabay.com/data/2018/06/06/from-the-archives-the-original-story-of-the-rosewood-massacre/.

Mottram, James, "Interview with Darren Aronofsky," BBC, January 16, 2001. https://www.bbc.com/films/2001/01/16/darren_aronofsky_requiemforadream_160101_interview.shtml.

Mottram, James. "Darren Aronofsky: Requiem for a Dream." BBC. January 16, 2001. https://www.bbc.co.uk/films/2001/01/16/darren_aronofsky_requiemforadream_160101_interview.shtml.

Moviefone. "Here's Why Guillermo del Toro's *Mimic* (Barely) Survived Development Hell." August 21, 2017. https://www.moviefone.com/news/guillermo-del-toro-mimic-20th-anniversary/.

Moyer, Justin. "As 'Slacker' Turns 20, Director Linklater Reflects on the Film." *Washington Post*, July 15, 2011. https://www.washingtonpost.com/lifestyle/style/as-slacker-turns-20-director-linklater-reflects-on-the-film/2011/07/07/gIQAzUxcGI_story.html.

Murray, Noel. "Wes Anderson," *AV Club*, December 4, 2008. https://www.avclub.com/wes-anderson-1798215291.

Neff, Renfreu, and Daniel Argent. "Remembering Where It All Began: Christopher Nolan on *Memento*." *Creative Screenwriting*, July 20, 2015. https://www.creativescreenwriting.com/remembering-where-it-all-began-christopher-nolan-on-memento/.

Nelson, Daryl. "Ice Cube Explains How a Chance Meeting with John Singleton Landed Him a Role in 'Boyz n the Hood': 'I'm Just Real Thankful.'" *Atlanta Black Star*, June 21, 2019. https://atlantablackstar.com/2019/06/21/ice-cube-explains-how-a-chance-meeting-with

-john-singleton-landed-him-a-role-in-boyz-n-the-hood-im-just-real-thankful/.

Newman, Jason, "Phillip Baker Hall Remembers 'Genius' Philip Seymour Hoffman," *Rolling Stone*, February 3, 2014. https://www.rollingstone.com/tv-movies/tv-movie-news/philip-baker-hall-remembers-genius-philip-seymour-hoffman-176570/.

Nolan, Nathan, "Memento Mori," *Esquire*, January 29, 2007. https://www.esquire.com/entertainment/books/a1564/memento-mori-0301/.

O'Neal, Sean. "Thirty Years After 'Slacker,' the Film Is an Austin Time Capsule—and a Hopeful Tribute to Its Spirit." *Texas Monthly*, July 20, 2021. https://www.texasmonthly.com/arts-entertainment/30th-reunion-of-slacker-film/.

Obias, Rudie. "15 Facts About Rushmore." *Mental Floss*, December 11, 2018. https://www.mentalfloss.com/article/56236/21-things-you-didnt-know-about-rushmore.

Ornelas, Joseph. "Kevin Williamson's Alien Horror Movie Makes a Perfect Double-Feature with 'Scream.'" *Collider*, February 4, 2024. https://collider.com/the-faculty-horror-movie/.

Owen, Dan. "Retrospective: 'From Dusk till Dawn.'" *Medium*, January 17, 2021. https://medium.com/dans-media-digest/retrospective-from-dusk-till-dawn-33b28612348f.

Parker, Ryan. "Salma Hayek Details Her Traumatic Experience Shooting 'Desperado' Love Scene." *Hollywood Reporter*, February 15, 2021. https://www.hollywoodreporter.com/movies/movie-news/salma-hayek-details-her-traumatic-experience-shooting-desperado-love-scene-4133064/.

Paste. "Salute Your Shorts: Wes Anderson's 'Bottle Rocket.'" November 12, 2009. https://www.pastemagazine.com/movies/wes-anderson/salute-your-shorts-wes-andersons-bottle-rocket.

Peers, Meah. "10 Wild Quentin Tarantino-esque Movies His Fans Need to Watch." *Screen Rant*, September 12, 2020. https://screenrant.com/best-quentin-tarantino-style-movies/.

Peirce, Nev, "Forget the First Two Rules of Fight Club," Total Film, April 2006.

Pelan, Tim. "Paul Thomas Anderson's 'Hard Eight,' AKA 'Sydney': 'It's Always Good to Meet a New Friend." *Cinephelia and Beyond*, accessed November 22, 2024. https://cinephiliabeyond.org/hard-eight-aka-sydney/.

Pirnia, Garin. "13 Oversized Facts About Boogie Nights." *Mental Floss*, October 10, 2017. https://www.mentalfloss.com/article/72860/13-oversized-facts-about-boogie-nights.

Price, Michael, "A Gritty Look at the Skin Trade," *Fort Worth Star-Telegram*, September 22, 1995. https://www.newspapers.com/article/fort-worth-star-telegram-seven/144218887/.

Pulver, Andrew. "Fight the Good Fight." *Guardian*, October 29, 1999. https://www.theguardian.com/film/1999/oct/29/1.

Raftery, Brian. "The First Rule of Making 'Fight Club': Talk About 'Fight Club.'" *Ringer*, March 26, 2019. https://www.theringer.com/movies/2019/3/26/18281406/fight-club-davis-fincher-making-of-brad-pitt-edward-norton.

Rausch, Andrew J. "The Maddest Story Ever Told: An Interview with Director Jack Hill." *Shock Cinema*, no. 59 (2021).

Rebello, Stephen. "Playboy Interview: David Fincher." *Playboy*, September 17, 2014, 57–60, 134–36.

Ressner, Jeffrey. "The Traditionalist." *DGA Quarterly* (Spring 2012). https://www.dga.org/craft/dgaq/all-articles/1202-spring-2012/dga-interview-christopher-nolan.aspx.

Rhys, Timothy. "Hanging Out with Richard Linklater: On Directing *subUrbia* and Ensemble Casts." *MovieMaker*, updated January 31, 2023. https://www.moviemaker.com/hanging-out-with-richard-linklater-on-directing-suburbia-and-ensemble-casts/.

Richardson, John H. "The Secret History of Paul Thomas Anderson." *Esquire*, September 22, 2008. https://www.esquire.com/news-politics/a4973/paul-thomas-anderson-1008/.

Rickey, Carrie, "Fight Club," *Philadelphia Inquirer*, April 22, 2013.

Rodrigues, Rene, "Stylish Seven scores with a smart script and electrifies with a shocking resolution," *Miami Herald*, September 22, 1985. https://www.newspapers.com/article/the-miami-herald-seven/144219145/.

Rooney, David, "Bottle Rocket," *Variety*, February 4, 1996. https://variety.com/1996/film/reviews/bottle-rocket-1200445150/.

Rosenbaum, Jonathan, "2 Days in the Valley," *Chicago Reader*, September 24, 1996. https://jonathanrosenbaum.net/2020/08/2-days-in-the-valley/.

Rosenbaum, Jonathan, "From Dusk Till Dawn," *Chicago Reader*, January 16, 1996. https://jonathanrosenbaum.net/1996/01/from-dusk-till-dawn/.

Rosenbaum, Jonathan, "Mr. Jealousy," *Chicago Reader*, June 8, 1998. https://chicagoreader.com/film-tv/mr-jealousy/.

Rosenbaum, Jonathan. "Reasons for *Kicking and Screaming*." *Criterion*, August 21, 2006. https://www.criterion.com/current/posts/440-reasons-for-kicking-and-screaming.

Rothkopf, Joshua. "David Fincher Talks Us through the Off-Screen Torture of Making 'Seven.'" *Los Angeles Times*, April 18, 2024. https://www.latimes.com/entertainment-arts/movies/story/2024-04-18/david-fincher-seven-imax-tcm-classic-film-festival-interview.

Rotten Tomatoes, "Desperado Consensus," https://www.rottentomatoes.com/m/desperado.

Salisbury, Mark. "Seventh Hell." *Empire* 80 (February 1996).

Savlov, Marc, "Boyz n the Hood," *Austin Chronicle*, July 19, 1991. https://www.austinchronicle.com/events/film/1991-07-19/boyz-n-the-hood/.

Savlov, Marc, "Jackie Brown," *Austin Chronicle*, December 28, 1987. https://www.austinchronicle.com/events/film/1997-12-26/jackie-brown/.

Savlov, Marc, "Pi," *Austin Chroncicle*, July 31, 1998. https://www.austinchronicle.com/events/film/1998-07-31/138517/.

Savolv, Marc, "The Faculty," *Austin Chronicle*, December 25, 1998. https://www.austinchronicle.com/events/film/1998-12-25/the-faculty/.

Scheck, Frank, "Rushmore," *Hollywood Reporter*, December 11, 1998. https://www.hollywoodreporter.com/movies/movie-news/rushmore-review-wes-anderson-movie-1235719144/.

Scott, A.O., "'The Virgin Suicides': Evanescent Trees and Sisters in an Enchanted 1970's Suburb," *New York Times*, April 21, 2000. https://archive.nytimes.com/www.nytimes.com/library/film/042100virgin-film-review.html.

Seal, Mark. "Cinema Tarantino: The Making of Pulp Fiction." *Vanity Fair*, March 2014. https://archive.vanityfair.com/article/2014/3/cinema-tarantino-the-making-of-pulp-fiction.

Seitz, Matt Zoller, "Slouching toward Hollywood," *Dallas Observer*, September 7, 1995. https://www.dallasobserver.com/news/slouching-toward-hollywood-6398279.

Sennett, Shae. "Filming Rushmore Was an Unexpected Homecoming for Wes Anderson." *Slash Film*, October 6, 2022. https://www.slashfilm.com/1042308/filming-rushmore-was-an-unexpected-homecoming-for-wes-anderson/.

Sheffield, Rob. "How Richard Linklater Created a Legend with 'Dazed and Confused.'" *Rolling Stone*, November 19, 2020. https://www.rollingstone.com/culture/culture-features/richard-linklater-dazed-and-confused-oral-history-1092607/.

Sherlock, Ben. "10 Behind-the-Scenes Facts About From Dusk till Dawn." *Screen Rant*, July 25, 2020. https://screenrant.com/from

-dusk-till-dawn-behind-scenes-facts-quentin-tarantino-robert-rodriguez-vampire-movie/.

Sherlock, Ben. "10 Crazy Behind-the-Scenes Stories from Kevin Smith's Clerks." *Screen Rant*, September 17, 2019. https://screenrant.com/kevin-smith-clerks-crazy-behind-the-scenes-stories/.

Sherlock, Ben. "Bottle Rocket: 10 Ways It Established Wes Anderson's Style." *Screen Rant*, January 24, 2021. https://screenrant.com/bottle-rocket-wes-anderson-directorial-debut-filmmaking-trademarks/.

Sherlock, Ben. "Clerks: 10 Ways It Established Kevin Smith's Style." *Screen Rant*, January 13, 2021. https://screenrant.com/clerks-ways-established-kevin-smith-style-filmmaking/.

Shulgasser, Barbara, "He's Got a Passion for 'Pi'," *San Francisco Chronicle*, July 24, 1998. https://www.sfgate.com/news/article/he-s-got-a-passion-for-pi-3077762.php.

Simpson, Jonathan "Jono." "Desperado (1995): 25 Years Later." *Medium*, August 24, 2020. https://medium.com/framerated/desperado-1995-25-years-later-48e03641410a.

Smith, Gavin. "Inside Out: David Fincher." *Film Comment* (September/October 1999). https://www.filmcomment.com/article/inside-out-david-fincher/.

Smith, Kevin. "The Hows and Whys of *Chasing Amy*." *Criterion*, June 26, 2000. https://www.criterion.com/current/posts/79-the-hows-and-whys-of-chasing-amy?srsltid=AfmBOor6RuhAr32SVqQfb_0PDQuIVNdp_WnCq4A63oGzFhkjSu6QOVeK.

Southgate, Martha. "Boyz II Man." *Premiere* 6, no. 12 (August 1993).

Spencer, Ashley, "Before Sunrise: The Making of an Indie Classic," *New York Times*, January 22, 2020. https://www.nytimes.com/2020/01/22/movies/before-sunrise-ethan-hawke-julie-delpy.html.

Spencer, Ashley. "'Before Sunrise': The Making of an Indie Classic." *New York Times*, January 22, 2020. https://www.nytimes.com/2020/01/22/movies/before-sunrise-ethan-hawke-julie-delpy.html.

Spitz, Marc. "An Oral History of 'Dazed and Confused.'" *Maxim*, December 26, 2013. https://www.maxim.com/entertainment/oral-history-dazed-and-confused/.

Spry, Jeff. "25 Years Ago, Guillermo del Toro's First Sci-Fi Blockbuster Changed Monster Movies Forever." *Inverse*, updated February 20, 2024. https://www.inverse.com/entertainment/mimic-movie-interview-tyruben-ellingson-guillermo-del-toro.

Stack, Peter, "Grim Message of Suburbia," *San Francisco Chronicle*, February 14, 1997. https://www.sfgate.com/movies/article/Grim-Message-Of-SubUrbia-Linklater-s-latest-2854782.php.

Stack, Peter, "Sofia Coppola Creates a Dreamy, Lyrical World," *San Francisco Chronicle*, April 21, 2000. https://www.sfgate.com/movies/article/Sofia-Coppola-Creates-A-Dreamy-Lyrical-World-2763344.php.
Stark, Jeff, "It's a Punk Movie," Salon, October 13, 2000. https://www.salon.com/2000/10/13/aronofsky/.
Stark, Jeff. "'It's a Punk Movie.'" *Salon*, October 13, 2000. https://www.salon.com/2000/10/13/aronofsky/.
Stein, Ruthe, "Shaping Rushmore in His Own Image/Young filmmaker Wes Anderson finds inspiration close to home," *San Francisco Chronicle*, January 24, 1999. https://www.sfgate.com/entertainment/article/Shaping-Rushmore-In-His-Own-Image-Young-2950643.php.
Stern, Marlow. "'Dazed and Confused' 20th Anniversary: 20 Craziest Facts About the Cult Classic." *Daily Beast*, September 24, 2013. https://www.thedailybeast.com/dazed-and-confused-20th-anniversary-20-craziest-facts-about-the-cult-classic/.
Stice, Joel, "How Bottle Rocket Launched the Wes Anderson Brand of Whimsy," Uproxx. https://uproxx.com/movies/the-story-behind-bottle-rocket-wes-anderson/.
Stice, Joel. "How 'Bottle Rocket' Launched the Wes Anderson Brand of Whimsy." *Uproxx*, April 30, 2015. https://uproxx.com/movies/the-story-behind-bottle-rocket-wes-anderson/.
Strauss, Bob. "*Magnolia* Springs from Valley Roots." *Montreal Gazette*, December 19, 1999.
Strom, Heidi, "Desperado Burns Up Screen," *Daily Press*, September 1, 1995. https://www.dailypress.com/1995/09/01/desperado-burns-up-screen/.
Sundance Institute. "Interview: 20 Years Later, Richard Linklater on His Sundance Classic, 'Slacker.'" October 14, 2010. https://www.sundance.org/blogs/richard-s-linklater-s-slacker-no-longer-idle/.
SyFy Wire. "Everything You Didn't Know About The Faculty." October 9, 2019. https://www.syfy.com/syfy-wire/everything-you-didnt-know-about-the-faculty.
Taubin, Amy. "Twenty-First Century Boys." *Village Voice*, October 19, 1999.
Taylor, Charles, "The Faculty," Salon, January 15, 1999. https://www.salon.com/1999/01/15/reviewb_10/.
Taylor, Charles. "Gen X? Noah Way." *Boston Phoenix*, November 10, 1995.

Taylor, Trey. "The Secret History of Wes Anderson's Rushmore." *Dazed*, June 2, 2015. https://www.dazeddigital.com/artsandculture/article/24912/1/the-secret-history-of-wes-anderson-s-rushmore.

Tenreyro, Tatiana. "The Improbable True Story of How 'Clerks' Was Made." *Vice*, October 21, 2019. https://www.vice.com/en/article/an-oral-history-of-clerks-25th-anniversary/.

The Directors Series (blog). "Wes Anderson's 'Rushmore' (1998)." June 22, 2017. https://directorsseries.net/2017/06/22/wes-andersons-rushmore-1998/.

Thomas, Kevin, "'Following' the Twisted Path of Sinister, Neo Noir Intrigue," *Los Angeles Times*, June 4, 1999. https://www.latimes.com/archives/la-xpm-1999-jun-04-ca-43950-story.html.

Thompson, Rustin, "The Reformation of Rebel Without a Crew," *MovieMaker*, September/October 1995.

Total Film, Total Film Presents the Top 100 Movies of All Time, October 17, 2006. https://web.archive.org/web/20081230035420/http://www.totalfilm.com/features/100-greatest-movies-of-all-time.

Travers, Peter, "Fight Club," *Rolling Stone*, October 16, 1999. https://www.rollingstone.com/tv-movies/tv-movie-reviews/fight-club-96171/.

Travers, Peter, "Jackie Brown," *Rolling Stone*, December 25, 1997. https://www.rollingstone.com/tv-movies/tv-movie-reviews/jackie-brown-247090/.

Travers, Peter, "Memento," *Rolling Stone*, February 15, 2001. https://www.rollingstone.com/tv-movies/tv-movie-reviews/memento-105684/.

Travers, Peter, "Pulp Fiction," *Rolling Stone*, October 14, 1994. https://web.archive.org/web/20110415121356/http://www.rollingstone.com/movies/reviews/pulp-fiction-19941014.

Travers, Peter, "Requiem for a Dream," *Rolling Stone*, December 11, 2000. https://www.rollingstone.com/tv-movies/tv-movie-reviews/requiem-for-a-dream-118844/.

Travers, Peter, "Slacker," *Rolling Stone*, July 11, 1991. https://web.archive.org/web/20110531112308/http://www.rollingstone.com/movies/reviews/slacker-19910705.

Travers, Peter, "The Game," *Rolling Stone*, October 2, 1998. https://web.archive.org/web/20071120013907/http://www.rollingstone.com/reviews/movie/5948705/review/5948706/the_game.

Travers, Peter, "The Stoner Movie Hall of Fame," *Rolling Stone*, August 28, 2012. https://www.rollingstone.com/culture/culture-news/the-stoner-movie-hall-of-fame-186832/.

Tucker, Ken, "Rebel Highway," *Entertainment Weekly*, May 5, 2007.
Turan, Kenneth, "Mallrats No Match for Ultra-Low-Budget Clerks," *Los Angeles Times*, October 20, 1995. https://www.latimes.com/archives/la-xpm-1995-10-20-ca-59005-story.html.
Turan, Kenneth, "Obsession Gets a Comic Spin in Mr. Jealousy," *Los Angeles Times*, June 5, 1998. https://www.latimes.com/archives/la-xpm-1998-jun-05-ca-56702-story.html.
Turan, Kenneth, "The Gang That Couldn't Shoot Straight, or Think, Straight," *Los Angeles Times*, February 21, 1996. https://www.latimes.com/archives/la-xpm-1996-02-21-ca-38140-story.html.
Vilas-Boas, Eric. "'Following' First Taught Christopher Nolan How to Tame Time." *Observer*, August 28, 2020. https://observer.com/2020/08/following-christopher-nolan-time-analysis/.
Vincent, Mal, "Four Rooms Is Well Worth One Viewing," *The Virginia-Pilot*, January 1, 1996.
Walters, Chris, "Slacker: Freedom's Just Another Word for Nothing to Do," *Criterion*, September 13, 2004. https://www.criterion.com/current/posts/1059-slacker-freedom-s-just-another-word-for-nothing-to-do.
Weinraub, Bernard. "At the Movies; 'Boogie' Writer Back in the Valley." *New York Times*, October 8, 1999. https://www.nytimes.com/1999/10/08/movies/at-the-movies-boogie-writer-back-in-valley.html?searchResultPosition=2.
Weinraub, Bernard. "Stirring Up Old Terrors Forgotten." *New York Times*, February 19, 1997. https://www.nytimes.com/1997/02/19/movies/stirring-up-old-terrors-unforgotten.html?searchResultPosition=1.
Williams, David E. "AC Gallery: *The Game*." *American Cinematographer*, October 18, 2016. https://theasc.com/articles/ac-gallery-the-game.
Willmore, Alison. "An Oral History of Requiem for a Dream." *Vulture*, October 16, 2020. https://www.vulture.com/article/an-oral-history-of-requiem-for-a-dream.html.
Wisniewski, John. "Screenwriter Jim Uhls on Writing Fight Club." *AMFM Magazine*, March 17, 2021. https://www.amfm-magazine.tv/screenwriter-jim-uhls-on-writing-fight-club/.
World of Reel, "Tarantino's Sight and Sound Ballot," December 22, 2022. https://www.worldofreel.com/blog/2022/12/tuwtg8t58fez8m61supmc24ezcwbtp.
Zuckerman, Esther. "Clea DuVall on *Can't Hardly Wait*, *Buffy*, and How Cramps Almost Cost Her *Carnivàle*." *AV Club*, August 24, 2016. https://www.avclub.com/clea-duvall-on-can-t-hardly-wait-buffy-and-how-cramps-1798251486.

Documentaries, Commentaries, Podcasts, Television, and Radio

"AFI Harold Lloyd Master Seminar with John Singleton." March 1995.

"Antonio Banderas talks with Joe Leydon about Desperado," March 12, 2010. https://www.youtube.com/watch?v=JO1vOqUt-ZI&t=150s.

"DJ Sway in the Morning," September 22, 2011. https://www.youtube.com/watch?v=gj7vbIAp2Gw.

"Extended Interview with Guillermo del Toro." *Cronos*. DVD (region 2). 2006.

"Filmmaker Robert Rodriguez on the Humble Origins of His First Film," 2023. https://www.youtube.com/watch?v=Rk65Hqz_mFU&t=63s

"Guillermo del Toro Mimic The Directors Cut Toronto underground," September 2011. https://www.youtube.com/watch?v=oQTu-JD9gNN0&t=1130s.

"Guillermo del Toro's Interview on BBC Film," 2010. https://www.youtube.com/watch?v=FQCDdIfMJ54.

"Interview with Director of Photography Guillermo Navarro." *Cronos*. DVD (region 2). 2006.

"Revisiting Mr. Jealousy." *Mr. Jealousy*. Directed by Noah Baumbach. Lionsgate, 1998.

"Siskel & Ebert & the Movies," original air date unknown. https://www.youtube.com/watch?v=U6vzcdKJY3s.

"The Making of 'Requiem for a Dream.'" *Requiem for a Dream*, director's cut. DVD. Directed by Darren Aronofsky. Artisan, 2002.

"The Making of Alien 3 Documentary," 2017. https://www.youtube.com/watch?v=QTzrasBUOf4&t=617s.

"The Making of El Mariachi: The Robert Rodriguez Ten Minute Film School," 1998. https://www.bing.com/videos/riverview/related-video?q=the+making+of+el+mariachi&mid=FCC185708DD0665BF895FCC185708DD0665BF895&FORM=VIRE.

"The Making of Seven," Criterion, 1996. https://www.youtube.com/watch?v=vFKSnM6bWWE&t=2028s.

"Who Do You Think You're Fooling?", 1993. https://www.youtube.com/watch?v=7HgbSAL8OKY.

AMC Theatres. *Pi: The 25th Anniversary IMAX Live Pi Day Experience*. March 14, 2023. Video, 1 hr., 54 min. https://www.amctheatres.com/movies/pi-the-25th-anniversary-imax-live-pi-day-experience-72850.

Armchair Expert, "Salma Hayek," February 15, 2021. https://armchairexpertpod.com/pods/salma-hayek.

Benn, Colleen A., J. M. Kenny, Marian Mansi, and Rene Smallwood, prods. "*Mallrats*: The Erection of an Epic—The Making of *Mallrats*." *Mallrats*, 10th anniversary extended ed. DVD. Directed by Kevin Smith. Miramax, 2005.

Benson, Phil, dir. *Snowball Effect: The Story of Clerks*. Miramax, 2004.

Braverman, Barry, dir. *The Making of Bottle Rocket*. Criterion, 2008.

Brosnan, Michael, dir. *The Enduring Significance of Boyz n the Hood*. Columbia Pictures, 2011.

Cain, Lance, ed. *Anatomy of a Scene*. "Memento." Aired March 16, 2001, on the Sundance Channel.

Cohen, Lewis, dir. *The Vice Guide to Film*. Season 1, episode 3, "Quentin Tarantino." Aired March 17, 2016, on Apple TV. https://tv.apple.com/us/episode/quentin-tarantino/umc.cmc.2dh9j6swpji96dfw5vauwzfps.

Cohen, Lewis, dir. *The Vice Guide to Film*. Season 1, episode 4, "David Fincher." Aired March 18, 2016, on Apple TV. https://tv.apple.com/us/episode/david-fincher/umc.cmc.47jrykfxgv6gui1nnimy0iw12.

Coppola, Eleanor, dir. *Making of 'The Virgin Suicides.'* Paramount Pictures, 1998.

Entertainment Weekly. "'The Virgin Suicides' Roundtable: Sofia Coppola, Kirsten Dunst, and More: Entertainment Weekly." YouTube. Posted June 18, 2020. Video, 22 min., 53 sec. https://www.youtube.com/watch?v=MVfdxMOqwcE.

Film at Lincoln Center. "An Evening with Sofia Coppola." YouTube. Posted June 26, 2017. Video, 1 hr., 14 min., 34 sec. https://www.youtube.com/watch?v=1fbWzk_jZh4.

Fincher, David. "Commentary." *Se7en*. DVD. Directed by David Fincher. Criterion, 1995.

Gross, Terry, host. "How a Heart Attack Brought Antonio Banderas Closer to 'Pain and Glory.'" *Fresh Air*. Aired January 31, 2020, on NPR. https://www.npr.org/2020/01/31/801559096/how-a-heart-attack-brought-antonio-banderas-closer-to-pain-and-glory.

Gross, Terry, host. "Wes Anderson, Creating a Singular 'Kingdom.'" *Fresh Air*. Aired February 15, 2013, on NPR. https://www.npr.org/2013/02/15/172006736/wes-anderson-creating-a-singluar-kingdom.

Hard Eight (Philip Baker Hall's commentary), Columbia/Tri-Star, 1999.

Maron, Marc, host. *WTF with Marc Maron*. Episode 565, "Paul Thomas Anderson." Aired January 5, 2015. https://www.wtfpod.com/podcast/episodes/episode_565_-_paul_thomas_anderson?rq=paul%20thomas%20anderson.

MediaMikesPresents. "Sean Gullette Reflects on the 25th Anniversary of Pi, Working with Darren Aronofsky and Directing!" YouTube. Posted July 20, 2023. Video, 26 min., 47 sec. https://www.youtube.com/watch?v=c7pOfw7kte4.

Morgan, Barbara, Miguel Alvarez, Sonia Onescu, Maya Perez, and Erin Hallagan, prods. *On Story*. Season 6, episode 10, "Se7en: Script to Screen with Andrew Kevin Walker." Aired June 17, 2016, on PBS. https://www.pbs.org/video/-story-se7en-script-screen-andrew-kevin-walker/.

Museum of Modern Art. "Requiem for a Dream: Cast and Crew Reunited Twenty Years Later." YouTube. Posted October 9, 2020. Video, 40 min., 29 sec. https://www.youtube.com/watch?v=XtR-uepL_mQ.

NPR, "How a Heart Attack Brought Antonio Banderas Closer to 'Pain and Glory'," January 31, 2020. https://www.npr.org/2020/01/31/801559096/how-a-heart-attack-brought-antonio-banderas-closer-to-pain-and-glory.

Otesanek Productions. "Wes Anderson in Conversation with Noah Baumbach." New York Public Library. Posted November 9, 2009. Video, 1 hr., 36 min., 25 sec. media.nypl.org/video/live_2009_11_09_anderson_baumbach.mp4.

Rance, Mark, dir. *That Moment: Magnolia Diary*. New Line Cinema, 2000.

Rodriguez, Robert, dir. *The Robert Rodriguez Ten Minute Film School*. Columbia Pictures, 1998.

Rose, Charlie, host. *Charlie Rose*. "Paul Thomas Anderson." Aired October 30, 1997, on PBS.

Singleton, John. "Commentary." *Boyz n the Hood*. DVD. Directed by John Singleton. Sony Pictures, 2003.

Singleton, John. "Commentary." *Higher Learning*. DVD. Directed by John Singleton. Sony Pictures, 2001.

Singleton, John. "Commentary." *Poetic Justice*. DVD. Directed by John Singleton. Sony Pictures, 1999.

Singleton, John. "Commentary." *Rosewood*. DVD. Directed by John Singleton. Sony Pictures, 2007.

Smith, Kevin, dir. *Chasing Amy*. Miramax, 1997. DVD liner notes.

Stewart, Jacqueline. "Interview with John Singleton." Television Academy Foundation, New York, September 24, 2016. https://interviews.televisionacademy.com/interviews/john-singleton.

StudioBinder. "7 Ways Sofia Coppola Captures Isolation—Directing Style Explained." YouTube. Posted October 23, 2023. Video, 24 min., 55 sec. https://www.youtube.com/watch?v=_6fqTXhUPY8.

The Game (David Fincher's commentary), Criterion, 2012.

The Newton Boys: Portrait of an Outlaw Gang, Texas Commission of the Arts, 1976.

Turner Classic Movies. "Pulp Fiction Cast on Meeting Quentin Tarantino and Changing Film History: TCMFF 2024." YouTube. Posted April 19, 2024. Video, 29 min., 53 sec. https://www.youtube.com/watch?v=r2ycpVYNTXE.

Vice. "Christopher Nolan on 'Following'—Conversations Inside the Criterion Collection." YouTube. Posted August 24, 2014. Video, 26 min., 29 sec. https://www.youtube.com/watch?v=jUpA7Qma_9E.

Winfrey, Oprah, host. "John Singleton." *Oprah Winfrey Show*. Aired June 10, 1991, on ABC.

Additional Resources

Internet Archive. https://www.archive.org.
Internet Movie Database (IMDb). https://www.imdb.com.
Metacritic. https://www.metacritic.com.
Rotten Tomatoes. https://rottentomatoes.com.
Wikipedia: The Free Encyclopedia. https://wikipedia.org.
YouTube. https://youtube.com.

Index

Aaton XTR Prod camera, 221
Abduction, 48
Academy Award nominations, 109, 204; for *Boogie Nights*, 201; for *Jackie Brown*, 66; for Nolan, 217; for *Pulp Fiction*, 60
Academy voters, 204
acting: by Coppola, S., 234–35; Method, 227–28; by Tarantino, 52, 135
actors: Aronofsky with, 223; auditioning, 185; bonds of, 167–68; cadence of, 195; coaching, 238, 240; extra takes for, 215; singing on film, 205; stunts done by, 130–31; working with, 130. *See also specific actors*
Adams, Joey Lauren, 154–55, 156
aesthetics: of Anderson, P., 207; visual, 106, 188–89
Affleck, Ben, 13–14, 151, 156, 157
AFI. *See* American Film Institute
AIP. *See* American International Pictures

Alien 3, 98–99; filming, 100–101; production of, 101; reviews for, 101–2; scripts, 99–100
Allain, Stephanie, 33
Alphaville Films, 12
Álvarez, Javier, 91
Amber Waves (character, *Boogie Nights*), 198
American Film Institute (AFI), 219
American Gothic (TV series), 78
American International Pictures (AIP), 125
American New Wave filmmakers, 4
Anders, Alison, 61
Anderson, Jeff, 146
Anderson, Paul Thomas, 83, 205; aesthetics of, 207; *Boogie Nights*, 197–201; *Cigarettes and Coffee*, 192; directing style, 194–95; early life of, 191–92; *Hard Eight*, 193–94; *Magnolia*, 201–6; *Midnight Run*, 192–93; Reynolds and, 200, 204; themes by, 206

Anderson, Wes, 175; *Bottle Rocket*, 178–83; early life of, 177–78; post '90s films, 189; *Rushmore*, 184–88; visual aesthetics, 188–89
Angelou, Maya, 39, *40*
Aniston, Jennifer, 170–71
Arkoff, Lou, 125
Arkoff, Samuel Z., 125
Aronofsky, Darren: early life, 219; *Pi*, 219–25, *222*; post '90s films, 231–32; *Proteus*, 225–26; *Requiem for a Dream* (film), 226–31; working with actors, 223. *See also specific films*
Arquette, David, 126–27
Arriflex 16BL camera, 211
Arriflex 16 mm camera, 9
The Arsenio Hall Show (TV show), 31
audience expectations, 110
audience reactions: to *Memento*, 215–16; to *Se7en*, 107
Austin, Texas, 7–8
Austin Film Society, 7
Austin Stories (short films), 122
Avary, Roger, 69–70
Avellan, Elizabeth, 131
Avid, 224

Baby Boy, 47
Bancroft, Anne, 227
Banderas, Antonio, 127, 131
Barrymore, Drew, 198
Battat, Stacey, 239
Baumbach, Noah, *168*; early life, 163–64; Ernie Fusco pseudonym, 174; *Highball*, 173–74; *Kicking and Screaming*, 164–66; *Mr. Jealousy*, 169–71; post '90s, 174–75; script writing, 164–65, 166–67

Beals, Jennifer, 61
Beatty, Warren, 198–99
Beautiful Girls, 4
Bedhead, 122
Before Midnight, 20
Before Sunrise, 15–20, *17*, 26
Before Sunset, 20, 26
Belic, Roko, 209
Bell, Ross Grayson, 112
Bender, Lawrence, 50–51, 57, *58*, 62, 70, 136
Berkman, Bo, 164
Bernstein, Steven, 166–68, 172
Best Director award, Singleton nomination, 37
Best Original Screenplay nomination, 201
Bethany (character, *Dogma*), 158
Black community, representation of, 32
Black filmmakers, 35, 47–48
Bogdanovich, Peter, 171
Bogosian, Eric, 20–22
Bolex 16 mm wind-up camera, 211
Bolex H16 camera, 221
bonds, of actors, 167–68
Bonham Carter, Helena, 115–16
Boogie Boy, 70
Boogie Nights, 197; casting for, 198–99; editing, 200; filming, 200; reviews for, 201; test screening for, 200
Boondock Saints, 80–81
Boondock Saints II: All Saints Day, 82
Borden, Bill, 129
Bottle Rocket, *180*; casting, 180–81; editing of, 182; filming of, 179–80, 181; music for, 181–82; reviews of, 183–84; script for, 178–79; test screenings for, 182

Boyhood, 27
Boyz n the Hood, 32–37
Bread and Chocolate, 77
Brook, Claudio, 88
Brooks, James L., 178–80, 182
budget: for *Dogma*, 159; for *Slacker*, 8–9
Bunker, Edward, 51
Burstyn, Ellen, 227, 228
Buscemi, Steve, 128–29, 131
Butch Cassidy and the Sundance Kid documentary, 97

CAA. *See* Creative Artists Agency
Caan, James, 180–81
cadence, of lines, 195
Calderon, Paul, 61
Camberos, Guadalupe Gomez, 86
cameras: Aaton XTR Prod, 221; Arriflex 16BL, 211; Arriflex 16 mm, 9; Bolex H16, 221; SnorriCam, 230; Super 8, 7, 209
Cameron, James, 94–95
Campbell, Neve, 227
cancer, 204
Cannes Film Festival, 59, 169
Carson, L. M. Kit, 178
Cassavetes, Zoe, 234–35
casting: for *Boogie Nights*, 198–99; for *Bottle Rocket*, 180–81; for *Clerks*, 146–47; for *Cronos*, 87–88; for *Dazed and Confused*, 12–13; for *Dogma*, 158–59; for *From Dusk till Dawn*, 135; for *The Faculty*, 140–41; for *Fight Club* (film), 113–15; for *The Game*, 109–10; for *Jackie Brown*, 63–65; for *Magnolia*, 203, 204; for *Mallrats*, 151–52; for *Memento*, 214; for *Mimic*, 93; for *Mr. Jealousy*, 170–71; for *Pulp Fiction*, 56–57; for *Requiem for a Dream* (film), 227; for *Roadracers*, 126–27; for *Rushmore*, 185–86; for *Se7en*, 104–5; for *Things to Do in Denver When You're Dead*, 74; for *The Virgin Suicides* (film), 238–39
Castle Rock, 21, 24
Catholicism, as inspiration, 86–87
Catholic League for Religious and Civil Rights, 159
celluloid film, 217
Chaffin, Ceán, 111
Chappelle, Dave, 227
chapters, use of, 67
character study, 241
Chasing Amy, 157; audience response to, 157–58; filming of, 156–57; script for, 155
Chattaway, Peter, 221
Chechik, Jeremiah, 102–3
Cigarettes and Coffee, 192
The Cinema of Generation X (Hanson), 3
cinematography, 65–66, 90
City on Fire, 53–54
Clark, Larry, 4
Clerks: casting for, 146–47; earnings for, 150; editing, 147–48; filming, 147; funding for, 145–46; production of, 145–46; rating for, 149–50; at Sundance Film Festival, 149
Clooney, George, 135
coaching actors, 238, 240
colors, in film, 58–59
Columbia Pictures, 33, 36
Columbine tragedy, 116
Connelly, Jennifer, 227

Cook, A. J., 239
cop character, 203
Coppola, Francis Ford, 233
Coppola, Roman, 240
Coppola, Sofia, 185, *237*;
    acting, 234–35; early life,
    233–34; music used by, 242;
    screenwriting, 235–36; *The
    Virgin Suicides* (film), 235–41,
    240
costume design, 92–93, 159, 240
Creative Artists Agency (CAA),
    33
critics, 36, 108
Cronenweth, Jordan, 100
Cronos, 86, 90, 95–96; casting,
    87–88; editing, 91; music for,
    91; paying for, 89; reviews for,
    91–92
Cruise, Tom, 204

Dafoe, Willem, 82
Damon, Matt, 158
Daniel, Lee, *9*, 9–10
Daniel, Sean, 12
Dante (character, *Clerks*), 148
Dazed and Confused: casting for,
    12–13; filming, 13–14; test
    screening for, 14–15
Dead Man, 199
Delerue, Georges, 172
Delpy, Julie, *17*, 17–18
del Toro, Guillermo, 6, 85, *88*;
    childhood, 85–86; *Cronos*,
    86–92, 95–96; *Mimic*, 89, 92–96;
    post-'90s filmography, 96;
    writing scripts, 86
DeLuca, Mike, 103, 107, 197, 198
De Niro, Robert, 191
design: costume, 92–93;
    production, 106

Desperado, 127; casting for, 128–29;
    filming, 130–31; release of, 132
The Devil's Backbone, 88, 90
dialogue, 9, 51–52, 67
Diaz, Cameron, 127
Dick, Philip K., 221
directing style, Anderson, P.,
    194–95
director's cut, *for Mimic*, 95
Dirk Diggler (character, *Boogie
    Nights*), 192, 198
The Dirk Diggler Story
    (mockumentary), 192
documentary, 97
Dog Day Afternoon, 4
Dogma: budget for, 159; casting
    for, 158–59; editing of, 159;
    religious outrage about, 159–
    60; reviews for, 160
Doherty, Shannen, 151
D'Onofrio, Vincent, 24
Doodlebug, 210
Do the Right Thing, 148
Douglas, Michael, 109
dreams, lucid, 85
drug usage, depictions of, 56, 58
Duffy, Troy, 80–82
Dunaway, Faye, 227
Dunst, Kirsten, 238
Dust Brothers, 116
DuVall, Clea, 140

Earl Partridge (character,
    Magnolia), 204
Ebert, Roger, 26, 35–36, 47;
    on *Boogie Nights*, 201; on
    Dogma, 160; on *From Dusk till
    Dawn*, 137–38; on *Kicking and
    Screaming*, 169; on *Magnolia*,
    206; on *Mimic*, 94; on *Se7en*,
    107–8

editing: *Boogie Nights*, 200; *Bottle Rocket*, 182; *Clerks*, 147–48; *Cronos*, 91; *Dazed and Confused*, 14; *Dogma*, 159; *Hard Eight*, 195–96; *Pi*, 224–25; *Requiem for a Dream* (film), 229–30; *Slacker*, 9, 9–10; *Suicide Kings*, 79
'80s filmmaking, 2–3
Ellingson, TyRuben, 92–93, 94
Epps, Omar, 227
Ernie Fusco (Baumbach pseudonym), 174
Escape from New York, 121
Esposito, Jon, 134
Eugenides, Jeffrey, 235, 236–37
expectations, of audience, 110

The Faculty, 139; casting for, 140–41; reviews for, 141–42; soundtrack for, 141
fake movie trailers, by Rodriguez, 122
Ferguson, Larry, 100
Ferrara, Abel, 73
Ferrer, Miguel, 192
ferris wheel scene, *Before Sunrise* (film), 18–19
Fifth Year (script), 164–65
Fight Club (film), 112; casting, 113–15; filming of, 115–16; premier of, 116–17; reviews of, 117–18; script for, 113, 114
Fight Club (Palahniuk), 112–13
film: celluloid, 217; reformatting, 196
filming locations, 124, 136, 152, 223–24
film ratings, 149–50, 230
film school, Singleton in, 31–32
Fincher, David, *118*; early life, 97–98; *Fight Club* (film),
112–18; on filmmaking, 118–19; *The Game*, 109–11; *Se7en*, 102–9
Fiorentino, Linda, 158
First Blood, 121
Fishburne, Laurence, 30, 35
Fisher, Terence, 89
Flack, Sarah, 239
Flanery, Sean Patrick, 78, 82
flashback scenes, 168–69
Fleder, Gary, 74–75
Following, 210; editing of, 211–12; at festival circuit, 212
Fonda, Bridget, 64, 170, 172
Forster, Robert, 63, 66
Foster, Jodie, 110
Four Brothers, 48
Four Rooms, 61, 92, 133
Franchise Pictures, 82
Frankenstein, 89
Franklin, Scott, 221
Frank "T. J." Mackey (character, *Magnolia*), 204
Freeman, Morgan, 105, 107
French New Wave, 16, 172
Fried, Robert, 81
From Dusk till Dawn, 56, 133; casting for, 135; filming of, 135–37; reviews of, 137–38; script for, 134
funding, 7–8; for *Clerks*, 145–46; for *Pi*, 221

Galecki, Johnny, 79–80
Gallardo, Carlos, 121, *123*
The Game: casting, 109–10; reviews of, 111
gang members, films about, 36
gang violence, 36
Garofalo, Janeane, 114
Generation Tarantino, 2
Generation X, 1, 3; *Slacker* and, 11

Geometria, 86
Gersten, Jenny, 233–34
Gersten, Jilian, 233–34
Ghigliotti, Marilyn, 146
Gibson, William, 99
Gladstein, Richard, 51
Gleiberman, Owen, 26
Glenn, Scott, 238
The Godfather, 233
The Godfather Part III, 234
Goldberg, Adam, 13
Gomez, Nick, 236
Gordon Gecko (character, *Wall Street*), 109
Gore, Chris, 3
Graham, Heather, 198
Gramercy Pictures, 14
Grier, Pam, 63, 64–65
Griffith, D. W., 5
Grindhouse, 138
Gullette, Sean, 220, 222, 222
The Guy from Down Under, 122

Haig, Sid, 65
Hall, Philip Baker, 191, 192, 193–94, 195, *196*; in *Magnolia*, 203
Hamann, Craig, 49, 58, 70
Hanley, Chris, 236
Hanson, Peter, 3
Hard Eight, 193; casting for, 194; editing for, 195–96; release of, 196; reviews for, 196–97
Hartnett, Josh, 140, 239, 240
Hawk, Bob, 148
Hawke, Ethan, *17*, 17–18, 20, 24
Hawkes, John, 126
Hayek, Salma, 126–27, 131, 135–36, 141
Haygood, Jim, 116
Hayman, Leslie, 239
Heal, Gareth, 211

Hellman, Monte, 7, 51
Henry, Buck, 113
Herzfeld, John: on Tarantino, 77; *2 Days in the Valley*, 76–78
Highball, 173–74
"high-concept" films, 3
Higher Learning, 41–45
Hill, Debra, 125
hip-hop filmmaking, 224
hip-hop generation, 37
Hoffman, Philip Seymour, 194
horror genre, 86

IATSE. *See* International Alliance of Theatrical Stage Employees
Ice Cube (rapper), 31, 34–35, *35*
ILM. *See* Industrial Light and Magic
improvisation, 76–77, 173
Independent Spirit Awards, 225
industrial films, 209–10
Industrial Light and Magic (ILM), 98
Inside Monkey Zetterland, 234
International Alliance of Theatrical Stage Employees (IATSE), 136
International Film Festival Rotterdam, 212
It's Impossible to Learn to Plow by Reading Books, 5, 7

Jack Horner (character, *Boogie Nights*), 198–99
Jackie Brown, 62; Academy Award nomination for, 66; casting for, 63–65; reviews of, 66–67
Jackie Brown (character), 63, 64–65
Jack Nicholson Writing Award, 31

Jacks, James, 12, 150
Jackson, Janet, 37–38, 39
Jackson, Samuel L., 56, 64, 67
James, Peter, 25
Jane, Thomas, 199
Jarmusch, Jim, 199
Jay (character, *Clerks*), 150, 152
Jean-Baptiste, Marianne, 171
Jeremy, Ron, 199
Jesús Gris (character, *Cronos*), 87–88
Jim Kurring (character, *Magnolia*), 203
Jimmy Gator (character, *Magnolia*), 203
J. Sloan's pub, 80, 81
Jules Winnfield (character, *Pulp Fiction*), 56, 57–58
Julia, Raul, 127–28

Kael, Pauline, 188
Kagan, Jeremy, 193
Kastelberg, Joe, 165
Katt, Nicky, 22
Keaton, Michael, 65
Keitel, Harvey, 51, 53, 57, 135
Kicking and Screaming: Fifth Year (script), 164–65; financing for, 165–66; reviews of, 169; script for, 164–65, 167–68
Kids, 4
Killing Zoe, 69–70
Killshot, 62
King, Rodney, 39
King, Viki, 33
King of New York, 73
the Kinks, 187
Klein, David, 146, 147
Koepp, David, 102
Kopelson, Arnold, 102–4
Korty, John, 98

Krizan, Kim, 16
Kurosawa, Akira, 34
Kurtzman, Robert, 133–34

LaGravenese, Richard, 193, 194
Lam, Ringo, 53–54
Lane, Anthony, 19
LaSalle, Mick, 201
Last Exit to Brooklyn (Selby), 226
Leary, Denis, 78–79
Lee, Jason, 151–52, 156
Lee, Spike, 5, 30
Lehrhaupt, Amy, 16, 18
Leonard, Elmore, 62
Leonard Shelby (character, *Memento*), 214
Leto, Jared, 227–28
Libatique, Matthew, 220
"Life Without Zoe," 234
lighting, 90
Linklater, Richard, 5–7, 9; *Boyhood*, 27; *Dazed and Confused*, 12–15; *Before Midnight*, 20; *The Newton Boys*, 20, 24–26; *School of Rock*, 26; *Slacker*, 8–12; *SubUrbia*, 20–23; *Before Sunrise*, 15–20; *Before Sunset*, 20; *Tape*, 27; *Waking Life*, 27
locations, filming, 124, 136, 152, 186
Lombardi, Louis, 79
London, Jeremy, 151
Lopez, Jennifer, 171
Los Angeles National Cemetery, 76
Love, Courtney, 115
Love and a .45, 71–73
love scene, filming, 131
Lucas, George, 30
lucid dreams, 85

Luppi, Federico, 87–88
"Lux Aeterna," 230
Lynch, David, 143

Macy, William H., 197–98
Mae Day: The Crumbling of a Documentary, 144
Maggart, Mike, 177
Magnolia, 201, 205; casting, 203, 204; filming, 205–6; Reilly and, 203; release of, 206; reviews for, 206; title meaning, 203–4; writing for, 202–3
Magnum Force, 4
makeup, prosthetic, 87
makeup effects, 159
Making of Alien 3 (documentary), 99–100
Making of Seven (documentary), 106
Mallrats, 161; budget for, 152–53; casting for, 151–52; earnings for, 153; reviews for, 153–54
"The Man from Hollywood," (segment), 61
Mann, Aimee, 202, 205
Mansell, Clint, 224, 230
Margulies, Julianna, 25
El Mariachi: filming of, 124; premier of, 125; script for, 123–24
Marin, Cheech, 129, 131
marketing, 25–26
Marla Singer (character, *Fight Club*), 114, 115
Maron, Marc, 197
Martin, Steve, 165
masculinity, toxic, 117
massacre, Rosewood, 44–45
Maverick, 199
Max (character, *Rushmore*), 184

Max, Arthur, 106
Max Cherry (character, *Rum Punch*), 63
McConaughey, Matthew, 13, 24
McGuire, Tobey, 227
Mean Streets, 36
Mechanic, Bill, 24, 114, 117
Mehring, Margaret, 31
Memento, 211, 215; audience reactions to, 215–16; casting for, 214; at film festivals, 216–17; inspiration for, 212–13; reviews of, 216–17; script for, 213–14
"Memento Mori" (story), 212–13
Method acting, 227–28
Mewes, Jason, 146, 152
The Midnight Club (screenplay), 76
Midnight Run, 191, 192; script for, 193
Mifune, Toshiro, 29, 34
Mimic, 89, 92, 96; casting for, 93; director's cut for, 95; reviews of, 94
"Mimic" (*Four Rooms* segment), 92
Miramax, 56, 74, 81; *Four Rooms* and, 92; *Mimic* and, 93
mixtapes, for actors, 13
mockumentary, 191
Molina, Alfred, 199
monologues, 52
montages, 229
Moore, Julianne, 198, 205
Moritz, David, 182
Mosier, Scott, 144, 155
Moss, Carrie-Anne, 214
Mothersbaugh, Mark, 181
Motion Picture Association of America (MPAA), 131, 149, 230

movie plots, 193
MPAA. *See* Motion Picture Association of America
Mr. Jealousy, 169; casting for, 170–71; filming of, 170–71; music for, 172; release of, 172–73; reviews for, 173
Murray, Bill, 185, 186–87
music: for *Bottle Rocket*, 181–82; Coppola, S. using, 242; for *Cronos*, 91; for *Dazed and Confused*, 14; for *Mr. Jealousy*, 172; for *Pi*, 224; for *Requiem for a Dream*, 230; for *Rushmore*, 187
My Best Friend's Birthday, 49–50

Natural Born Killers, 50
Navarro, Bertha, 87
Navarro, Guillermo, 65, 87, 90–91; Rodriguez working with, 129–30, 136–37
Neil, Chris, 238
Network, 205
Neuwirth, Bebe, 141
New Line Cinema, 202
Newmarket, 214
Newton, Willis, 23
The Newton Boys, 20, 24–26
Newton Gang, 23–24
New York, filming in, 169, 223–24
New York Film Festival, 200–201
Nicotero, Greg, 140
'90s, 1–2
no-budget movies, 49–50
Nolan, Christopher: Academy Award nomination for, 217; early life, 209; at film school, 210; *Following* (film), 210–11; giving actors extra takes, 214–15; *Memento* (film), 211–17, *215*; post-'90s films, 217

nonlinear style storytelling, 213, 216
Norton, Edward, 114
Nosferatu (film), 90
nu metal, 2

O'Donnell, Ernest, 146
O'Fallon, Peter, 78–80
O'Halloran, Brian, 146
O'Neal, Tatum, 198
One Flew over the Cuckoo's Nest, 4
The Open Road (script), 50
Ordell Robbie (character, *Jackie Brown*), 64
Owens, Bill, 239

Palahniuk, Chuck, 112
Paltrow, Gwyneth, 105, 194
Panaflex camera, 192
Pan's Labyrinth, 90
Parker, Alan, 192
Patrick, Robert, 141
Pearce, Guy, 214, *215*
Pee-wee's Playhouse (TV show), 30
Penn, Sean, 110
Penta Film, 102
The People vs. Larry Flynt, 114
Peppe, Chris, 79
Pereira, Vincent, 143–44
Perlman, Ron, 88, 89
Peters, Jon, 44
photography, 239–40
Pi, 219, 222; awards for, 225; debut of, 225; editing, 224–25; filming of, 222–23; funding for, 221; lack of permits for, 222–23; music for, 224; reviews of, 225; writing, 220–21
Pierson, John, 148
Pitt, Brad, 104, 107, 113–14
plots, movie, 193

Poetic Justice, 37–41, *40*
politics, studio, 14
porno films, 199
Posey, Parker, 22
Price, Frank, 33
production, of *Alien 3*, 101
production design, *Se7en*, 106–7
prosthetic makeup, 87
Proteus, 225–26
Pulp Fiction: Academy Award nominations for, 60; casting for, 56–57; reviews on, 59–60; script for, 55–56
Pulver, Andrew, 118

Quiz Kid Challenge (TV show), 203

Rabisi, Marissa, 13
racial violence, 44–45, 47
racism, 36, 44–45; Tarantino and, 67–68
Raftery, Brian, 115
Raging Bull, 38
Rahad Jackson (character, *Boogie Nights*), 199
Raiders of the Lost Ark, 30
ratings, film, 149–50, 230
Rebel Highway (movie series), 125–26
Red, Eric, 99
Redford, Robert, 19
Reedus, Norman, 82
reformatting film, 196
Reilly, John C., 193, *196*; *Magnolia*, 203
Reitman, Jason, 10–11
Requiem for a Dream (film): casting for, 227; editing of, 229–30; festival circuit, 230; filming of, 228–29; music for, 230; reviews of, 231; script for, 226–27

Requiem for a Dream (Selby), 226
Reservoir Dogs, 50–54, *53*
Return of the Jedi, 98
reviews: *Alien 3*, 101–2; *Before Sunrise*, 19; *Bottle Rocket*, 183–84; *Boyz n the Hood*, 35–36; *Cronos*, 91–92; *Dazed and Confused*, 15; *From Dusk till Dawn*, 137–38; *The Faculty*, 141–42; *Fight Club* (film), 117–18; *Four Rooms*, 61; *The Game*, 111; *Hard Eight*, 196–97; *Jackie Brown*, 66–67; *Kicking and Screaming*, 169; *Magnolia*, 206; *Mallrats*, 153–54; *Memento*, 216–17; *Mimic*, 94; *Mr. Jealousy*, 173; *The Newton Boys*, 26; *Pi*, 225; *Poetic Justice*, 39–40; *Pulp Fiction*, 59–60; *Requiem for a Dream* (film), 231; *Rosewood*, 47; *Rushmore*, 188; *Se7en*, 107–8; *Slacker*, 8, 11–12; *SubUrbia*, 22–23; *2 Days in the Valley*, 77–78; *The Virgin Suicides* (film), 241
Reynolds, Burt, 199; Academy Award nomination for, 201; Anderson, P., 200, 204
Ribisi, Giovanni, 22, 227
Rice, Wayne, 78
Rickman, Alan, 158–59
Riley, Robert, 20
rip-offs, of Tarantino, 69–71, 82
Roadracers, casting, 126–27
Road Warrior, 121
Robards, Jason, 204, *205*
Rockwell, Alexandre, 61
Rodriguez, Robert, 61, *128*, 212; *Austin Stories*, 122; *Bedhead*, 122; *Desperado*, 127–32; *From Dusk till Dawn*, 56, 133–38; early life, 121–22; *The Faculty*,

139–42; *El Mariachi*, 123–25; Navarro working with, 129–30, 136–37; *Roadracers*, 126–27; Tarantino and, 132, 134
Rohmer, Éric, 16
Rosenberg, Scott, 4, 73, 75–76
Rosewood, 44–47
Rosewood massacre, 44–45, 46
Ross, Anne, 239
Roth, Tim, 53, 61
The Royal Tenenbaums, 189
rules, for writing, 220
Rum Punch (Leonard), 62
Rushmore, 184; casting for, 185–86; location for, 186; music for, 187; premier of, 187–88; reviews of, 188
Ryder, Aaron, 214
Ryder, Winona, 114, 234

Sadler, William, 126
Sam Houston University, 7
San Francisco International Film Festival, 212
San Francisco location, 110
Savides, Harris, 110
Sayles, John, 24, 93
Scalia, Pietro, 79
Scent of a Woman, 194
School of Rock, 26
Schwartzman, Jason, 185–86
sci-fi movies, 139
Sciorra, Annabella, 171–72
Scorsese, Martin, 36, 224
Scott, Darin, 72
Scott, George C., 204
Scott, Ridley, 99
Scream 2, 139–40
screenings. *See* test screenings
screenplay. *See* scripts
screenwriting. *See* scripts

scripts, 9; *Alien 3*, 99–100; Baumbach writing, 164–65, 166–67; *Before Sunrise*, 16–17; *Boondock Saints*, 80–81; *Bottle Rocket*, 178–79; *Chasing Amy*, 155; del Toro writing, 86; *From Dusk till Dawn*, 134; *Fight Club* (film), 113, 114; *Kicking and Screaming*, 164–65, 167–68; *Magnolia*, 202–3; *Memento*, 213–14; *Midnight Run*, 193; *Natural Born Killers*, 50; *The Newton Boys*, 24; *The Open Road* (script), 50; *Poetic Justice*, 41; *Pulp Fiction*, 55–56; *Requiem for a Dream* (film), 226–27; *Reservoir Dogs*, 50; *Se7en*, 103–4; *True Romance*, 50; *2 Days in the Valley*, 76–77; *The Virgin Suicides* (film), 236
Selby, Hubert, Jr., 226, 229, 231
Se7en, 102; audience reactions, 107; casting, 104–5; production design, 106–7; reviews for, 107–9; scripts, 103–4
'70s filmmaking, 2–3, 4
Shaft, 47
Shakur, Tupac, 38–39
Shenkman, Ben, 222
"She Watch Channel Zero?!," 230
Shoaib, Samia, 22
Silent Bob (character, *Clerks*), 146, 150, 156
Singer, Bryan, 83
singing on film, actors, 205
Singleton, John: Best Director nomination, 37; on Black filmmakers, 47–48; *Boyz n the Hood*, 32–37; critics praising, 36; early life, 29–30; in film school, 31–32; *Higher Learning*, 41–45;

Jack Nicholson Writing Award, winning, 31; *Poetic Justice*, 37–41, *40*; *Rosewood*, 44–47
Siskel, Gene, 36
Slacker, 8–13, 143
Sleep with Me, 165
Smith, Kevin, 143; *Chasing Amy*, 155–58; *Clerks*, 145–50; *Dogma*, 158–60; *Mallrats*, 152–54, 161; on relationships, 154–55; as Silent Bob (character, *Clerks*), 146, 150, 156; Vancouver Film School, 144
SnorriCam camera, 230
Soderbergh, Steven, 5, 65, 93
Solondz, Todd, 4
Sorvino, Mira, 93
soundtrack, for *The Faculty*, 141
Spacey, Kevin, 105
Spader, James, 76–77
Spiegel, Scott, 50
Spielberg, Steven, 25, 30, 34
Stanush, Claude, 23
stealing ideas, 54
Stoltz, Eric, 170–72
storytelling, nonlinear style, 213, 216
studio politics, 14
stunts, actors doing, 130–31
SubUrbia, 20–23
Suicide Kings, 78–80
Sundance Film Festival, 183, 225; *Before Sunrise* at, 19; *Clerks* at, 149; *El Mariachi* at, 125; *Reservoir Dogs* at, 52; *Slacker* at, 10, 12; *The Virgin Suicides* at, 241
Sundance Film Institute, 51
Super 8 camera, 7, 209
Superman Lives (script), 138
Supermarket Sweep, 219

Talkington, C. M., 71–73
Tape, 27
Tarantella, 209
Tarantino, Quentin, 1, 15, *58*, 131–32; cinematography and, 65–66; *Four Rooms*, 61; *Jackie Brown*, 62–66; on *Love and a .45*, 72; "The Man from Hollywood," (segment), 61; *My Best Friend's Birthday*, 49–50; *Natural Born Killers*, 50; no-budget movies by, 49–50; *The Open Road* (script), 50; own acting, 52, 135; *Pulp Fiction*, 55–60; racism and, 67–68; *Reservoir Dogs*, 50–54, *53*; rip-offs of, 69–71, 82; Rodriguez and, 132, 134; script writing, 134; stealing ideas, 54; *True Romance*, 50
Tarantinoesque films subgenre, 70–71, 73, 82, 83
Tarantinoesque word, 60, 69
test screenings: for *Boogie Nights*, 200; for *Bottle Rocket*, 182; for *Dazed and Confused*, 14–15
Theron, Charlize, 76–77
Things to Do in Denver When You're Dead, 4, 73–76
Thomas, Emma, 210
Thomson, Desson, 26
Thurman, Uma, 57, 58
Tichenor, Dylan, 200
Tiger Award Prize, 212
Toronto International Film Festival, 187, 200–201
toxic masculinity, 117
Travolta, John, 56, 57, 59
Trejo, Danny, 129
Troublemaker Studios, 142
True Romance, 50

Turner, Guinevere, 155
Turner, Kathleen, 237
20th Century Fox, 100
2 Days in the Valley, 76–78
2 Fast 2 Furious, 48
Twohy, David, 99
Two Women, 38
Tyler Durden (character, *Fight Club*), 113

Uhls, Jim, 113
Ulrich, Skeet, 24
University College London, 209
University of Southern California School of Cinema-Television's Filmic Writing Program, 30
University of Texas at Austin, 177
The Usual Suspects, 83

Vancouver Film School, 144
Van Sant, Gus, 10
Venice Film Festival, 116–17, 216
Vienna, Austria, 16, 17
violence, 67; gang, 36; racial, 44–45, 47; *Reservoir Dogs*, 50; *Rosewood*, 46–47
The Virgin Suicides (film), 235, 240; atmosphere on set, 239; casting for, 238–39; filming, 240; release of, 241; reviews of, 241; script for, 236–37
visual aesthetics, 106, 188–89
visual effects, 116

Wahlberg, Mark, 198, 201
Waking Life, 27
Walken, Christopher, 78
Walker, Andrew Kevin, 102, 104, 108, 114
Walker, Clark Lee, 23–24
Walters, Melora, 201
Ward, Vincent, 100
Warzone, 49
Watson, Eric, 220
Wayans, Marlon, 227–28
Weaver, Sigourney, 100
Weinstein, Bob, 139
Weinstein, Harvey, 59; and *Boondock Saints*, 81–82; *Chasing Amy*, 155–56; del Toro and, 94–95
Whale, James, 89
White, Mike, 53–54
Who Do You Think You're Fooling? (documentary), 53–54
Williamson, Kevin, 139, 140
Willis, Bruce, 61
Wilson, Luke, 179, *180*
Wilson, Owen, 177–79, *180*, 184
"Wise Up," 205
Woods, James, 237, 239
writing, rules for, 220
Wuthering Heights, 85

Yoakam, Dwight, 25

Zahn, Steve, 22
Zellweger, Renée, 12–13
Ziskin, Laura, 112, 116